TACIT KNOWLEDGE
IN
ORGANIZATIONS

Tacit Knowledge in Organizations

Philippe Baumard

Translated by
Samantha Wauchope

SAGE Publications
London • Thousand Oaks • New Delhi

Originally published as *Organisations Déconcertées: La gestion stratégique de la connaissance* © Masson, Paris 1996

English translation © Philippe Baumard 1999

This edition first published 1999

 SAGE Publications Ltd
6 Bonhill Street
London EC2A 4PU

SAGE Publications Inc.
2455 Teller Road
Thousand Oaks, California 91320

SAGE Publications India Pvt Ltd
32, M-Block Market
Greater Kailash – I
New Delhi 110 048

British Library Cataloguing in Publication data

A catalogue record for this book is available
from the British Library

ISBN 0 7619 5336 1
ISBN 0 7619 5337 X (pbk)

Library of Congress catalog card record available

Typeset by Mayhew Typesetting, Rhayader, Powys
Printed and bound in Great Britain by Athenaeum Press, Gateshead

Contents

Acknowledgements

I owe much more than I can ever say to Bill Starbuck and the late Jérôme Nésa, but there comes a time when everything which has been happily kept tacit has to be made explicit. For both intellectual stimulation and a friendship respectful of tacit understanding, I will always be grateful to Bill and for what is yet to come, I will always be grateful to Jérôme, who has been more than a father and a guide in my life.

I am also grateful to colleagues whose suggestions and support are implicit throughout the book. They include Bo Hedberg, J.C. Spender, Gérard Koenig and Patrick Fridenson. Gérard Koenig was my research advisor when I undertook this work on tacit knowledge in 1991. I have benefited greatly from his wisdom and its renowned intellectual rigour.

I am also much indebted to the Faculty of the Department of Management of New York University, who have given us – the young and ethusiastic scholars – the most detailed and productive research environment. To colleagues in Australia, at the University of Sydney (UTS) and at Qantas, I owe a special debt of thanks. Allan Moore, from Qantas, gave me a real opportunity when he arranged for me to be able to stay in the Qantas offices – everyday if I wished, to observe freely the managers of the company. Alongside Qantas, the contents of this book owe much to the managers at Pechiney, Indosuez and Indigo who gave their time over to relentless interviews.

The professional staff at Sage are truly extraordinary and I am especially grateful to Rosemary Nixon, for her patience and commitment to this project, Seth Edwards, the books' production editor, and the most precise and efficient copy-editor I ever met, Ms. Beth Humphries. Also, I would like to gratefully thank my translator, Samantha Wauchope who dedicated two years to the translation of this book from its intricate French version.

There are many others . . . from whom I assimilated experiences, lessons, failures and emotions.

Introduction

We must head for there . . .
Where reason likes to be in danger.

Gaston Bachelard

Organizations all experience periods of difficulty, from which they generally recover. We often attribute these 'recoveries' to wise strategic choices, to the personality of a particular manager, or to a coincidence of fortunate events – that is, to *serendipity*, or *happenstance*. The title of this work is born of a bias: that of an interest in finding in the organization itself, and more precisely in its knowledge, the dynamics of this recovery. This is not to dispute the validity of chance events, nor to argue against the influence of inspired leadership, nor again against a positivism that would see in strategy the source of all organizational direction, but to include in our understanding of organizations a consideration of substance and process, of the existing and the created, the acquired and the revealed, of the tangible and the intangible.

Organizations may end up in situations they did not expect, yet that they precisely enacted. No matter how effective their self-knowledge, they might end up facing themselves as their worst enemy. Organizations that demonstrate the most accomplished codification of their knowledge may well be the most prone to overlook large bodies of their inner knowledge that escape this intensive care. When Microsoft, a temple of knowledge codification, faced Senate investigations for wrongful behaviour, its Chief Executive Officer appeared the least knowledgeable person on his own premises, as the audience listened, astonished by bewilderment about facts they had all taken for granted. Were they witnessing an outrageous volte-face, a deliberate attempt to escape their grips? Or was Bill Gates truly puzzled by the discovery of a situation he had genuinely overlooked?

The answer to this question may well lie in the organizational attributes of the giant software firm: a palace of ruled, archived, and organized knowledge, where loose coupling may well be discouraged as a sin. Hence, organizations can overlook knowledge as they end up sitting on a vast, ignored body of knowledge that they use, transform, and mine without knowing its true boundaries.

When these puzzled organizations eventually recover from these unexpected pitfalls, their ability to come up with sound explanations for these turnarounds is as puzzling as the fiascos themselves. This book is about organizations that recovered from puzzling situations, but still do not know how they did it. They attribute these recoveries to wise strategic choices, yet are quite unable to tell how they got there in the first place, and where they found the knowledge to escape the turmoil. People did 'unlearn', but do not know exactly what they unlearned. If asked, they would reinvent both the processes that put them into trouble, and the processes that got them out of it.

A candid explanation could be that people cannot tell how they unlearned and changed, because at the time, in the midst of the crisis, they really did not know. Traditional perspectives on change and reorientation clearly recommend developing managers' awareness of their frames, biases, preconceptions and single-loop learning. The managers did try, but became even more perplexed. Yet they had articulated the knowledge necessary to escape puzzlement and to get back on the right track. The resource-based view of the firm acknowledges that idiosyncratic know-how can explain unusual success, but how this is done is often a mystery left to the imagination. Theories of organizational change somehow easily accommodate this black box in human cognition, and leave the mystery for neural and cognitive scientists to struggle with.

Ambiguous events foster indecisiveness, and leave people powerless despite their heavy baggage of superfluous codified knowledge. People use this ambiguity in turn as a shield and as an opportunity to experiment. As a shield, it protects them from scrutiny by keeping their role definitions ambiguous, or by allowing them to avoid awareness of failure by describing their personal situations in ambiguous terms. Used as an experiment, ambiguous definitions or orders leave open different options for action. Ambiguity is a means of creating purposeful flexibility and loose coupling between organizational members. Ambiguous events, uneven acts and equivocal behaviours allow for several possible meanings, lead to uncertain interpretations, and allow for contradictory settings to prevent over-tight scrutiny and dissension. Purposeful ambiguity in language supports equivocal processes between organizational members. Unintentional ambiguity, on the contrary, may fossilize these loose couplings, and lead organizations to inaction. Behind both purposeful and unintentional ambiguities lies a knowledge that cannot be articulated or stabilized. On one hand it is implicit knowledge, that is something we might know, but we do not wish to express. On the other hand, it is tacit knowledge, that is something that we know but cannot express.

Puzzled organizations

Crises are very unusual events, while puzzling situations are very common to organizational life. What is a 'puzzled organization'? It is an organization that cannot find its way, that finds itself in a fog, of which it cannot determine the thickness, the extent or the duration. It is an organization whose members can find neither a foothold nor a guiding rail, who have nothing to grasp at, who have difficulty in identifying patterns. The organization in these circumstances is confronted with a number of different, ambivalent interpretations of events among which it is difficult to choose, the predominance of one over the other seemingly impossible to determine.

What should organization members do? Follow Bachelard's advice, and 'head for . . . where reason likes to be in danger' (Hölderlin, 1987) – that is, should they explore the ambiguity, dive into it, embrace it? Or should they, on the contrary, take refuge in the tangible, the established, the explicit and the stable; and try to carry out a step-by-step engineering of their decisions? However much managers may wish to avoid ambiguity, they encounter the problem of managing knowledge *in motion* in perilous situations, when explicit knowledge cannot be applied. How does organizational knowledge endure lasting ambiguous settings? How knowledge is mobilized, not only at the height of confusion, but equally at its outset; during the subtle and pervasive growth of ambiguity, is the concern at the heart of this book.

That which is mobilized in our knowledge, both explicit and tacit, individual and collective, remains a mystery. We do not know whether one form of knowledge is more appropriate than another to get us out of our dilemma. We do not know what is the nature, the form or the dynamic of the relations that are established between individual and collective knowledge once a situation becomes dramatically disturbing. We either take refuge in excessive explanation (explicitation) or we find refuge in the unsaid, in the tacit circulation of our knowledge, in order to grapple with a situation which is far too disturbing. We may act solely on the basis of our own knowledge or we may prefer, when faced with ambiguity, to rely on collective knowledge, but in either case there is a connection and a transition between 'modes of knowing'. This central idea leads to the question of whether one can identify enough coherence and permanence in the employment of one form of knowledge rather than another to permit us to identify links between these ways of knowing and their particular adaptation to the crisis or the organization under study. What are the mechanisms of the passage from one mode to another?

An investigation into tacit knowledge in its real life settings

This book unveils case studies of four organizations in which certainties suddenly wavered, in which the very core of their knowledge vanished in doubt, in rancour, in agitation. These firms are not exemplars of knowledge management. In fact, none of the studied firms had ever heard of knowledge management at the time of observation, or intended to handle their puzzling situation by modifying their knowledge. To have announced to these organizations that their knowledge was going to be the centre of attention might well have impeded the gathering of data. Likewise, there is an unavoidable paradox in attempting to study tacit knowledge by means of codification. The initial assumption is that this inquiry requires immersion in the companies, repeated return to the actors involved and the (at times disturbing) questioning of their stated positions. At the same time the study undertakes direct observation of their behaviour, their attitudes, of objects displaced, of spaces modified. Most observations were therefore non-participative, yet everyday presence in the studied organizations was a condition that they all kindly accepted. If tacit knowledge was to be embodied in socialization, the research design had to reflect this; hence, extended observations were to be conducted in the field.

Different situations were observed: these called for different types of knowledge and led to the analysis of various patterns, deliberate or spontaneous, which organizations followed while they struggled with ambiguity. In bringing together direct observations, in-depth interviews and secondary data, particular attention was given to the formats of the knowledge which was employed, and to the tacit knowledge which was circulated. More than 200 interviews – involving multiple returns to take into account deceptive statements, omitted facts and forgotten episodes – were conducted.

The difficulty has been to observe organizations *while they are experiencing* this instability and ambiguity. Voluntary research into organizations has been difficult. The case method disturbs organizations by its investigative nature, its high cost in terms of hours of interviews, and the difficulty of promising quantifiable results. Spending time within a company encourages it to expose itself to the researcher's scrutiny, which company directors are not generally favourable to; and executives themselves are reticent about responding to an investigation which is interested in the manner in which they acquire and manage their knowledge during difficult periods.

The initial idea was to research organizations which were collapsing, which were losing their market, their *purpose*; organizations that had to change their way of seeing their environment in order to survive: for example, to cooperate so as to better enter into competition (Perlmutter and Heenan, 1986). Organizations which were facing a rapid and disturbing shift of their market, e.g. those which were suffering sudden deregulation, could also provide revealing illustrations (Ohmae, 1989; Parkhe, 1991). This was the case with Qantas Airways in Australia when the company had to weather two successive mergers in one year; first integrating with the domestic Australian Airlines, and then ceding

25 per cent of its capital to British Airways not long after, in the spring of 1993.

To gain a more specific picture of tacit knowledge, organizations whose attempts at learning new skills came up against disputes within their workforce also appeared appealing (Shenkar and Zeira, 1992), as they usually provoke conflict, 'divorces' between partners (Savona, 1992), departures, and the serious undermining of hierarchical structures. This was the case, in the United States, with the Indosuez Bank, which attempted to expand into sectors of activity which were new to it. To achieve this it recruited a team of experts from a rival financial institution. But relations between the bank and the new arrivals were difficult, and the situation quickly became disconcerting.

To get a wider picture of how organizations were transforming their knowledge on a long-term basis, cases were sought in the arena of historical pitfalls: organizations who were caught up in the torments of history (Bowman and Kunreuther, 1988); who were witness to regional conflicts or political disputes; whose assets were nationalized; who had to negotiate with host governments (Fagre and Wells, 1982) – those whose industry was experiencing profound changes which could constitute a threat to their permanence (Yates, 1983). This was the case with Pechiney, not in its recent development, but during the decolonization period in Guinea. Historical research made sense as most witnesses to and actors in the events were still alive, and quite accessible with the help of the company, which opened its archives, memos and reports covering the period from 1942 to 1968.

Finally, by contrast, it seemed interesting to look at organizations for whom ambiguity is their 'daily bread', organizations whose occupation is to make sense of equivocal environments. These are organizations strongly dependent on knowledge, who market their faculty for comprehension and expertise, until the day when events go beyond their comprehension. We find here, too, upheavals that are specific to their environment – for example the confusion which followed the fall of the Berlin Wall, hindering any simple interpretation of the macro-environment (Sigurdson and Tågerud, 1992). This was the case with the Indigo company, which specialized in writing and publishing confidential newsletters, and which had to confront a complex, slippery and often puzzling environment.

Hence, cases were chosen for both their variety and their exemplary nature: a situation of evident challenge for Qantas, of deliberate learning for Indosuez, an unexpected emergent challenge for Pechiney, and a permanent turmoil for Indigo. All of these situations took place in industries that were undergoing profound transformation: the deregulation of the airline and financial industries, the challenge to their access to natural resources in the mining industry at the end of the 1950s, the dubious opening up of the geopolitical spectrum at the end of the 1980s, creating great disarray in the intelligence community. All involved complex operations: managing an airline company (Weick and Roberts, 1993), directing a financial institution while acquiring new aptitudes (Bantel and Jackson, 1989), managing an almost vertical integration in the production of aluminium (Barrand, Gadeau et al., 1964), and acquiring intelligence and making sense of a reality which is rather evasive, if not cryptic (Aguilar, 1967; Wilensky, 1967a, 1967b).

This work is addressed to organizations that are entering a complex twenty-first century, in which rapid and multiple transformations – which will overturn all they have taken for granted – will impede their learning curves, and necessitate a capacity 'to learn and unlearn' relying on a management that is aware of the full extent of their knowledge. Organizations for which ambiguity is an everyday fact.

1

Knowledge within Organizations

Organizing as sense making

The organization is often likened to a 'black box', with a constant and diverse input and output of information. In this vision managers, in accordance with their bounded rationality and in the context of a search for a local solution, select a particular information set on which they base their decisions. 'Knowledge' is primarily exogenous, or developed from a base of exterior elements (see, e.g., Cyert and March, 1963; March and Simon, 1956). Recently, however, an opposing perspective has emerged from research into organizational knowledge, protesting that human beings are not just data processors; more importantly, they are creators of knowledge (Nonaka and Kenney, 1991: 67). In this case an organization's primary function, rather than to process information, would be, as Nonaka (1991b) suggests, to generate knowledge.

Organizations in fact work intensely to create, to preserve and to protect their knowledge. The dominant paradigms of organizational theory, nevertheless, are alike in their representation of firms as 'interpretation systems' which process information and so resolve problems. Like Daft and Weick (1984), they regard the firm's mode of interaction with its external environment as dependent upon both the thoroughness of its intrusions into this environment and the degree to which management believes in the environment's 'analysability'. Very little attention, though, has been given to the dynamics of knowledge itself. Studies of organizational scanning analyse an enterprise's involvement as a physical phenomenon. How many agents did they send into the environment (Wilensky, 1967a)? What monitoring services did they employ (Thomas, 1980)? They grant knowledge its explicit dimension only, whereas in reality that 'which can be expressed in words and numbers represents only the tip of the iceberg of the entire body of knowledge' (Nonaka, 1992: 14–37).

The very nature of expertise lies in the reduced effort of 'searching' required of an expert to solve a problem. A chess grand master considers far fewer alternatives when making a move than does an amateur player (even an excellent amateur) (De Groot, 1965; Newell and Simon, 1972). The grand master's knowledge of the probability of success or failure of different plays is tacit. That is, the search for solutions is selective, calling upon implicit memory against having to reiterate arguments in full; eventually to the point where the player no longer needs specifically to recall each step of those alternatives which lead to failure: as Polanyi (1966a) puts it; we know a lot more than we can express. Like chess players, people in organizations spend a lot of time investigating the likely consequences of movements they are considering deploying, and for this they too use all the knowledge, tacit and explicit, of which they are aware – whether it be drawn from within or outside the organization, or from their memory, or that of others. All organization is thus founded on differing degrees of knowledge intensity.

Nonetheless, not much seems to have been done to cultivate knowledge's tacit dimension (Spender, 1993). In the chess game we look for continuities, but are limited by our aptitude to perceive them: the player notices only a small proportion of the considerable number of possible plays, and ignores a large number of valid moves (Newell and Simon, 1972: 775). People in organizations behave in the same manner, and fail to recognize a large number of strategic alternatives – there is little they can do 'until they perceive how much their incapacity to perceive fashions their thoughts and their engagement' (R.D. Laing, cited in Goleman, 1985: 24). Distortions in perception, in the attribution of sense, in prediction, or the attribution of causality, affect the taking of strategic decisions in numerous unsuspected ways.

Knowledge strategies thus become crucial for any accurate understanding of the way organizations work, and a mastering of the dynamics of knowledge can determine the competitiveness of an economic agent. When confronted with market globalization, industries often take to coordinating their knowledge to ensure its predominance over that of others, and for this they employ strategies, ruses, intelligence – a complex and coherent body of practical knowledge. Like chess players, organizations too have a memory, a capacity to learn, a mode of knowing. Yet, of the four fields of research into organizations introduced by Cyert and March, there is only one that academic study seems to have neglected over the last 30 years: the 'search' that individuals carry out as they try to understand and interact with their environment.

Organizations have limited time in which to construct cohesive, 'objective', interpretations of their environment. Vast, fragmented and multidimensional institutions, they have to locate, capture, filter and interpret information on the 'outside world' through something akin to a nervous system, at the core of which choices are made. In this way, organizations can be considered as immense interpretation systems, reconciling their intrusions into the environment with the confidence they have in their capacity to interpret it (Daft and Weick, 1984). Understanding the way in which it filters and analyses its environment therefore becomes a key element in understanding a firm. Organizations very often act on projections of themselves.

The reduction of complexity and of uncertainty are the two most frequent goals of the research that organizations themselves undertake. As part of the organization's interpretation process, many of these researchers have distinguished individual from collective cognition, asking if a sum of individual cognitions could effectively lead to a 'group cognition': the question (as posed by Schwenk and Lyles, 1992) being whether phenomena of cognition at the individual level can contribute to strategies at the organizational level. Others, *a contrario*, confer on the organization itself a cognitive system and a memory. They point out that, although individuals may come and go, an organization preserves its knowledge, its behaviours, its norms and values: as Daft and Weick (1984) suggest, a cognitive map endures in an organization beyond the movements of its members.

Managers, whether by deploring the fact or encouraging it, traditionally equate 'the company's interpretation' to that of its directors. They assume that, below the directorial and presidential levels, company personnel do not have access to environmental interpretations concerning the future of the organization as a whole (Aguilar, 1967). However, many authors, such as Weick (1979), view an organization's understanding of its environment differently, and interpretation is often categorized according to whether it is passive or whether the company actually generates its relationship with its environment. Consequently, an organization's interpretation system can be characterized as a succession of three steps: scrutiny (understood as an acquisition of data); conferral of sense to the information obtained; followed by organizational learning, defined as the process by which certain knowledge about action dominates the organization's relationship with its environment (Daft and Weick, 1984: 286). It would seem that interpretation is to be understood as both a process and a product. Understood as a product, it serves as a basis for the taking of action, and so precedes organizational learning (Argyris and Schön, 1978). Understood as a process, interpretation is the sequence through which a signification is given to information and through which actions are chosen (Daft and Weick, 1984). The tendency is then to attempt to establish a retroactive relationship between each step; interpretation influencing scrutiny, learning through action influencing interpretation.

Daft and Weick further develop this three-step process of interpretation with the addition of two key dimensions:

1   Management's belief in the feasibility of interpreting a particular environment (its 'analysability'), and
2   The extent to which the organization has intruded into its environment in order to understand it.

If management considers an environment to be 'un-analysable' it will proceed incrementally; by trial and error. In this way the organization constructs – actually forces – an interpretation, and to an extent creates an environment in accordance with a desired interpretation. Daft and Weick see this process as being more personal, less linear, more ad hoc and improvised than the interpretation of an 'analysable' environment.

One should be wary, though, of differentiating between enterprises or industrial sectors on the basis of the 'analysability' of their respective environments. An environment which is changeable, subjective, or difficult to penetrate will accordingly be perceived as less 'analysable'. Correspondingly, petroleum companies, associated as they are with broad trends – demographic growth, and the volume of vehicle registrations – once considered themselves to be positioned in 'analysable' environments; and many studies were written within this perspective before the 1973 and 1979 oil crises, and the recession which is having an appreciable impact on car registrations today (e.g. Aguilar, 1967). I am interested in isolating the endogenous and exogenous dynamics of knowledge and seeing how they interrelate, rather than in making any, perhaps rash, presumptions about environments.

Daft and Weick's perception of 'intrusion' enters into the organizations-as-processors tradition: theories which take it for granted that organizations are 'systems', which find solutions to problems by 'processing' information. I will persist in challenging this premise.

To measure the extent of intrusion, Daft and Weick rely on the existence of research departments, on the organization's subscription to monitoring services, or its sending out of agents into the field. 'Intrusion' in this sense can go as far as manipulation when organizations break the presumed rules of an environment in order to modify them or impose new ones. However, a physical interpretation of intrusion is ineffective in explaining a number of organizational phenomena, and can be contrasted with a more qualitative approach. For example, according to Daft and Weick's outline IBM should have had a much greater 'intrusion' into the environment than its Asian clone-producing rivals (being up to 1,000 times the size of them), and so should easily have been able to hold its own against them. This of course was not the case. It is for this reason that I feel it is more interesting to question the phenomenology of knowledge than to view organizations simply as information processors.

Awareness of knowledge rather than availability

The number of intrusions into its environment undertaken by an organization is therefore of little real importance. A company may be inundated with information yet be incapable of formulating knowledge, and even if it were capable of formulating knowledge, it could still be unaware of the knowledge it has. If we are to better establish the relationship the organization has with its environment we have to introduce the concept of 'awareness'.

We can distinguish between two levels of awareness: self-awareness and 'collective awareness' – or 'collective consciousness'. We define ourselves *vis-à-vis* a sense of self (awareness of an identity) and a sense of belonging to a group (social or collective identity). We make a distinction between that to which we belong (a country, a group, a company, a profession) and that which belongs to us (tradition, expertise, material possessions, achievements). The combination of awareness and identity leads to different attitudes towards knowledge, and different abilities to formulate strategies on the basis of knowledge. For example, the combination of a weak collective consciousness and a strong social identity produces a conservative force. People in this category find their identity in a feeling of belonging to a particular representation of the world, a representation which they want to preserve exactly as it is (Curle, 1972: 9).

In his work on mysticism and militants, Adam Curle shows how a wide awareness and a weak identity (a weak sense of belonging) are the vectors which support the emergence of militant movements. Curle's works are based on his own experiences and observations of the phenomena he describes. Their interest lies in the light they shed on the interaction between a person's state of awareness, of alertness or proactive attention, on the one hand, and his or her identity or involvement in the external world on the other. Curle's notion of 'involvement in the external world' – which he describes as militancy – can be compared to Daft and Weick's concept of a firm's 'intrusion' and 'enactment' of its environment (see Figure 1.1).

The tyranny of the local environment

While Daft and Weick oppose passive organizations to those which generate their own environment, I will be interested in more limited, or local, zones of coherence. In this my reading aligns itself with that of March and Cyert. I will attempt to explain the genesis of passive zones within the organization, as well as trying to describe and explain the genesis of other more active, environmentally creative or manipulative, zones. This represents what Watzlawick (1976, 1984) recognized as an acceptance of the existence of multiple 'realities' within an organization;

SENSE OF BELONGING

		Weak	Strong
	Weak	Unfocused intrusion Incremental search	Contingent intrusion Reactive search
AWARENESS			
	Strong	Emergent intrusion Random search	Focused intrusion Purposeful search

Figure 1.1   *Belonging and intrusion*

multiple simply because individual actors carry out their interpretations within accepted limits, and in so doing act as 'test avoiders' (Weick, 1979) and reduce 'reality' to what is contained within limits that are self-imposed. Managers act not only according to local rationality, but equally within mental frames of reference which reduce their own liberty.

Organizations as irrational, ceremonial and manoeuvring

Because their intrusions do not mean that they are aware of reality; because they favour a local rationality; and because they obey mental models; organizations are fairly informal and non-systematic in their interpretation of their environment (Fahey and King, 1977). They lack time to understand their environment, and often act under pressure, overloaded with new information, reports and environmental stimuli. To add to the difficulty, most firms are, as Starbuck (1992b) recognizes, in competition with others who have at their disposal very similar knowledge, with which they too formulate their strategies. They make sense of their environment within the constraints of time and a bounded rationality (Cyert and March, 1963), and so frequently perceive only a reflection of their own beliefs (Starbuck and Milliken, 1988a). Organizations are thus vast, fragmented and multidimensional operative fields, with their own 'ceremonial conformity' (Meyer and Rowan, 1977).

A company's history, its past successes and failures, its archives, its internal mail, its customs and its rumours all act as guarantees of its identity. It is in this context that stimuli from the 'outside world' are captured, deformed and filtered: and so organizations act as 'mis-interpretation' systems, in which environmental scrutiny, action and learning are intimately linked (Daft and Weick, 1984). In this activity of knowing the external world there is an important key to understanding organizations. A firm is not a 'black box' whose informational input is identifiable, fitting into some sort of cycle or 'system'; rather it interacts with its environment in a social and historical continuity. Firms follow their industrial sector's tried recipes, including employing all available means to enact these recipes, with the objective of avoiding uncertainty: through professional unions, consultants, newspapers, and contacts with economic and political elites, firms negotiate their own environments (Cyert and March, 1963).

Constrained by urgency and a bounded rationality

In this negotiated environment, individuals act according to information which may be more or less reliable and complete. Collecting information within the constraints of time and pushed by a sense of urgency, actors look for the simplest means to reduce complexity based on the criteria on which they feel they are judged, so that amongst a number of decision-making criteria those thought to be closest to the aspirations of the hierarchy will be advantaged. A local coherence is sought, often without taking into account the global coherence of the organization. In response to a local rationality, the individual limits his or her own objectives to what is accessible *a minima*, preferring to apprehend a limited number of problems, and to have a limited number of objectives, in which his or her role will be contained *a minima*. The limits imposed by individual cognition, together with the difficulty of attaining collective cognition, mark out membership zones within a firm, as people make distinctions amongst themselves (as 'engineering people', 'management staff', etc.) even when these are not designated by others. To protect these fragile boundaries, task definition and accomplishment may be shrouded in 'fuzziness' and a perceptible wastage of resources. These 'fuzzy' zones contribute to organizational flexibility, as each person works out a personal space in which to organize any last minute manoeuvres – a blurred project definition concealing a personal strategy or a minimum zone of personal liberty within the social system. Resource-wasting manoeuvres also mask the intentions of one group from another (Crozier and Friedberg, 1980). This can involve the equipping of a particular office within a firm or the granting of a personal computer or a supplementary budgetary percentage 'with no specific designation'.

Bureaucratic demarcation of cognitive territories

Cognition then delimits a 'territory' that reflects what individuals perceive as well as what they fail to notice. Intrusion into 'cognitive territories' unknown to the person who ventures into them is difficult to represent in a system, and trial and error, chance or contingency are sometimes the only ways that new elements are discovered in an environment. Wastage manoeuvres and the maintenance of 'fuzzy zones'

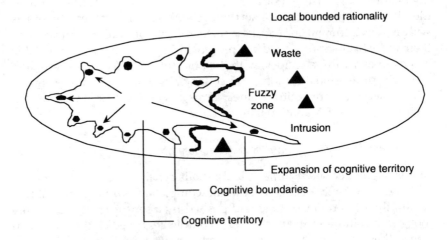

Figure 1.2   *Cognitive bulwarks and territories*

then take on another face. They provide a bulwark against the intrusion of others. As Figure 1.2 shows, organizational actors themselves can prove to be very prudent when it comes to being open to others' cognitive efforts. Knowledge and cognition are very often 'territorialized' in organizations, partly by the actors' bounded rationality, but equally by their determination to protect their knowledge, which they associate with their power and authority. Consequently, it is difficult not only to achieve a good circulation of knowledge, but equally to reach any consensus as to what constitutes a firm's generic knowledge.

Knowledge of organizational structure is therefore not uniform but polymorphous. A core of generic knowledge on which there is general consensus can exist at the same time as other elements of knowledge which support this core but on which there is no great consensus (Schwenk, 1989). In this perspective, the organizational knowledge system is a formation of connections between a knowledge core and its periphery.

The existence of perception models

In the same way that incongruity is defined in relation to a normality inscribed in models, the capacity to create connections is defined in relation to perception models. The behaviour of suppliers, competitors and consumers is 'modellized' by agents, so that future perception of their actions is dependent on the *ideas* agents have constructed of their past behaviours. There exists thus a cognitive approach to the problem of competition definition, as decision-makers already have an image of their rivals and of the dimensions of the possible confrontation before

they define a competitive strategy. Competition definition is as important as it is problematical (given the great number of organizational
conventions and of decisions taken by a firm), which leads actors to
employ simplified mental models of the rivalry. In internalizing a
mental classification of organizational forms, strategists can simplify
their perception of their environment by regrouping organizations
taxonomically (Porac and Howard, 1990).

For example, in its annual report of 1992, General Electric included
as a priority the modification of its managerial staff's framing of their
environment. General Electric's president, John Welch, drew up a series
of questions addressed to managers, and invited them to question
reality and the interpretations they make of it. He had a double objective: to enable himself to see through his own personal 'doctrine' on
rivalry and, above all, to invite his managers to question theirs. Few
CEOs put into practice such an awareness of the critical role of
knowledge interpretation.

Models that emerge within a community of cognition

The construction of mental models is a learning process. An underlay of
models is derived from education and culture, and mental models particular to a firm's specific culture are then superimposed on this
foundation. These models are born from organizational learning and
interactions between agents, from a cognition established within a
community of action and reflection with its own rites and beliefs and its
own tools.

Because of its small size and long tradition, Scotland's knitwear sector
was chosen by Porac, Baden-Fuller and Howard (1989) for a study of the
role of shared beliefs within a community. Over a six-month period they
interviewed directors of 35 per cent of these companies, discovering that
the sector owes its existence as such in Scotland today to mental models
of transactions and to habitual strategic decisions which assert themselves on the market. The identity of the generic knowledge core,
together with its associated causal beliefs, allows the directors of these
networks to delimit their competitive activity and to make sense of
interactions taking place within these boundaries. Technical choices are
made that serve to strengthen the cognitive community while forcing
information flows to return to the original decision-makers – so limiting
their vision of the market to that which already was in common belief.
One can, though, question the external validity of the 'cognitive community', as Baden-Fuller, Porac and Howard acknowledge in their work.
We cannot be sure, however, that these modes of action and interpretation are particular to the knitting industry, and not to Scotland itself. As
part of our analysis, the question of the actual existence of 'cognitive
communities' must be considered.

The creation of organizational knowledge

Creation, application, preservation and association

A less cognitive, less structural, approach to organizational knowledge
is to examine its three elementary dynamics: its creation, its application,
and its preservation. Those who are specifically responsible for knowledge management within firms (researchers, attorneys, experts . . .),
define these dynamics in a variety of sometimes surprising ways.
William Starbuck notes that 'creating, applying, and preserving inter-
twine and complement each other. At least over long periods, merely
storing knowledge does not preserve it. For old knowledge to have
meaning, people must relate it to their current problems and activities'
(1992a: 722). Knowledge is thus a mutable and fragile organizational
entity. Its sense is derived from its application, and is lost once it is
removed from the context of its utility: out of the dynamics of its
utilization, there is no knowledge which is more or less intense, or
valuable, than any other. As Starbuck stresses, 'ambiguity about the
meaning of knowledge creation implies a weak tie, if any, between
knowledge creation and knowledge intensity' (1992a: 723).

The creation of organizational knowledge appears more and more to
be a process that is at once visible and invisible, tangible and intangible,
stable and unstable. It can be described as the capacity to create connections where previously there were none either obvious or foreseeable. At the same time, we find that these connections cannot be pulled
out of thin air. Before beginning any analysis of an environment there
must be pre-existent strategy, a desire to find some sense that will
strengthen or contradict a sought direction. Firms make sense of their
environment by using indicators, whether quantitatively (to measure
performance, for example), qualitatively (for self-appraisal, to position
themselves and see themselves more clearly), or in a Boolean fashion
(making logical connections between a given signal and an action).
Together, these tools for the management of organizational knowledge
regulate and condition the way in which actors relate to each other.
Perceived environmental events are either integrated or rejected by the
firm depending on whether or not they are compatible with its version
of 'reality' – there is not really any knowledge without a *raison d'être*.

Management tools and knowledge

A study of the role of management tools in firms makes it clear that
actors act according to factors on which they feel they are locally judged
(Berry, 1983; Cyert and March's 'bounded rationality', 1963). In large
organizations, agents are involved in complex management situations
and are led to make decisions and choices when the information at their
disposal is incomplete and its reliability uncertain; in addition, limitations on the amount of time they can devote to a particular problem,

combined with the sense of urgency that often presides over the implementation of an action leaves them very little room in which to move. In
any case, many acknowledge making decisions and choices without
having had time to make these as informed as they should have been.

If the reduction of complexity appears then as 'an operation which is
at once necessary and perilous', it has the particular effect of conferring
sense on an agent's environment by 'limiting what is good and true',
which – although perhaps not faithful to reality – at least has the merit
of maintaining social control and productivity levels; in other words,
maintaining an 'anti-learning' organization.

Thus reality is often formulated by the organization's normative
aspect: agents will use very small amounts of information, privileging
that on which they feel they are judged, while respecting the rationality
of their relationships with other agents of their local environment. It is
precisely because organizations generally reduce the wealth of their
knowledge to *information*, *measures* and *standards* that they curtail its
dynamics. Knowledge and management tools will of course have certain common characteristics: they translate a symbolic hierarchy (access
to knowledge denotes hierarchical privilege) and crystallize power
struggles (holders of knowledge dominate the process in which a body
of perceptions is translated into a strategy). Yet knowledge can easily be
ossified by an unresponsive supplies office, or by imperatives to answer
to objectives on which agents will feel themselves judged: agents will
avoid straying too far from the limited scope of their missions.

One can, however, expand the question of the responsiveness of the
supplies office to the question of economy in the broad sense. This is
demonstrated in the works of Ronald V. Jones in which, going
somewhat off the beaten path, he develops his theory of practical joking.
Jones was inspired by the conclusion of Freud's *Jokes and their Relation to
the Unconscious*, in which Freud states:

> The pleasure in jokes has seemed to us to arise from an economy in expenditure
> upon inhibition, the pleasure in the comic from an economy in expendi-
> ture upon ideation (upon cathexis) and the pleasure in humour from an
> economy in expenditure upon feeling. In all three modes of working of our
> mental apparatus the pleasure is derived from an economy. (quoted in Jones,
> 1975: 10–17)

Jones, a physicist, wondered if there could be a connection between
scientific method and practical jokes. He found that the nature of joking
is, in effect, 'the creation of an incongruity in the normal order of events'.
Pleasure is derived from the psychological economy of having created a
signifier that is strong and incongruous – comical – by twisting
perceptions and using an economy of signs. We can make two analogies
here with knowledge creation. Firstly, the production of knowledge
underlies the reduction of complexity, as the object of a reduced number
of signs is to transmit meaning by extracting it from its receptacles (data,

different possibilities and probabilities, fuzziness). Secondly, knowledge too answers to a principle of multiple economies. While humour represents economy of language (suggestion) together with a psychological economy (the creation of incongruity against the normal order without having to define normality itself), knowledge creation arises from an economy of the organization's resources (creating sense in order to meet urgent demands, or to finish one task and move on to the next) and, at the individual level, from psychological economy (creating sense in order to manage the uncertain).

The same principle of economy presides over the vigilance, or watchfulness, of actors with regard to their environment. Next to knowledge, vigilance seems a restrictive notion, yet one finds there too the idea of interpretation and comprehension of the environment. Vigilance is a response to an economy linked to a local agenda, and so defines local crisis as a confrontation of agendas with different imperatives, necessitating different interrelations with the environment. In Jones's works, incongruity itself is found in knowledge: the unexpected connection made between two events is an incongruity next to the usual order of events within the organization. It would be wrong to consider this example of Jones as simply a deviation. In the wordplays studied by Jones, there is sense-making as well: non sense or sense are used to correct incongruities by triggering our tacit understanding. This spawning of enlightening connections remains the profound mystery of knowledge creation. Are its foundations to be discovered in tacit knowledge? What then are the factors which permit an agent to draw connections they have never drawn previously? Is knowledge revealed to us by its familiarity or by its incongruity?

In his paper, Jones looks at different forms of incongruities. He finds that joking attracts us by drawing our attention to the unusual connection – the incongruous connection – contained in a message that does not openly expose it as such, but suggests it with an economy of signs. This is exactly what happens in reality when an agent discovers an incongruous but sense-laden connection between two events in their environment. The first type of incongruity described by Jones is the 'mismatch of scale'. The second type is that from which irony proceeds: a communication that is the opposite of what is meant. The third class of incongruity arises when an entirely normal situation takes place where an incongruous situation was expected. In each case, incongruity is defined in relation to a model: the joke reveals the existence of the model by being out of line with it.

Knowledge and information

Although the terms 'knowledge' and 'information' are commonly used interchangeably, a clear distinction exists between the two concepts. Information has been variously defined as: a flow of messages that increases knowledge, restructuring and modifying it (Machlup, 1983); a raw material capable of yielding knowledge; and a signal carrying information from which we can learn (both Dretske, 1981). Following this through, knowledge would be a representation of representations: a belief derived from information. I cannot be in full agreement with this definition. While information establishes itself in the sphere of common understanding, knowledge derived from it is subjective in nature, and intimately linked to the individual or the group of individuals generating it. For example, 'the Berlin Wall has fallen' is information. But this chunk of data will transform itself into different representations according to the actor or the group of actors receiving it. The information will modify the *knowledge* of the actors in different ways, according to whether they are, for example, Russian or German, scientists or labourers, political decision-makers or research workers. We are once again in the realm of knowledge being taken as *representation*. This way of viewing knowledge is nevertheless thoroughly limited, because the idea of representation embraces a principle of universal intelligibility. We cannot distinguish what fundamentally differentiates information from knowledge if we limit ourselves to the level of the image. What is more, what would tacit knowledge be then? A representation that cannot be represented? Clearly this idea fails to embrace all of knowledge's dimensions.

As soon as we evoke a representation we suggest the existence of a bi- or tri-dimensional reality in which this knowledge could be encapsulated. But in the same way that light is both a wave (an abstraction) and a particle in motion (solid matter), knowledge is at once a representation and a substance. The refusal to accept knowledge as a substance comes from both the Judaeo-Christian heritage and from a pretension on the part of humankind to want to separate itself from the inert and common element that matter can be. Nonetheless, within the human brain knowledge is very much the consequence of a modification of matter (cerebral matter); and therefore *physically* existent. Without entering into a digression for which this is not the place, it is necessary simply to accept the idea of substance because this accommodates itself better to the sentiments, the impressions, the intuitions, the premonitions that are all part of knowledge, and which the idea of 'representation' would not be able to convey faithfully. In any case, one cannot put representations on one side and substances on the other, as if a Cartesian dichotomy existed between, for example, that which is felt in substance, and that which is foreseen. If we take the example of premonition, we can no more maintain that it is just a representation than that it is a substance. Knowledge is the object of a continuum that extends from interpreted information (such as a simple pencilled diagram) to the non-representable (premonitions, for example).

To prefer to study knowledge rather than information within the organization entails a willingness to respect this continuum. Research focusing on what is properly information will lead to a theorization of information management processes, neglecting knowledge's inclusionary dimension. Information is but a medium to initiate and formalize knowledge. Most theories of information direct all their attention to the manner in which it is transported, distributed or exchanged, while it remains necessary to develop a theory that looks more closely at the *sense* of the information and the *messages* that convey information in organizations. It is without doubt the vanity of 'I think therefore I am' that has made us forget 'I think therefore I act'. The desire for representation, of which knowledge is unceasingly the object, is similar to the human desire for intelligibility – to apprehend ourselves and everything around us through Reason. This vain yearning to represent, to assert a penetration of the mind on the times, diverts us from the wealth of our intangible and conjectural knowledge. As Détienne and Vernant put it, it allows:

> the gulf that separates man from beasts . . . to dig itself deeper, and human reason to appear ever more distinct from animal behaviour . . . but is this not also, and more especially, a sign that the concept of Platonic Truth, in relegating to the shadows a whole plain of intelligence with its own kinds of understanding, has never really ceased to haunt Western metaphysical thought? (1978: 306)

Knowledge and competitive advantage

We encounter this 2,000-year-old inheritance when we look at the organizational conception of knowledge: in patents, formulas, plans, designs and products. When we question firms about what knowledge they see as being a source of competitive advantage, these are invariably the first elements that spring to mind. Following them there is 'know-how' – but when it comes to describing this, the terms 'engineers', 'researchers' and 'technical expertise' predictably crop up. If we take the questioning further, and ask why their engineers are better than their competitors', they talk of 'rigorous selection processes', 'the best schools' or 'technical excellence' – and so we remain steadfastly within the boundaries of what the Greeks named *techne* and *episteme*: expertise and science. That said, the Greeks never dissociated expertise and science from *phronesis* – wisdom acquired through socialization.

One finds this cumbersome metaphysical paradigm in a company's own examination – when this actually occurs – of its knowledge. Managers believe that knowledge that cannot be generalized or encapsulated in a series of technical recipes can only be individual and singular. If they want to protect knowledge that is non-codified and non-codifiable (and so cannot be locked in a safe), they think immediately of either the handiwork of such-and-such an engineer, and reinforce the protection clause in their contract; or of the 'talent' of a particular marketing executive, and so increase their salary. If non-codifiable knowledge does exist, this can only be because of the singular character of a particular individual, who will then be classed as 'high potential' (HP) and rewarded with a comfortable career under the best security conditions (to prevent their escape). Here we are not far from Greek mythology and the concept of beings endowed with *mètis*. Rather than managing knowledge, organizations manage its codifications. The uncodified is left to mythology.

The idea that non-codifiable knowledge could be collective is rarely present in the mind of company directors. They follow an ideology in which expertise is either codifiable and collective (e.g. patents), or non-codifiable and individual (e.g. high potential). So we have two tenuous no man's lands: the non-codifiable collective, and the codifiable individual. This brings us to another taboo: the idea that collective thought that is superior to individual thought could exist within the organization (Sandelands and Stablein, 1987). From a Cartesian perspective it is impossible to imagine an organization having a 'virtual brain' born of the jostling (or confrontation) of human brains, an image that would appear grotesque to any company director, even more grotesque than talk of a 'planetary brain'. Here again we see a desire for representation: if there were collective knowledge, we would immediately want to represent it as a mechanism, a machine, whereas there could very well be collective knowledge without it being simply a unilateral mechanism for cognition, interpretation and sense attribution. We can distinguish between collective knowledge and collective cognition. The existence of collective knowledge does not presuppose the homogeneity of this knowledge. It may be entirely heterogeneous, but nonetheless belong integrally to a community, whether because it would disintegrate if the community itself was broken up, or because the same team would lose its efficiency if it were positioned in another organization.

Any knowledge or know-how that a firm has which its rivals do not is at stake in the competition. A pharmaceutical firm, for instance, depends on the uniqueness of its formulae to maintain its competitive advantage. The aluminium conversion know-how possessed by France's Pechiney is another example. Since Pechiney's foundation, this know-how has been central to its competitive dynamics, notably in its relationships with its American rival, Alcoa. The ideology of knowledge as I have described it above makes the firm manage its knowledge within a 'codifiable/non-codifiable' dialectic; wherein the codifiable is 'battened down', and care is taken to prevent the escape of the non-codifiable. This dichotomy brings the firm to mobilize all of its resources in the codification of the knowledge in its possession – as it is easier to 'batten down' codified knowledge than to identify and win over 'non-codified' knowledge. In doing so it comes up against two obstacles. The first is that there is some knowledge that is not, and never will be, codifiable, for the simple (and good) reason that once identified it is generally lost. The leitmotiv 'you don't change a winning team' is a response to the fear of breaking up

non-codifiable knowledge that has shown itself to be successful. Similarly, firms are well aware that knowledge – even if it isn't codifiable – is
sensitive to the effects of ageing. From this, they understand equally that
it is necessary to 'renew' teams or to 'inject new blood' into the organization. It is here that the firm is confronted with the second obstacle; as
it usually has to effect this renewal with that which it has mastered, that
is to say, using its codified knowledge. It is a classic story: the company
retains its most qualified experts and expels the black sheep (those 'too
old', 'not dynamic enough', etc.) only to realize, a posteriori, that the
renewed team no longer functions at all. Thus, the firm's competitive
advantage depends on tacit knowledge which it doesn't know how to
manage, or which it manages indirectly through the distorting mirror of
codification.

We must also differentiate between two types of knowledge: that
which the firm wants to keep for itself, and that – call it 'environmental'
– which circulates in the environment, allowing itself to be exchanged,
imitated, exhausted and appropriated. It is not enough to promote
organizational learning, to evoke 'learning organizations', if it does not
retain acquired knowledge and derive strategic advantage from it
(Spender, 1993: 37). The difficulty is of course linked to the nature of this
knowledge. Scientific, explicit, universal knowledge – that which Greek
philosophers would describe as *episteme* – can be written, recorded,
validated and protected by a firm; either by patent or by secret. Know-
how, the capacity to accomplish a task that others cannot accomplish –
what Greek philosophers call *techne* – can also be protected and safe-
guarded. When this concerns technical know-how, it can be protected as
belonging to the firm. When it is a question of an engineer's experience,
attentive management of human resources and the establishment of
contractual bonds can again preserve this knowledge. But when knowledge cannot be recorded or documented, when its tangibility is only
ephemerally perceptible, when that knowledge is *tacit*, it becomes
difficult for a firm to truly know what it is in the process of acquiring, to
preserve it or use it to construct a competitive advantage.

How can we apprehend tacit knowledge?

The maintenance of organizational flexibility is one of the essential roles
of tacit knowledge. The knowledge that actors have of each other, of
each other's intentions, stakes, private goals and 'territories', is not
expressed, recorded, universal knowledge. *Phronesis* is born from the
experience of social practice; it provides markers for what can be said
and what cannot; as when a discussion is directed according to the
personality of a colleague, according to what tacitly one knows to be
the approach that has the best chance of gaining an attentive ear.

Tacit knowledge appears then as an essential and daily element of
the management of organizations. Empirical studies have demonstrated

that there is a very weak correlation between profits and the formal-ization of planning within a firm (Grinyer and Norburn, 1975). In other words, formalization, or putting knowledge into explicit terms, does not automatically mean higher profits, any more than it does greater losses. The correlation rate is so weak that it brings into question the necessity of a planning department (if not of strategy itself insofar as it is practised). On the contrary, patents, by articulating tacit knowledge of technique and explicitly mastered knowledge, contribute to the preser-vation of a firm's knowledge, perhaps even to the development of an 'appropriation regime' (Teece, 1987). Explanation can in this way enable diffusion and imitation of techniques. Tacit knowledge is thus a reser-voir of wisdom that the firm strives either to articulate or to maintain if it is to avoid imitation. In an example given by Nonaka, a Japanese firm sought to discover the secret of the art of bread-making so as to arti-culate the master baker's tacit rules, with the objective of imitation. To achieve this, it was obliged to send someone to work alongside the baker, to 'learn by doing'.

Knowledge is therefore not only objective and social, but very often personal and subjective. Scribner (1986: 13–30) saw the nature of exper-tise as lying in the capacity to correctly formulate problems, requiring the mobilization of all forms of available knowledge about the work-place: the expert is seen as one who, with little apparent effort, per-tinently formulates a problem faced by all. This apparent facility seems to be a characteristic of tacit knowledge. The great strategist or the great chess player also seems to choose with facility among a large number of alternatives, selecting those they estimate to have the best odds for success. Here, what distinguishes tacit knowledge from objective knowl-edge is its characteristic quality of non-communicability. Many studies of directors' agendas, governmental decisions and decisions made in emergencies show that decisions are taken largely on a tacit basis. It is in fact the interaction of explicit and tacit knowledge that allows firms to make sense of their environment, by appealing as much to the exercise of moderation, to control and modellization, as to organizational memory, to their experience and that of others, and to intuition.

The conversion of organizational knowledge

Transition mechanisms

We have explored the complex nature of organizational knowledge. In doing this, we discovered its polymorphism, its multiple faces, its rules, ceremonies, regulations, its intuition, communities of practice and social contracts. During its creation, organizational knowledge may be held by experts, and later either diffused or preserved. We noted that its durability lies in its usage, but that this is subjected to 'local tyrannies',

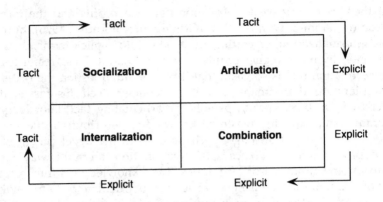

Figure 1.3 *From tacit to explicit (Nonaka, 1990a)*

to a bounded rationality, and to the existence of mental models. How are all of these linked together? How can organizational knowledge be consistent?

Organizational knowledge's coherence and consistency are found in the dynamics of its conversion. If rules are laid down without systematically provoking revolution, it is because there has already been a tacit absorption of them before their institution is made explicit. In this way shared and explicit elements of knowledge can gradually 'crystallize' out of the tacit emergence of collective needs. Vice versa, once the rule is laid down members of the organization do not become 'robots'; the rule and its usage differ, and sometimes differ so much that 'jurisprudence' becomes stronger than 'law'. Rules may be read from different angles, in different lights. One has to be wary of explicit terms; as Berger and Luckmann (1966) have shown, words often have a particular signification within the social construction they stem from. Thus the initial explicit form of a rule will evolve into a web of collective interpretations. These will in turn become the 'tacit' rule – the rule as it is understood. This process of conversion of the explicit to the tacit is what we call *internalization*.

Because the rules are internalized, each person adopts the new interpretation and makes it part of their personal tacit knowledge. Organization members regulate each other's behaviour by articulating their tacit knowledge of the way one should comport oneself *explicitly* in different types of situation. Nonaka has developed a dynamic diagram to represent the transitions between these two forms of knowledge, tacit and explicit (see Figure 1.3).

TACIT TO EXPLICIT: ARTICULATION The conversion of tacit knowledge into explicit knowledge is realized daily in organizations. The institutionalization of tacit rules as internal regulations is a good example. That which is commonly known, and which we could call 'common knowledge', is gradually articulated into explicit knowledge. Rumours that circulate tacitly can, by their articulation, become hard fact – persistent and explicit organizational knowledge. One may find oneself reproached for being unaware of a reality widely accepted by organizational members. This reality, which was at first common tacit knowledge, has unwittingly become established fact. The emergence of organizational strategies is another phenomenon of the articulation of collective tacit knowledge 'on the way one should set about doing something' into an explicit formulation embracing a plan, actions, manoeuvres and tactics. The transformations that occur between tacit and explicit dimensions of knowledge are shown in Figure 1.3.

EXPLICIT TO EXPLICIT: COMBINATION   The conversion of explicit knowledge into another form of explicit knowledge is a question of combination:

> Individuals exchange and combine their knowledge through mechanisms such as telephone conversations. The combination of existent information can be facilitated by the selection, addition, grading, and categorization of explicit knowledge; as typically realized in computerized databases. (Nonaka, 1992: 13)

In the explicit combinative, as this example suggests, the logic of compatibility, or 'fitting together', predominates. This is allied to the modellization of molecular structure: one series of characteristics is compatible with another series of characteristics. Within the firm, the architecture of the information system is a combination of elements which are open to each other without the need of interpretative intervention. The combinative logic is therefore mechanistic, as opposed to the articulative logic, which – as we will see later – is organic. Another example of explicit combination is the programming and provision of tasks as part of industrial planning, through operational research aimed at controlling the management of time and space in order to closely coordinate tasks and the physical spaces available for their realization.

EXPLICIT TO TACIT: INTERNALIZATION   Foucault's panoptic prison, in which 'the potentiality of inspection replaces its deployment', provides an exemplary illustration of internalization (Foucault, 1977; for a detailed analysis see Baumard, 1991a: 147–56; 1991b: 96–104). The panoptic prison is circular, made up of open cells through which light passes in order to sharply outline the silhouettes of the prisoners. The warden is lodged in a tower at the centre of the circular building, which is fitted with blinds enabling him to 'see without being seen'. In this context, prisoners have explicit knowledge of the surveillance tower. They recognize the possibility that they are being watched at any given time, without it being possible to know whether the warden is really looking at them or at something else. The prisoners 'internalize' this explicit knowledge, and turn it into tacit knowledge; they know tacitly that they may be watched at any time and accept the possibility. While the explicit expression of their knowledge amounts to a black tower at the centre of the building, their tacit knowledge has internalized the 'presence' of the warden within this obelisk.

All of the visual, and so explicit, information available in an organization is internalized by organizational members in the same way. The expressions on the faces of colleagues leaving a meeting communicate a message of 'success' or 'failure' without them having to put this into words; the explicit knowledge stemming from the meeting is internalized even before the results are announced. Only too often do we hear the words 'I knew it'. The aggregate of such internalizations of events that are explicitly brought to the attention of organizational members forms part of what we refer to as an organization's 'atmosphere'. Tacit knowledge develops from an observation of the movements of explicit knowledge. In the interpersonal communication described by Edward T. Hall in *The Hidden Dimension*, explicit manifestations that can be read in the body language or facial expression of the interlocutor are unconsciously internalized by the speaker. Folded arms will be internalized as a sign of discomfort. At no point is this discomfort explicitly mentioned, although the speaker immediately takes it into account.

TACIT TO TACIT: SOCIALIZATION   This mode of knowledge conversion allows us to pass tacit knowledge on:

> An individual can acquire tacit knowledge directly from another without the use of language. Artisans live with their masters from whom they learn their art not through language but through observation, imitation, and practice. In the organization, on-the-job training follows the same principle. Tacit knowledge conversion is based on the sharing of experience. (Nonaka, 1992: 13)

Communities of practice, organizational thought, and collective or organizational memory are all phenomena studied in management in which the circulation of tacit knowledge through socialization comes into play. The principal characteristic of socialization is its resistance to codification. A source of competitive advantage when this resistance to codification is central to the development of know-how (for example, the master baker's), this resistance can also be an obstacle when it comes to the imitation of this know-how.

An integrated process

These four types of knowledge conversion are widely studied in organizational theory under numerous labels. The conversion of knowledge by socialization is intimately linked to theories of organizational culture.

Indeed, organizational culture is above all a 'tacit system' of knowledge conversion and regulation. As for conversion by combination, one can refer to bureaucratic theories, or to the bodies of work concerned with organizational information systems or institutionalization.

As for the transformation of tacit knowledge into explicit knowledge (articulation) and the transformation of the explicit into the tacit (internalization), these are the two engines of organizational learning; although the articulation of tacit knowledge into explicit knowledge seems to have been somewhat neglected by theories of organizational learning (Nonaka and Sullivan, 1986).

The creation of organizational knowledge is the integration of these four processes, and develops along two dimensions: epistemological (tacit and explicit); and ontological (from the individual to the organization, then to the inter-organizational domain). As Nonaka found, 'none of these four modes of knowledge is sufficient in itself. They are mutually complementary and interdependent processes. The creation of organizational knowledge takes place within a continual organizational management of these modes, and forms a continual cycle' (1992: 17).

If this cycle is continual, there can however exist a sequential order in which the different modes of knowledge come into play in the creation of organizational knowledge. Taking the development of an innovative home bread-making machine by a team at the Matsushita Electric Company as an example, Nonaka shows how such a sequence can operate, and how these different forms of knowledge interact. In order to learn the skill of kneading, one of the members of the product development team, Ikuko Tanaka, suggested they study the technique used by the bakery at the Osaka International Hotel, which was renowned for producing the best bread in Osaka. Tanaka, who was not a trained baker, apprenticed herself to the bakery. While working with the head baker she noticed he had a very particular method of stretching the dough while he kneaded it. Although as an apprentice she found it was difficult to take notes while working, there being always work to be done that could not wait, Tanaka was able to share her experience and her observations with the Matsushita product development team when she returned to the organization. After having incorporated a number of modifications in the design of the bread-making machine, Matsushita succeeded in recreating the baker's method of twisting the dough while it was being stretched, and so released on the market a new machine that beat previous sale records. We can distinguish four sequences in Tanaka's story. (This idea of 'sequences' will be central to our analysis when we study concrete cases of firms mobilizing their organizational knowledge to face puzzling situations.) The following four sequences are identified by Nonaka:

1   Ikuko Tanaka learns tacit know-how from the baker at the Osaka International Hotel (socialization).

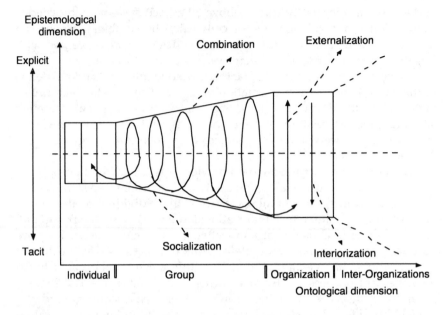

Figure 1.4   *The spiral of organizational knowledge creation (Nonaka, 1992)*

2   She then translates the baker's secret into a form of explicit knowl-
    edge that she can communicate to her team, and to others at
    Matsushita (articulation).
3   The team standardizes this knowledge, and brings it together with
    the body of knowledge they have acquired – firstly in a manual,
    and then in a product (combination).
4   Finally, thanks to the shared experience of creating a new product,
    Tanaka and her team have enriched their own tacit knowledge
    bases (internalization). In particular, they have come to an extremely
    intuitive understanding of how products like bread-making machines
    can produce authentic quality. In fact, the machine should produce
    bread that tastes as good as the baker's.

It is interesting to note in this example the dominance of certain
modes of knowledge, according to whether they are more or less
appropriate to the actors' objective. When the environment does not
permit Tanaka to employ an explicit transfer of knowledge (in the bakery
where she is only an apprentice), she observes attentively and learns
implicitly. When the need is felt to 'put things down on paper'
(debriefing), Tanaka articulates her tacit knowledge, and the team's
knowledge mode bends in line with the explanation. For knowledge to
be truly organizational, a certain number of interactions must be set in
place 'to connect' the modes of knowledge in a durable manner (Nonaka,
1991a). This process resembles that shown in Figure 1.4.

INDIVIDUAL   COLLECTIVE

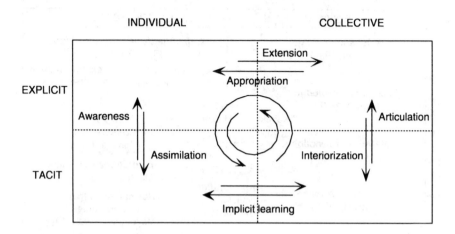

Figure 1.5   *Knowledge transitions*

A diagram of organizational knowledge

We can thus identify *knowledge modes* on the one hand (for example, explicit-collective) and modes of passage from one form of knowledge to another (for example, the *extension* of explicit-individual knowledge into explicit-collective knowledge) on the other. We can note, for example, that the transition from tacit-individual knowledge to explicit-collective knowledge necessitates two conversions; whether this occurs in the form of a chain of events (tacit-individual becoming explicit-individual becoming explicit-collective), that is to say, by articulated implicit learning; or whether, hypothetically, the two conversions occur simultaneously. Figure 1.5 articulates the different forms of organizational knowledge in a single representation. More particularly, the accent is on the conversion of organizational knowledge and on the dynamics of organizational knowledge creation.

We have up to now presented and questioned prevailing ideas of current knowledge theory. We will now try to regroup the different forms knowledge takes. The aim of this summary is to establish a reference matrix which will enable the comparison of case analysis results with existing theoretical ideas.

In Figure 1.6, transitions between modes of knowledge are indicated by arrows, acknowledging the relevant works to which these may be attributed (for example, 'extension' refers to Nonaka and Hedlund, 1991). Two new transitions are introduced. The first I have entitled 'conscience', with reference to the passage from unconscious knowledge to knowledge of which we are aware (from tacit-individual to explicit-individual). For the reverse transition I have used the term 'assimilation'. In opposition to the idea of tacit knowledge as being purely

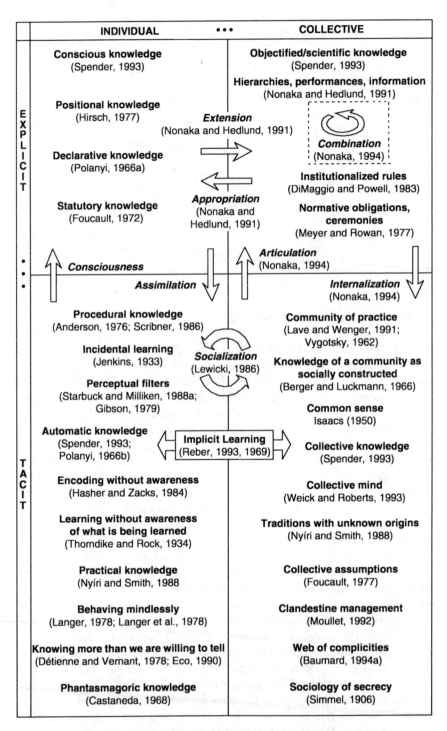

Figure 1.6 *The diversity of tacit and explicit knowledge embodiments in organizations*

automatic, I have included (at the bottom of the tacit-collective classification) some forms of tacit knowledge that are not necessarily
unconscious; these signify the difference between 'knowing more than
one can express' (Polanyi, 1966a) and 'knowing more than one wants to
say'. These works are concerned with 'clandestine management' and the
sociology of the implicit-collective, wherein interlocutors employ tacit
allusions and tacit references to suggest knowledge without making it
explicit.

'LOOPING' THROUGH KNOWING MODES   Figure 1.6 illustrates the
richness of the knowledge dynamic within the organization. It may
be read in a number of ways. As well as showing that there is no
knowledge which is free from the dynamics of its own transitions and
conversions, in reading the table we can follow the movements of
organizational knowledge. The organization's objective and collective
representations of its knowledge; its hierarchies, its performances, and its
information (at the top right of the table), will be *appropriated* by
individuals (at the top left of the table) – enabling them at once to
express statutory knowledge, and to become aware of the role this plays
in the organization, and to 'position' themselves with regard to these
explicit indicators *vis-à-vis* their peers. These actors are then going to
assimilate their explicit role in the organization into their personal and
tacit perceptual filter (at the bottom left of the table). This assimilation
accomplished, they will act according to forms linked to their role, but
without being consciously aware of these forms (coding without being
aware of it). It is because of this assimilation that they will be able to
learn *implicitly* to integrate themselves into a workgroup and to participate in the socialization necessary to establish the collective behaviour
of the organization (bottom right). But in order to ensure the smooth
running of this community of practice, actors will each then *articulate*
their particular singular and tacit knowledge in a collective codification,
enabling them to position themselves according to common objectives
(return to top right).

And so we have come full circle: we have returned to management
tools, to the collective measurement of production. From there, we can
head off towards a new assimilation of the role of each actor, then pass
by routine, move on to automatic knowledge then, by collective organization, to new social norms, which will quickly become institutionalized. These are the dynamics that are studied in the remainder of this
work (see Figure 1.6).

Conclusion

Why do we create and accumulate knowledge? How do we realize this
creation and this accumulation? Several elements can be brought in to

Table 1.1   *Organizational knowledge*

	Traditional theories	Nonaka (1990–94)
What is organizational knowledge?	A feeling of belonging (Curle, 1972) An unconscious scheme or schema (Goleman, 1985) Simultaneous representations (Watzlawick, 1984) Belief derived from information (Dretske, 1981) A psychological economy (Jones, 1975) A source of power (Zand, 1981; Crozier and Friedberg, 1980)	It is made up of four types of knowledge: – tacit and individual, – tacit and collective, – explicit and individual, – explicit and collective. It is dynamic.
Why do organizations accumulate knowledge?	To solve problems (Cyert and March, 1963) To assert predominance (Teece, 1987; Winter, 1987) To manipulate the environment (Kotter, 1979) To learn and unlearn (Hedberg, 1981)	The organization's object is to create knowledge (Nonaka and Kenney, 1991). Knowledge is at the centre of the organizational dynamic.
How do organizations create knowledge?	Through intrusions into their environment (Wilensky, 1967b) By strategizing with the same information as their competitors (Starbuck, 1992b) By creating links and discovering incongruities (Jones, 1975) By being informal, non-systematic (Fahey and King, 1977) By obeying local rationality (Cyert and March, 1963; Berry, 1983) By creating consensual knowledge on the one hand and peripheral knowledge on the other (Schwenk and Lyles, 1992) By using a bounded rationality (Cyert and March, 1963) By being either passive or generative of their environment (Weick, 1979)	They obtain their knowledge either through socialization or through appropriation of collective explicit knowledge. They can then effect combinations of their explicit knowledge, or articulations of their tacit knowledge. Socialization, combination, exteriorization and internalization are the mechanisms of knowledge creation.

the *why* and the *how* of organizational knowledge. Table 1.1 summarizes the major points.

From these first observations, I have presented an integrative model of organizational knowledge. The different knowledge forms analysed have been united in the framework of a summary matrix.[1] It remains for us now to observe this matrix 'in action', and to establish connections between the various modes of knowing included in it.

Note

1 I have based this particularly on the analyses of Nonaka (1990a, 1992, 1994); Teece (1987), Spender (1993), Baumard and Spender (1995), Winter (1987) and Reber (1993).

2

Tormented Knowledge

Knowing is almost the opposite of existing.

Georges Poulet

We have no other possibility than the impossible.

Georges Bataille

'It's beyond my control'

Behaviour in the face of the unpredictable

The life of an organization is permeated with unforeseen events that ruffle the equanimity of its decision-makers. We have only to be confronted with an event not familiar to us to feel nonplussed, at a loss as to how to act. Such a phenomenon is not restricted to individuals, however, and when its compass stretches to include the greater part of an organization we can describe the organization as 'puzzled'. There are various degrees of 'puzzlement'. For example, the unexpected loss of a market will no doubt provoke great distress, while the failure of a market entry attempt will give rise to a less agitated reaction.

Here I have singled out two examples from opposite ends of the continuum that extends from total surprise to non-surprise, or expectation. Total surprise is that which disconcerts actors immediately and unilaterally, whereas non-surprise is the progressive – emergent – advent of an unsettling situation. The first belongs to the realm of the unforeseeable, and the second to that of the unforeseen. Our first question is the following: 'What behaviour does one observe in a puzzled organization?' In this the moot point is: 'Does unforeseeability modify behaviour?'

I begin my analysis with a detour by way of the extreme, into human and natural catastrophes. This represents a concern on my part to differentiate between organizations puzzled by events over which they have no control, and organizations disorientated by events whose genesis they themselves have brought about. Natural catastrophes are the territory of the unpredictable. While we may estimate the probability of their advent, we can neither prevent their arrival nor modify their course as they unfold. Human catastrophes, on the other hand, are not unpredictable but unforeseen. Their advent stems from human error, a hapless admixture of events in which actors, as viable thinking and acting beings, have not noticed the threatening evolution, and have perhaps even accelerated its realization. What concerns us here is not what the actors 'did not notice' – because in this case there would be no ambiguity – but what actors, even while having noticed, were incapable of identifying as a threat: because they could not make any clear sense of it, because they were overtaken by the ambiguity of events.

Disaster situations have the advantage of presenting us with dynamic ambiguity: if one does not act, one does not survive. They tolerate neither a 'wait-and-see' policy, nor the maintenance of the status quo. Disaster situations enable us to approach our concept differently, no longer in terms of a 'blocking' reality, but in terms of behaviour dynamics and the mobilization of knowledge. To understand their mechanisms we must plunge headlong into the harshest of situations in order to retrace events, and attempt to follow knowledge transformations as the situation gets more and more disconcerting.

AN ILLUSTRATION: A TORNADO IN ARKANSAS   The tornadoes that regularly sweep the American continent are violent and inescapable phenomena, and the scientific and sociological works on the subject abundant and rich.[1] For our purposes we have chosen to recount the passage of a tornado in Arkansas in 1952, selected because the sociological data amassed on it appeared sufficiently dense and detailed.[2]

At Little Rock that Friday evening the sky darkened and a violent gale set in. In 1952, telecommunication systems were little developed in rural zones, and only a third of the population were lucky enough to receive advance warning. We are going to examine the behaviour of the two-thirds of the population warned by the tornado itself. In the panic, people try to shelter by huddling in corners. Houses give way before the storm, as walls collapse or fly off. Many homes are simply blown away. It is impossible to understand what is going on as everything happens so quickly; in the commotion, all that can be made out is the immediate environment: the closest piece of furniture, a section of wall still standing, the grasping hand of a loved one. Striving to retain self-control, landmarks linked to the familiarity of home and family become the only points of reference. Everyone tries to act swiftly, to take refuge in whatever place seems the most secure. Later, victims recall 'not having had time to think', reacting 'by relying on memory'. They were no longer seeing, but knowing.

In the midst of the tornado people see only their immediate environment. Paradoxically, their behaviour rarely becomes uncontrolled. We can, in fact, identify 'islands of certainty' in the behaviour of every one of the families questioned. People managed to successfully orientate themselves, even though the electricity was cut, yet there was no time to bring any strategies into play to achieve this. A tornado, as John O'Toole points out in *Tornado! 84 Minutes, 94 Lives*, moves at such a speed (crossing a state in less than an hour and a half) that its passage through a single home takes only a matter of seconds, a minute at most (O'Toole, 1993).

IN LESS THAN A MINUTE, CHAOS   While awareness of such a phenomenon is immediate, there is insufficient time available for any rationalization of the situation; behaviour is thus shaped by instinctive reflexes (and in this it approaches 'animal instinct') and guided by unconscious repertoires of actions.[3] We can, however, distinguish between the responses of two categories of victims: those who are living through the phenomenon for the first time, and those who have already been through a similar experience. While the first apprehend the phenomenon in an entirely instinctive manner, the second seem to repeat behaviour they have already had the opportunity to test out. Because of the disaster's emotional impact, though, neither group of victims was later able to be explicit about their behaviour during the tornado's onslaught (according to Fritz and Marks's 1954 study, almost 10 per cent of the men and 20 per cent of the women were still in a state of shock, incapable of movement or speech, half an hour after the tornado's passage). Nevertheless, we can identify a certain 'rationality' in what they were able to report: hugging up against supporting walls, sheltering under tables, protecting loved ones. The number of victims – only 7 per cent of those in the impact zone were seriously hurt – was relatively low in comparison with the magnitude of the material damage. Six hundred homes were entirely destroyed, and more than 800 seriously damaged.

When disasters are sudden and unilateral, organizational mobilization should be rapid, adequate, efficient and precise. Reality is only too often far from this. Allen Barton, in *Communities in Disaster: A Sociological Analysis of Collective Stress Situations* (1969), notes that in normal situations individual behaviour is regulated 'by social roles which guide it and make it predictable to others, and equally by emotions and personal preferences which will perhaps be predictable on the whole but can vary dramatically from one individual to another' (1969: 126). Although in an emergency, reality is no longer what it was in the framework of its routine social construction, even in the thick of the general disorder we can identify very coordinated, very consistent, subsystems working to modify the erratic and uncontrollable mass phenomena taking place. As people attempt to coordinate their actions, we witness a tremendous oscillation of improvised behaviour, coherent then incoherent, divergent and convergent, within a time span that leaves little scope in which to formulate understanding. 'Organizations can have difficulties in making decisions and directing personnel in such unexpected conditions. . . . They cannot define the situation when they are asked to intervene' (Barton, 1969: 129). The competence map becomes confused and, as Barton continues, 'the establishment of valid symbols of competence becomes difficult' (p. 143). Cyert and March's bounded rationality has become a microcosmic rationality. Organizational prescriptions based on institutional values are pushed aside to make way for more basic priorities such as survival, protection of a space, or protection of someone close. 'There is a difficulty in coordinating activities under the pressure of emergency, together with the rupture of usual channels of communication. . . . Some organizations will simply attempt to furnish a taskforce, while others will try to define a role for themselves with regard to the disaster' (Barton, 1969: 163).

Suddenness and physical and social proximity to the disaster all condition individual and organizational responses. In his study of Social Darwinism in the United States, Hofstadter observes that the social estrangement of the poor, brought on by factors such as ethnic or educational differences, together with their corresponding physical distance from major urban centres, serves to justify the absence of reply to the growing human disaster of poverty in the US (1955: 10). Poor people were thus, in this Darwinist period, considered 'negligent, obstinate towards change, ineffective, unreasonable and imprudent'. Similarly, although to a lesser scale, the perception of disasters occurring within an organization can prove to be very 'selective', according to the social, hierarchical or educational schisms that divide members of the organization. Notwithstanding, contact with victims has been found to profoundly alter this perception (Barton, 1969: 259).

In situations of extreme emergency, and in the context of survival, two phenomena are therefore observed: (1) a tacit organization between individuals instinctively reappears; and (2) the social organization of individuals remains ever present. The tacit regains the upper hand over the formalized. In any case, the speed of the phenomenon leaves neither space nor time for commentary or rationalization.

Human and natural catastrophes do not limit themselves to physical devastation, to material havoc; they also act upon the social, cognitive and behavioural structures of communities. The psychology of those who have lived through them is deeply altered, and often remains so throughout their life. Most of the survivors of the bombing of Hiroshima 'believe that they still suffer from an "atomic illness" that has left them permanently weakened and accelerated their aging'(Barton, 1969: 33), yet measurement of this proves contentious: the proportion of cancer-related deaths is higher in Hiroshima than in the rest of Japan, but only by 20 per cent. While this is a substantial figure, the number of cancer victims still bears little correspondence to the far higher number of people who complain of debility. A psychological study carried out more than 20 years after the atomic explosion, however, showed that survivors still suffered from a loss of faith in the very structure of their existence (Lifton, 1967: 482). A tacit repository of interpretation and behaviour inscribes itself permanently on the consciousness of everybody involved.

In this first example the advent of the disorientating situation is sudden and its source exogenous. During the tornado individuals do think in terms of the knowable, but at that moment the knowable is limited to what is already known tacitly – the spatial organization of a room, or an unfolding and instinctive coordination of the small organization that is the bewildered family. For want of the ability to construct knowledge appropriate to the situation, it is mustered from the unconscious, from the primary (tacit) knowledge whose articulation lies in a search for familiar elements. While the explicit dimension is in a state of pandemonium, it is in the unconscious and tacit dimension that individuals seek and find the resources they need to meet the confusion.

Behaviours that lead to the unforeseen: *Challenger*

Works in the field of management studies have shown a strong interest in natural and human disasters. The Bhopal Union Carbide disaster of 1984, the explosion of the space shuttle *Challenger* in 1986, the 1977 aerial catastrophe involving the collision of two Boeing aircraft (KLM and Pan Am), the earthquake in the San Francisco Bay area in 1989, the tragedy of KAL flight 007 – destroyed by the Soviet Aerial Defence in 1983 – and, more recently, floods in the American Midwest and the attack on the World Trade Center in New York are some of the natural or human disasters that have opened the way for a deeper understanding of crisis management.[4]

THINK THE UNTHINKABLE The tragedy of the *Challenger* space shuttle explosion on 28 January 1986 shows us the complex, devious and furtive logic of the elaboration of a disaster. As Starbuck and Milliken remind us:

> Organizations often communicate imperfectly, make errors of judgement, and provide playing fields for control games. Organizations often interpret past successes as evidencing their competence and the adequacy of their procedures, and so they try to lock their behaviours into existing patterns. Organizations often try to generalize from their experiences. Organizations often evolve gradually and incrementally into unexpected states . . . [such are the effects] of repeated success, gradual acclimatization, and the differing responsibilities of engineers and managers . . . [that] it is easy to believe that success demonstrates competence, whereas failure reveals deficiencies [under the simple presupposition that experience should result in better performance]. . . . Better, however, may mean either more safely or less so, depending on the goals and values that guide efforts to learn. If better means more cheaply, or quicker, or closer to schedule, then experience may not rise the probability of safe operation. (1988b: 320–3)[5]

In the case of the *Challenger* tragedy:

> As successful launches accumulated, these managers appear gradually to have lost their fear of design problems and grown more confident of success . . . Thiokol's engineers based the design of the shuttle's SRB [solid rocket booster] on the Air Force's Titan III because of the latter's reliability. The Titan's case was made of steel segments, with the joints between segments being sealed by rubber O-rings. The Titan's O-rings had occasionally been eroded by the hot gases inside the engine, but Thiokol's engineers did not regard this erosion as significant. Nevertheless, to make the shuttle's SRB safer, Thiokol's engineers put a second, presumably redundant, O-ring into each joint. (1988b: 324)

From this small change there followed a non-linear series of redesigns requested by NASA, beginning with the thickening, then the readjustment of the joints. In November 1981, an O-ring in one of Titans' joints was eroded by hot gases:

> but this event made little impression: NASA's personnel did not discuss it at the next flight-readiness review and they did not report it upward to top management. The three flights during 1982 produced no more evidence of O-ring problems. (1988b: 325)

Little more thought was given to the problem of the potential rotation of the joints. In 1982, an engineer proposed a new design that would inhibit rotation but, as the proposal would have added 300 kilograms (600 pounds) to each Solid Rocket Booster, NASA's engineers decided to continue using the old joint design, in conjunction with a new case material: carbon filaments in epoxy resin. The changes proposed by Thiokol thereafter were aimed at improving the rocket's efficiency; they in fact modified the structure, the form and the power of the shuttle, indirectly putting more pressure on the joints: 'but the reclassification document, written by a Thiokol engineer, implied the risk was small'. Subsequent alterations, in regard to the joints, comprised of adjustments to their width in accordance with 'acceptable erosion'. As testing of the SRB continued so did the erosion of the rings, without any adverse effects on the success of the shuttle flights. By September 1984, the idea of 'allowable erosion' had been admitted. In other words, in rendering the problem explicit, the normality of its existence was also accepted, a normality that was institutionalized without delay. Once the presence of erosion was normalized, it no longer presented any incongruity. Despite several initiatives directed at changing the joints, or proposing alternative designs, little by little the idea became installed that the file was closed.

> Success breeds confidence and fantasy. When an organization succeeds, its managers usually attribute this success to themselves, or at least to their

organization, rather than to luck. The organization's members grow more confident, of their own abilities, of their managers' skill, and of their organization's existing programs and procedures. They trust the procedures to keep them apprised of developing problems, in the belief that these procedures focus on the most important events and ignore the least significant ones. (1988b: 330)

NASA was the administration that had put men on the moon, and returned them safely to Earth, it was the administration whose leitmotiv had historically been 'We can do anything.' On top of this, after a quarter of a century of rocket launching experience, there was a widespread belief that the space shuttle had become an 'operational' technology. The devious and furtive logic of disasters seems to be the simple logic of 'thinking in terms of the thinkable.' Despite the accuracy, the precision and the repetition of the scientific work carried out, the decision to categorize the risk associated with the joints as 'acceptable' seems to be based more on the common meaning of the word 'acceptable' than on any scientific definition. There is no equivalent to the 'acceptable' in other areas of exact science – it is a value judgement, not a measure. This suggests that, if 'reality is hidden by measures' (Berry, 1983), measures too may be sometimes hidden by reality. The road to disaster in the *Challenger* shuttle case was clearly of social construction.

The notion of 'acceptability' was, in effect, a social construction developed in the context of an organization in which the perception of risk thresholds had been modified by the routinization of the mastery of a complex technology. If the O-ring problem had been brought to the attention of an untrained public it would quite probably have provoked an animated reaction. In a different social context it would have been found entirely 'unacceptable' to launch space shuttles with joints that risked giving way, whatever the level of this risk. The same phenomenon holds true for nuclear plants, in which reality is differently constructed according to whether one works there or is simply an outside observer. In many human disasters, those accused of negligence very often plead 'not guilty' without being dishonest with themselves or with the public.

That which appears negligent from outside its operational social construct could quite reasonably not have appeared so from within it. What from one side seems to have been an incredible freedom and disorder is quite likely to have been only a very slight variation of the routine order 'from the other side of the mirror'.

Ad hoc triumph or organized débâcle?

In the preceding discussion we have looked at two very different puzzling (and disconcerting) situations: one in which the actors had no control over events, and the other brought on by the actors themselves. In each of these cases, for each of these puzzled organizations, there is a 'reality' which eludes the actors. Within the framework of these two events we have studied the comportment of puzzled organizations: family units, towns and emergency assistance organizations in the first case, and NASA in the second. We have seen how, in the face of general confusion, people have organized themselves, garnering what knowledge they have and constructing new knowledge in provision for any future analogous situations. We have witnessed how people can generate disconcerting situations by 'constructing' a reality (the notion of the 'acceptability' of the space shuttle joints) which then moves beyond their control. Faced with disorder and a reality which they have difficulty making sense of, they try to master the situation: they try to understand this puzzling reality so as to manage their confusion and re-establish an 'organized' reality. This question of a 'puzzling reality' leads us to the more fundamental question of reality itself.

Is not all reality by nature 'puzzling'? Is not the distinctive feature of the action of 'organizing' the conferral of sense on to the puzzling? We could avoid this question, and equally avoid tackling the definition of reality, but in so doing we would be leaving ourselves open to criticism from all sides. Adherents of social construction, drawing inspiration from Berger and Luckmann, could argue that we do not know what we are studying, all reality being a social construction, all puzzling situations being themselves the object and the outcome of such a construction. Others would see in our puzzled organizations temporarily unstable states within a stable whole. But in our case studies we observe managers who have feelings of impotence when confronted with puzzling situations. They are engaged in a dynamic of order and disorder, in which they seek a way out, an 'honourable' exit from an oppressive situation. It is this dynamic of stability and instability, inertia and mutation, that we want to examine here. Is it part of the nature of organizations themselves? Is it a social construction? (If so, order and disorder would not exist as absolutes, but only as actors' different perceptions of *degrees* of order or disorder: 'What to you is disorder is perhaps order for me. What to me is order is perhaps disorder for you'.)

We should point out at once that the trap – and all the seduction – of social construction lies in its undeniability. One will find no area, in those inaccurate sciences that are the social sciences, wherein the constructivist approach cannot interpose itself. There is no situation in which we cannot say: 'What is true for you perhaps is not for me.' To all attempts at rationalization or the isolation of objective knowledge, social constructivists can raise their hand and say: 'How do you define this? It is entirely possible that this is only a social construction.' Yes, 'ambiguity' can definitely be a social construction. According to our various degrees of experience, the weight of our expertise, the familiarity of our environment, what is ambiguous for me may not be so for you.

To the constructivism that sees order and disorder as two inter-changeable constructions, interchangeable according to the construct in which one is placed, we will contrast another paradigm, that of chaos theory. Here too we could have let sleeping dogs lie; avoided its evocation, passed by any attempt at its explanation, and continued the study of our 'puzzled organizations' without, for that matter, as much as a mention of order and disorder, or of objective reality nor con-structed reality. We were not forced to discuss the existence of any sphere wider than the field of our investigation. To sum up, our unit of analysis is the organization, and we could have been content with an organizational horizon for our conclusions.

To contrast these two theories may seem surprising, but do they not propose opposite explanations of reality? It is not our intention here to say that 'this puzzled organization, this ambiguous situation, is con-structed', nor that 'this puzzling situation is chaotic'. The interest in the comparison – or the opposition – is in the common ground of these two theories: they both deal with puzzlement.

Social constructivism studies the actor whose 'relationship to the surrounding environment is everywhere very imperfectly structured with his own biological constitution'; whose 'instinctual organization may be described as underdeveloped, compared with that of the other higher mammals'; whose survival from infancy 'is dependent upon certain social arrangements'; and who 'lacks the necessary biological means to provide stability for human conduct' (Berger and Luckmann, 1966: 47–51). Actors become disorientated when they are out of their social context – without their 'symbolic universe', their institutionalization, their religions. Social construction does not take reality for granted, it places the sociology of knowledge at the centre of organizational phenomena and their comprehension, by calling for 'the systematic accounting of the dialectical relation between the structural realities and the human enterprise of constructing reality-in-history' (Berger and Luckmann, 1966: 186). Chaos theory, on the other hand, shows that a simple relationship that is deterministic but not linear can give rise to a number of very complex relationships at once (Baumol and Benhabib, 1989: 77). In a single instant chaos theory reconciles a puzzling non-linearity with order, with recog-nizable forms – stressing the idea that a change to, say, the fifth decimal point of a single parameter can completely transform the qualitative character of the whole. It hierarchically orders a group of non-linear elements and it reconciles determinism and chance.

This investigation of puzzled organizations is also the construction of a theory in response to my own puzzlement at how to wrestle with ambiguity and how to mobilize knowledge – and what knowledge at what moment? – in order to counter disorientation. What was our perception of light before we discovered that it is at once a wave and a particle in motion? A mysterious phenomenon for some, but symbolic and/or religious for others.

Whereas some could find no satisfactory explanation for it, to others it was entirely explicable. It was a polemic subject, as was 'sound' and 'noise': while some will perceive in the music of Boulez only an agglomeration of 'noise', others, whose ear is perhaps more initiated to this form of expression, will discern a sequence of 'sounds', they will hear 'phrasing' and 'music'. Some writers, the more determinist, will advance the hypothesis that these people possess a 'musical intelligence'. They will even go so far as to suggest that there are multiple intelligences: spatial intelligence ('the ability to form a mental model of a space and to be able to maneuver and operate using this model'); linguistic intelligence (of poets); logical intelligence (and they will not hesitate to accuse Piaget of having studied only this); kinetic intelligence (that 'of dancers, athletes and surgeons'); and interpersonal intelligence (or 'the aptitude to understand others: what motivates them, how they work, and how to work with them') (Gardner, 1993). This theory is definitely disturbing. Although we recognize the interest of introducing the notion of intellectual plurality, we can only be disquieted by the suggestion of superior discrimination that it seems to introduce in the area of the arts.

Defenders of this new theory waste no time in contradicting it elsewhere. To introduce 'musical intelligence' Gardner quotes the following example:

> From when he was three years old, Yehudi Menuhin was always discreetly introduced by his parents into the concerts of the San Francisco Orchestra. The sound of Louis Persinger's violin filled the young child so much that he insisted on having a violin for his birthday, and Louis Persinger as his teacher. He got both. Before he was ten years old, Menuhin was performing on the international scene. (1993: 17)

And the author concludes: 'the musical intelligence of the violinist Yehudi Menuhin was manifest even before he had touched a violin or received any music lessons. His powerful reaction to this particular sound and his rapid progress with the instrument suggests that he had been biologically prepared for this destiny.' Putting aside the questionable Darwinian implications of gracing violin aptitude with a genetic code – which will not fail to shock those who have invested tens of years in learning the instrument – the contradiction is evident. If the violin produces a 'sound' and not a 'noise' to the ear of the young Yehudi, this is simply because he has learnt its language at an age when one learns to speak. That he is attracted by the instrument is no more surprising: it is difficult to abandon a second mother tongue.

This short example only adds weight to the thesis of the constructivists in the polemic of order and disorder. The art of ordering noises into a 'language' – music – is for the young Yehudi a reality constructed by his social environment. Having mastered the language, a number of musical phrases that will seem to the novice to be 'disordered' will for Yehudi be simply phrases that are differently articulated.

The limits to the constructivist interpretation of order and disorder are found in the area of understanding. If one follows constructivist thought through, there can be no objective sense; all meaning must be socially constructed ('what is true for me is perhaps not for you'). If we take a step back and proceed adductively, this means that all meaning must be justifiable in any given social construction that actually exists.[6] In other words, 'All roads lead to Rome', a proposition that equally includes its antithesis: 'No road leads particularly to Rome.' The multiplication of meanings – the multiplication of the real – entails the disappearance of all meaning (Rosset, 1977, 1985, 1991). To take an example that concerns us particularly, if ambiguity is a social construction, which we will not deny, then it is a social construction for everybody. One can therefore speak of 'ambiguity' in general and refer to a single concept. Languages are also social constructions; nevertheless, we may speak the same language.

We can say the same for order and disorder. By taking the initiative, managers create an internal disorder for those who do not share the 'language' of their intervention. In the apparent disorder, in the multiplication of meanings, there perhaps exists the meaning the manager is seeking. For the manager, this 'disorder' would thus have sense. It may be transitory, and the manager's belief in the attraction of the meaning that he or she seeks over other possible meanings will be able to support this transition. Then again, the desired meaning may not appear. The manager's intervention then creates disorder for him or herself. It has not led to the expected results, but in modifying the organizational dynamics it will perhaps have meaning for another manager. In this succession of order for some, disorder for orders, it is difficult to maintain that the organization is following any 'pattern' or 'plan', as chaos theory asserts it is. Is it not, anyway, contradictory for a theory that deals with 'chaos' to rest on the deterministic idea of the existence of defined patterns?

ALLEGORICAL TRAPS   To reply to this question necessitates the avoidance of a classic trap, a trap encountered very often in management literature. The 'chaos' of which mathematicians have elaborated the theory is not the turbulent, incomprehensible, infernal fury that imagination and common sense may suggest. We must differentiate between the allegory that suggests turbulent disorder and the abstraction that tries to decipher the functioning of non-linear dynamic systems.

The definition used by mathematicians to characterize 'their' chaos is: 'a stochastic behaviour that takes place within a determinist system', the said system being called determinist 'when it contains no random exogenous variables'. An observable behaviour – the first stumbling block – in a dynamic system is called 'stochastic' when the transition of this system from one state to another can receive only a probabilistic description, as in the case of that completely random phenomenon, the spin of a roulette wheel. (Although this example could be debated: one remembers the affair at Cannes's Palm Beach Casino, in which two scientists had misappropriated a Cray calculator to predict results: they escaped with several million French francs.)

The aim of chaos theory is therefore – and we are here far from its furious allegory – to reconcile the random and the determined. It attaches itself to observable facts, to that which exact science knows how to manipulate. The first pitfall of its application to management is that many aspects of the organization's world are not observable, other than in their consequences: here we include beliefs, myths, tacit knowledge. The first challenge posed for the theory: can we reconcile the random and the determined in the play of stability and instability of managers' beliefs?

In the context of such a theory, if a system is not chaotic and it has complete knowledge at its disposal it becomes partially foreseeable. But in the organizational domain the question is no longer even posed: the idea of 'complete knowledge', or 'complete information' was abandoned a long time ago. As for a chaotic system, whatever amount of time is spent on accumulating data, it will not give rise to any exact prediction of the system's transition from one state to another. In this case a probabilistic approach is employed; the fact that chaotic systems are unpredictable in the long term is side-stepped by predictions that are more or less exact in the short term.

The idea that simple non-linear dynamic systems could present complex and apparently random behaviours had already been discovered by Poincaré at the beginning of the century. The arrival of computers and powerful calculation capacities in the 1960s was to contribute to a forward leap for the theory. Numerical investigations of models of atmospheric turbulence are an example of this. Lorenz's (1963) example of the fluttering of a butterfly's wing that eventually provokes a storm (after several months and a complex series of transitions between states) is without doubt the most well-known discussion of this phenomenon. While its purpose was to attract attention to the possibility of unsuspected complex relationships between very diverse elements, the article, despite itself, contributed to the encouragement of the allegorical movement in the years following the 1960s. In the same period, another important discovery was made: that of 'strange attractors'. Apparently random behaviours are attracted by one of these cells during a transition in which they remain for a period more or less stable. The 'strangeness' of these attractors comes simply from the particular and regular form of their mathematical modellization.

CHAOTIC TEMPTATION Chaos theory has extended its reach throughout the most varied areas of both the social and the exact sciences. A multidisciplinary team at the Santa Fe Institute has used it to trace an analogy between bacteria colonies and economics, hoping to explain why such complex adaptive systems seem to evolve towards a state lying on the boundaries of order and chaos. Their objective is to reconcile, within an evolutionary theory that takes both living and non-living systems into account, the articulation of linear and non-linear dynamic systems. In doing this they have discovered that molecules organize themselves into auto-reproducing proteins. These initial observations have also allowed them to establish the common characteristics of complex adaptive systems: they have found that these systems are 'self-managing' – that is to say, they consist of a number of 'agents' who act independently of each other, with no guidance from any central control. For example, within the human brain there are no 'super-neutrons', nor are there any parts of the brain that control the action of the brain's neurons. However, and this is the second characteristic, these 'agents' (neutrons) are capable of acting in cooperation: they seem to act as communities. Thus, a neuron outside the complex neuron system cannot accomplish the superior order of task that can be achieved collectively: that of human intelligence. Chaos theory is just as beguiling as that of social construction. While the one opposes any attempt at determinism with a wise relativity, the other opposes any attempt at reductionism with a broad holism. One can thus identify numerous chaotic temptations.[7]

Chaotic temptation arises with phenomena for which we have been unable to provide any simple models that allow for prediction. It tries to find answers to the mysteries of economic cycles, heartbeats, financial directions or technological breakdowns. 'The way in which scientists identify a system's prediction diagrams has been turned around completely. Instead of trying to break a system down into its components, and analysing the behaviour of these components separately – as in the reductionist tradition that has so influenced Taylor – many scientists have had to learn to approach phenomena in a holistic manner' (Freedman, 1992: 30). Rather than envisaging overall order as the *sum* of a number of particular orders (or separate mini-systems), the chaotic approach has the merit of considering the emergence of order as the indissociable *interaction* of particular orders. Chaos theory is most suited to complex systems in which the number of 'agents' is indefinite or indefinable. If the reservoir of agents is infinite or unknown, 'agents are not locked, in any permanent manner, into behaviours that were previously useful but have since become obsolete, which helps the system to adapt to change' (Freedman, 1992: 32).

If we try to employ a chaotic approach with a known and finite number of agents, we will come up against the philosophical question of the infinitely small and the infinitely large: in other words, that the finite does not exist, that there is in the infinitely small always another internal dimension, as there is another external dimension to the infinitely large. Another characteristic common to both social construction and chaos theory is the strong philosophical defence that both proffer to sceptics. On the side of social construction, this defence is existentialist; we are always able to say: 'This is not a pipe.' On the side of chaos theory, the defence is the limitations of comprehension, which presupposes the *de facto* existence, in a system whose dynamics are apparently linear, of a supplementary dimension in which chaos theory can conceal its validity. In essence, chaos theory shows that a simple relationship that is determinist but not linear can over time produce a very complex pattern. Thus, to prove that chaos appears or does not appear in economic phenomena is a speculative business. This enables us to draw not an analogy but a bridge between chaos theory and social construction: the chaotic reading can itself be a social construction.

This is not a difficult assertion to make, however (because, as we have already noted, the demonstration that a reality is not a social construction is a difficult art). What is undoubtedly interesting in 'chaotic temptation' is what it says by way of exposition about that which Foucault termed 'knowledge archaeology' (1972), for the social sciences in general, and management especially. Most people 'feel lost in the organization which they form part of. Managers are inundated with information from all sides, with too rapid changes, and too many conflictual demands', and this incapacity to confront complexity is 'the direct result of the traditional scientific approaches of a management . . . [that is] heir to Taylorism and nineteenth-century science' (Freedman, 1992: 33). Thus, chaos theory opens our eyes to the compartmentalized reality of management today. It states that each element is part of a whole, and that this whole replies to a non-linear dynamics. But we should not leave it at this, at the recording of stochastic phenomena in the belief of having uncovered all. This should encourage us to think: 'reality is elsewhere, reality is above us, reality is underneath us, reality is larger than this'.

IN THE ABSENCE OF EXPLANATIONS   This exploration of chaos and social construction has not been done without an ulterior motive. For Berger and Luckmann, there also exists an order above order; that of the symbolic universe that 'links men with their predecessors and their successors in a meaningful totality'. Only in this way can we make sense of the entire society of mankind: 'Particular institutions and their roles are legitimated by locating them in a comprehensively meaningful world. For example, the political order is legitimated by reference to a cosmic order of power and justice, and political roles are legitimated as representations of these cosmic principles.' Thus, 'the legitimization of the institutional order is also faced with the ongoing necessity of keeping chaos at bay. *All* social reality is precarious. *All* societies are constructions in the face of chaos.' And 'if man in society is a world-constructor, this is made possible by his constitutionally given world-openness, which already implies the conflict between order and chaos. Human existence is, *ab initio*, an ongoing externalization. As man externalizes himself, he constructs the world *into* which he externalizes himself' (Berger and Luckmann, 1966: 103).

The fundamental concept of social construction is then not completely at odds with that of chaos. We externalize ourselves in the worlds we build, within which we externalize ourselves anew, and again we build new worlds, within which to externalize ourselves. We find too in the idea of a socially constructed world the concept of patterns repeated to infinity. We also find a stochastic dimension – we are unable to predict what the next construction will be, to foresee the next world that will be created – and a determinism – the certainty that other worlds will be constructed within the new constructions.

Chaos theory could itself have seized upon social construction. Everything depends on the actual instant where one situates Berger and Luckmann's *ab initio*. One could quite easily consider the construction of reality as commencing not from the first instants of life, but before; that the formation of the cells and neurons are equally movements of construction. The construction of reality fits as much into chaos theory as chaos theory can fit into a theory of construction. Drawn together by the same fundamental hypothesis of universality, the two theories can however diverge when it comes to defining 'ambiguity'.

Organizations leave greater room for chance, unexpected connections and unpredictability than one might expect. They are complex entities, and this complexity can be baffling – anarchic and structured elements coexist, and in fact complement each other: 'The separation between manager as planner and organizer on the one hand, and as hesitant actor on the other, is artificial. Reality is more complex, interactive and dynamic than that presented in reduction models. . . . Reality contains elements of rationality, formality, and order mixed in with intuition, informality and disorder' (Thiétart and Forgues, 1993: 8). A chaotic conception of ambiguity would then be a repetition to infinity of patterns of ambiguity within the organization, and the chaos theorist's response to this ambiguity would be to approach it at the level of the dynamics of the organization as a whole – holistically. There is no such thing as isolated ambiguity; even those patterns which can be distinguished in the tangle of the organizational dynamics are transitory, existing in the same way as we can, with time, recognize in a non-linear dynamics the repetition of 'states' of like form. Such an approach would no doubt entail a recommendation such as Nonaka's: 'for an organization to continually evolve, it has to give some freedom to its constituent units, to generate creative conflicts between them' (1988a: 64). Another 'chaotic' perception of ambiguity lies in the potentiality of major, and far-reaching, consequences from a minor event (as in Lorenz's example of the flutter of a butterfly's wing provoking a tornado several months later); the ambiguity emerges from the impossibility of determining the consequences of an action, and so of choosing between two actions.

Organizational members are not completely incapable of knowing what tomorrow will bring, yet not only are they often surprised by events, the causes of which they are ignorant, they are also frequently confronted with the dilemma of having to make choices without being able to ascertain the full consequences of their decisions.

Conclusion

In the first part of this chapter two types of behaviour were discussed with regard to puzzled organizations: 'thinking within the thinkable' and 'thinking within the recognizable' (see Table 2.1). When the origins of the ambiguity and the puzzling situation are exogenous, and surprise people (as with the advent of the tornado), repertories of actions are brought into play which take refuge in the recognizable. However, when the ambiguity and the puzzling situation are endogenous to the organization, the repertories of actions invoked seek security in the thinkable; in the institutionalized, the recurrent, the usual and the constructed.

The analysis made in the first part of this chapter led us to consider why a situation, a reality, can be puzzling. To emulate a dialectic, we juxtaposed a relativistic conception of reality (social construction) with a more deterministic conception (non-linear dynamics).

There are a number of lessons to be learnt from this comparison, relevant to our study of puzzled organizations. From the constructivist approach we recognize that ambiguity can be socially constructed, that is, the same event can be perceived as ambiguous or clear according to the social reality in which one is situated. We realize also that

Table 2.1 *Behaviour of puzzled organizations*

	Puzzling situations	
	Sudden and exogenous: Tornados	Progressive and endogenous: *Challenger*
Behaviour observed in puzzled organizations	Tacit knowledge of spatial organization (habitat) enables orientation	Excess of confidence in behavioural patterns validated by the past
	Instinctive reflexes and improvised behaviour	Gradual acclimatization to the puzzling situation
	Familiar elements sought	Successive adjustments made
	Loss of faith in structures of existence	Social construction tending to 'normalize' disturbing events as 'acceptable'
	Islands of certitude	
	Simple rules	Excess of confidence in procedure
	Social and physical proximity condition responses	Circumvention, avoidance of disruptive events
Overall	Thinking within the recognizable	Thinking within the thinkable

Table 2.2　*Puzzling realities?*

	Through social construction	Through non-linear dynamics
How can we explain why reality may be puzzling?	All disconcerting situations are the result of a construction 'What is ambiguous for you may not be so for me', and vice versa (as with the music of Boulez) Language plays an important role (for example Yehudi Menuhin) Our relationship with our environment is by nature imperfectly structured (Berger and Luckmann, 1966) We are always disorientated outside our symbolic universe, our institutions, our symbols Societies are constructions in the face of chaos	A simple event may in time provoke very complex events (as with Lorenz's butterfly provoking a storm) Complex systems, which appear puzzling, can conceal an overall dynamic (as with molecular auto-reproduction: Ruthen, 1993) A system cannot be reduced to its component parts. The dynamics of the whole must be considered (Freedman, 1992)
What lessons are there in this for the study of puzzled organizations?	A sober relativity is conferred upon the interpretation All social reality is precarious. Judgements, repertoires of actions, perhaps even knowledge itself, can be dependent on constructed realities Language, social reality, and differences in representation, must be taken into account in the interpretation of observed phenomena	A 'holistic' approach to events is encouraged A systematic search for a global dynamics must be observed Every element is part of a whole; reality is always larger than it seems Models explaining the order/ disorder dialectic do exist within the determinist tradition

judgements, repertoires of actions, perhaps even knowledge itself, can be dependent on constructed realities.

We can also recall the example of the booster joints in the *Challenger* space shuttle, whose defects had been perceived as 'acceptable' by NASA engineers. From the study of non-linear dynamics we learn that a minor event can serve as the catalyst to very complex events, as in the example of the movement of a butterfly's wing provoking a storm.

Finally, this second chapter invites us to step back and consider observed reality (Table 2.2). Organizations may be puzzled because they perceive events in an ambiguous manner, or because they attribute to them a perplexing character that another organization would perhaps not have felt. We are also encouraged to incorporate the reality we observe into a larger reality; to uncover a broader dynamics that is not contained within the observable unit.[8]

Notes

1 For a numerical modelization see Wicker (1990); for discussions of relations between surface and structure, see Forbes (1978, 1979); for modelizations of hazardous phenomena, Coats (1985) and Hughes and Jefferson (1993); for studies on mobile homes see Jackson (1978); for an analysis of collective reactivity see Fischer (1992); and for a historical analysis see Brown and Webb (1941).

2 For the details of this case study we are indebted to Fritz and Marks's comprehensive work, *Human Reactions in Disaster Situations* (1954).

3 See Griffin (1982, 1984), for analyses of human reflexive behaviour.

4 Carney (1993); Mino (1983); Mitroff and Pauchant (1990a, 1990b); Ramanan (1992); Schut (1993); Schwartz (1987); Shrivastava (1985); Shrivastava and Siomkos (1989); Tranter (1989); Weick (1990).

5 This and the following discussion of the 1986 space shuttle *Challenger* explosion have been taken, with the kind permission of the authors, from Starbuck and Milliken (1988b).

6 'Adductively' refers to adductive thinking, i.e. a non-formal induction process, which permits the creation of an interpretation that corroborates a small number of pieces of evidence.

7 Among the domains in which chaos theory has tried to supply an explanation, we can cite: the development of psychological models of auto-managing systems (Barton, 1994); systems of instruction and education (You, 1993); entrepreneurship (Bygrave, 1993); the interpretation of literary works, through the opposition of contingency theory to chaos theory in George Orwell's *Nineteen Eighty-Four* (Argyros, 1993); explanation of the place of knowledge-placebos in the dynamics of knowledge (Kiresuk, 1993); the understanding of the fascinatingly erratic character of the beating of the human heart (Denton et al., 1990); organizational survival and strategic decision (Priesmeyer and Baik, 1989; Stacey, 1993; Toma and Gheorghe, 1992; Vinten, 1992); prediction of financial evolutions (Tvede, 1992); human resource management (Bailyn, 1993); explanation of economic directions and the achievement of equilibrium (Carrier, 1992; Griffith and Southworth, 1990; Savit, 1989); and explanations for technological breakdowns (Stambler, 1991).

8 When we personalize the organization by qualifying it as 'puzzled', we encourage a reading that attaches a cognitive phenomenon to the organizational. In this we do not intend to presume the existence of a collective cognition, even though that reading could be seen as *implicit*.

3

From Tacit to Explicit, the Conjectural Patterns of Knowing

The range of what we think and do
Is limited by what we fail to notice
And because we fail to notice
That we fail to notice
There is little we can do
To change
Until we notice
How failing to notice
Shapes our thoughts and deeds.

R.D. Laing

From abstract generalization to conjecture

In the second chapter we explored different types of puzzling situations in which organizations can find themselves. We looked at a natural disaster (a tornado in Arkansas) and a human disaster (the explosion of NASA's *Challenger* shuttle). Certain behavioural traits appear to be characteristic of puzzling situations: a loss of control or effectiveness, the privilege given in emergency to conjectural knowledge, the impossibility of defining a role for oneself, and acclimatization to an environment involving a possible risk of catastrophe. With the *Challenger* shuttle as an example, we discovered how the notion of acceptability, as used in relation to the joints that were to cause the explosion, was a social construction. This raised the question of whether ambiguity is itself a social construction. Finally, ad hoc triumph or organized débâcle, what is the reality?

This chapter is devoted to a delineation of the various forms knowledge may take, and we will later consider how these forms of knowledge are solicited in ambiguous situations. The first part of the chapter discusses knowledge's various epistemological dimensions, while the second part explores its tacit dimension.

We have only to call to mind Plato, Descartes, Locke or Hume to appreciate knowledge's breadth and diversity.[1] The search for knowledge has often been associated with the search for truth, animating a 1,000-year-old debate between empiricists and champions of the existence of a truth superior to that of experience. When the search for knowledge takes place in the territorial waters of the organization it of course becomes far more contextual than any absolute search for truth – in fact, within organizational reality truths are generated by those beliefs that actors are most committed to. Knowledge must then be understood as a *continuum*, and not as a dichotomy between the search for truth and the adjustment of beliefs.

For many people, knowledge refers to that which the positivist sciences define: knowledge is a model of reality, it is a sound representation of the world, tested and validated against the real; objective in the sense that it is independent of people. Yet a number of alternative definitions emerge once we recognize the weakness of this positivist approach, when we recognize that *uncommon* forms of knowledge exist, when we admit that the very term 'experience' papers over its own character, which is intuitive, tacit and unique. How, in a positivist approach, can we describe the 'lesson' we may learn from being involved in a road accident? Does not our knowledge of this accident differ from the general knowledge we have of the collision of two moving vehicles?

In a firm, will not the failure of a marketing venture be lived and translated in terms of 'knowledge' differently by the commercial superintendent who had been in charge of it than by his or her colleagues? Similarly, the experiencing of successive setbacks in the development of a new technique will result in a different knowledge for the engineer responsible for this development than for others who are less implicated. To reply to this knowledge dilemma, the Greek philosophers distinguished between four forms of knowledge:[2]

- *episteme* (abstract generalization)
- *techne* (capability, capacity to accomplish tasks)
- *phronesis* (practical and social wisdom)
- and *mètis* (conjectural intelligence)

Episteme can be defined as universal knowledge, that which we share and circulate, which we teach and preserve, and what is commonly understood by firms as their 'heritage'. *Episteme* is knowledge 'about' things, the opposite of *phronesis*, which is the result of experience and social practice. *Phronesis* is singular, idiosyncratic, it cannot easily be shared. It is personal, and has profound meaning only for the individual who has lived the experience. This non-scientific, practical, contextual knowledge is generated in the intimacy of lived experience. It is acquired by trial and error, through organizational and environmental learning, and is generally very difficult to analyse or test. Its intuitive content renders it difficult for organizational science to grasp.

One only needs to look at the characteristics of conjectural knowledge to grasp its importance. Conjectural knowledge is furtive, discretionary and simultaneous, it spurns idealizations and established representations – it provides a contrast to abstract generalization on every point. Where the one is hierarchical, the other is organic, indivisible, encapsulated in action. Where the one tends towards universality, the other chooses the ephemeral as its playing field (as it is only the tactical outcome that counts). Where the one seeks truth, the other seeks results. Where the one is the product of a long maturation, the other is unpredictable and intuitive. In short, where the one is analysable, the other is multiple and tacit. Conjectural knowledge is embodied into purpose, and does not make sense out of its instrumental boundaries. By bringing together different theoretical discussions of *episteme*, *techne*, *phronesis* and *mètis*, particularly those of Spender (1993), Détienne and Vernant (1978) and Reber (1993), we can establish the following table (Table 3.1).

The tacit resources of knowledge

Learning implicitly

Learning and unlearning are at the heart of the process we are studying. Before its appropriation by management studies, organizational learning was psychology's 'cognitive revolution' (Baars, 1986) – and one of the consequences of cognitive science's domination of learning is a tendency to apply a cognitive conceptual framework to all interpretations of learning (for example cognitive maps). Certain recent works, however, have advanced the hypothesis that there is a duality in learning, that there is a common process uniting abstraction and cognitive induction with conditioning and association. Notable champions of this line of thought are Holland, Holoyak, Nisbett and Thagard (1986), and Lewicki (1986). Nonetheless, contemporary cognitive research has focused on the representation and utilization of knowledge, neglecting the study of its acquisition in natural conditions. In his study of the relationship between learning and instruction (1990), Glaser too bemoaned this negligence, arguing that the emergence of the 'information sciences' was at the root of it. In our determination to control what we have, we have ignored its 'meaning'. Glaser suggests that 'human problem solving' leads us to a theory of knowledge based upon its representation, overlooking the importance of its acquisition.

THE DISCOVERY OF IMPLICIT LEARNING   Implicit learning means learning without being aware of what is being learnt. The first studies concerning the unconscious acquisition of complex information were carried out by linguists at the end of the 1960s (for inventories of existing theories see Reber, 1967, 1969; Reber and Millward, 1965). Other

Table 3.1 *Typology of categories of knowledge*

	Episteme	Techne	Phronesis	Mètis
Definition	Abstract generalization	Capability, task accomplishment	Practical and social wisdom	Conjectural intelligence
Cohesiveness	hierarchical	encapsulated	organic	mutable
Horizon	indeterminate	perennial	life	ephemeral
Field	universal	systems	people	situations
Structure	hard	hard and soft	soft	furtive
Nature	abstract and objective	abstract and practical	abstract and practical	practical, oblique
Goal sought	scientific truth	structure	wisdom	results
Emergence	maturation	experience	social interaction	unpredictable
Process	sequential	hybrid	hybrid	simultaneous
Elaboration	positive	hybrid	hybrid	relative
Method	abstraction, deduction, idealization	observation, study, recipes	learning socialization imitation	combination, regeneration, ruse, shortcuts
Preservation	laws, principles, representations	manuals, communities of practice accumulation	clans, culture, ethnic groups, personality initiation	discretionary, intimate, clandestine
State	substance			transient
Teaching or Initiation	analysable, easy to communicate, standard	hybrid, with a tendency towards the explicit	hybrid, with a tendency towards the tacit	complex, tacit, difficult to communicate

works in the field of perceptual learning have highlighted the existence of implicit rules and patterns of individual perception of which we have no awareness. These have all made a considerable contribution to the cognitive sciences without, unfortunately, having any great impact on our understanding of learning. If we want to find writers who have tried to bridge the divide between a behavioural and a cognitive approach we have to go back to the works of Jenkins in 1933, Thorndike and Rock in 1934, and Greenspoon in 1955.

Two notions were introduced in these works: learning with neither intention nor awareness of learning, and accidental learning. Most of the research was undertaken in the laboratory, where subjects were exposed to complex stimuli (generally linguistic). The aim of these studies was to determine whether subjects had unconsciously learnt behavioural patterns through repeated exposure to these complex messages. Unfortunately, disputes swiftly arose as to the 'accidental' nature of their exposure to these complex stimuli: when subjects come voluntarily to participate in a laboratory experiment, are they not already more alert than they would be under the normal conditions of daily life? The question was raised many times (see, e.g., Brewer, 1974; Eriksen, 1958; Osgood, 1953). These experiments finally failed to clearly identify and articulate the roles of conscious and unconscious processes in learning – it was the method itself which was most often discussed, prohibiting any real progression in the understanding of the phenomenon.

During the 1970s, implicit learning became increasingly associated with the study of the acquisition of complex information. The new school saw it as a process in which the effects of the situation are neutral. In other words, complex information is acquired with little awareness of the context in which it happens. There are many things we have learnt but cannot establish where or in what situation we have learnt them. Perhaps we have simply forgotten? Perhaps we have not forgotten, but this learning was unconscious and we will never be able to ascribe a place or context to it. Theorists took this second tack, but there again – as they were led by cognitive psychologists – the methods employed were those of the artificial learning of grammar, which installed a paradigm that is still very powerful today (Brooks, 1978; McAndrews and Moscowitch, 1985).

One of the variants explored was that of 'weak exhibition', what cognitive theory would call a 'weak signal'. This was a discovery that was not a discovery: it was expressed 2,000 years ago by the Latin proverb *Intelligenti pauca* – intelligence (here the capacity to make sense of things and to learn) proceeds from the slightest of things. Implicit learning's first five decades – from 1930 to 1980 – were thus dominated by a paradigm of laboratory and language, a paradigm based on the implicit assumption that the human animal is rational and seeks to understand and to make sense of things by summoning, consciously and unconsciously, patterns of discovery and recognition.

THE IMPLICIT AND THE NON-INTENTIONAL   History abounds in examples of decisions where it is difficult to find any 'rationality' behind them. It seems we are capable of solving very complex problems without following rational steps, or without being able to explain what information has really served as the basis for our decisions. Here it is not even a question of a 'bounded rationality', but of the apparent absence of all rationality. During the 1970s researchers become increasingly aware of this problem, and they actually began to be interested in human judgement, rather than in grammar. It was by studying their peers – mathematicians and statisticians – that researchers accomplished this twist in cognitive science's history. They discovered that the beings they had supposed to be guarantors of rationality and decisive rigour formulated choices that violated elementary rules, and that these choices, after the fact, proved to be good ones. In this way they showed that logic and rationality were largely independent of decision-making processes, and were often replaced by heuristic – that is, 'less optimal' – methods.

Another direction was opened up by social psychology, which examined how people make and justify their decisions in the 'real world'. We finally leave the laboratory to go out and see what actually happens in organizations – and the effort is rewarded. It was soon discovered that an important cognitive gap still remains between the knowledge (explicit) that we think we have used to come to our decisions, and the knowledge (implicit) that we have really used (more recent research undertaken by Starbuck and Milliken, 1988a on 'managers' perceptual filters' has confirmed these early discoveries). We explain our decisions after the fact using completely different knowledge from that which we initially used to reach them, and when we attribute sense, when we detect or fail to detect environmental stimuli, we are subject to a considerable number of distortions. Going even further, Ellen Langer and her colleagues at Harvard pointed out that a lot of our decisions are neither more nor less than mindless (Langer, 1978; Langer et al., 1978).

These Harvard researchers are notable for their introduction of the idea of 'placebo-information' in interpersonal interactions – we can only marvel that this was not thought of earlier. Placebo information is often used when we are asked to express ourselves: rather than being slaves to our words, the placebo allows us to fulfil our obligation to speak during an interaction, when we have to respond. We do this without deliberation, saying things that come into our heads spontaneously but which fulfil the same function as a placebo does in medicine. These placebos respond to a symptom without really having any intrinsic quality or specific connection to the question at hand. We also make use of 'placebo actions' and 'placebo decisions' without even being aware we are doing so, and these too come from our implicit knowledge system. They take place. We are the actors of them, but not really their

conscious formulators. They disappear from our memory of past
actions, and when we are asked to retrace the steps of our decisions
they escape our memory. Because the non-rational implicit will probably never penetrate the immediate level of consciousness we end up
justifying our actions with an explanation that has little in common with
our initial motivation, even though we could give no reason for wanting
to disguise the truth. We are simply unaware of it. Our motivation
escapes our conscious rationality, but this does not imply that it systematically responds to an unconscious rationality. At times we proceed
from a psychology that is implicit and non-intentional (Uleman and
Bargh, 1989; Wegner and Vallacher, 1977). These works made it clear
that cognition is often independent of what we believe to be rational
and of that which we are aware. In other words, we perceive more than
we think we perceive and, once perceived and assimilated, this
knowledge that is ours is not entirely known to us.

As Mace (1974) acknowledged, however, it is not what is in our
brain that is important, but where our brain is situated. We have an
awful predilection for the brain, a far from innocent desire to turn it into
a 'black box' that explains all, that solves all.[3] Everything is supposed
to be guarded carefully within it: memory, perceptual cards, filters,
assimilated and learnt rules, decisions, choices, etc. Yet it does happen
that we spontaneously adopt rules that are not ours. Those of our
siblings, our friends, or even those of people we have only the briefest
contact with. What exists outside our brain is not wholly external to us,
nor is it entirely ours. Our brain has 'legs'; it rests on a body which
moves in an environment that is probably without limits, but in which
the possibilities are very limited. These limits are physiological, biological, material, perhaps spiritual. We cannot physically be in two
different places at the same instant. The environment in which we
evolve presents a strong probability of stability and continuity: if I am
in one room at time t, the probability that I will be in the adjoining room
at time $t+1$ is far stronger than the probability that I will be in another
city and on another continent. We live in a world delimited by a series
of impossibilities that are more or less known to us, while leaving the
largest margin of possibilities. Our learning of existence is thus not
purely interior. Our daily environment offers many external factors that,
without being part of our knowledge or memory, are accessible to us at
any given moment. These external elements constitute a sort of reservoir
from which we draw, consciously or unconsciously, a basis of knowledge that is on the whole stable.

Knowing tacitly: knowledge's automatisms

WHAT WE KNOW TACITLY   Although a lot has been written on the
importance of knowledge in management, little attention has been given
to the manner in which knowledge is acquired and managed within

organizations. To approach this question, a distinction must first be made between *tacit knowledge* and *explicit knowledge*. For Polanyi, we know far more than we are prepared to believe. Polanyi differentiates knowledge that is explicit to us, that which is codifiable and transmissible in a formal and systematic language, from tacit knowledge, which is personal, difficult to convey, and which does not easily express itself in the formality of language.

Polanyi's principal argument is that tacit knowledge demonstrates the lack of pertinence of Gestalt psychology. Whereas Gestalt psychology argues that all images are contained in nature, Polanyi wants to demonstrate that human beings acquire knowledge through their engagement in the creation and organization of their own experiences. Although Polanyi orientates his analysis in the philosophical domain, it is possible to draw some lessons from it for an operational domain. There are two sides to tacit knowledge:

- a cognitive dimension: paradigms, mental models, representations;
- a technical dimension: know-how, expertise applied to a specific context.

As was later enlarged upon with reference to Kantian psychology (Piaget, 1980), the cognitive dimension of tacit knowledge refers to patterns that serve as a basis for the perception of and interaction with the external world. Thus it is only on a *selective* basis that we accept information to which we are exposed, staying faithful to our own preestablished cognitive patterns. Thomas Kuhn (1962) introduces the notion of 'paradigm' as a frame of reference, consisting partly of established scientific fact (realizing a convergence of meaning), and partly of modes of thought or beliefs of scientists, which underlie the development of the different families of science. Kuhn's works give an excellent example of the role that tacit knowledge can play in actors' formulation of strategies (here, strategies of research).

A 'mental model', on the contrary, is a personal representation of reality that affects the perception of the environment (Johnson-Laird, 1983). The hypothesis that underlies this definition is that human beings do not reason by following a formal logic, but by creating and by manipulating analogies in their mind. If one learns implicitly without being aware of it, or without even being aware what is learnt, it is because 'we know more than we are able to say'. Because we continually perceive stimuli of which we are not always aware, through our senses of sight, sound, smell, taste and touch – through sensation – we are continually learning. We automatically internalize what is brought to us through sensation, sharing with our environment an intimacy that goes well beyond what we usually consider to be 'intimate' to us. For example, the sensation of *déjà vu* that we feel in certain situations makes us ill at ease. We feel as if we are living a nightmare; we know what is going to be said, what is going to be done, and how all this will end for us. This sensation is nothing but a manifestation of tacit knowledge, a recognition of patterns whose shapes we have tacitly learnt without realizing it. We are surprised to find we know the solutions to problems that we believed were new to us. It is not the problem that we recognize, but its solution. As Plato underlines in *Nemo*, 'to seek the solution of a problem is an absurdity; because if you do not know truly what you are seeking, you will find nothing'. The answer to *Nemo*'s paradox is our unconscious knowledge of the problem's solution. This is what Polanyi calls 'tacit foreknowledge'. We share an underlying intimacy with a hidden dimension, which we cannot explicitly formulate a description of or give meaning to.

Within organizations, as recognized by Starbuck (1983), actors often invent problems to justify their solutions. It is simply that their knowledge in connection with what they believe to be the 'problem' is in fact intimately linked to what they know *tacitly* to be the solution. Institutionalization, common rules of behaviour and ceremonial customs forbid them however from announcing solutions that are not linked to an explicit reality of their particular organization. There is then 'invention' – or simply appropriation or diversion – of a problem.

Many organizational situations involve tacit knowledge. Very few managers or employees have actually read their company's internal regulations, yet they nevertheless seem to respect them from their first weeks. Their behaviour is not erratic, nor is it marginal; if they are remarked on at all it is because their face is unfamiliar, not because their behaviour differs fundamentally from that of others. They know tacitly how to behave in a context of socialization, whatever the organization is.

> This does not mean that we gain any understanding in our mind without any process of investigation, but that this investigation consists, as does scientific investigation, of noting the signs that presumably convey the presence of something else. And, as in scientific investigation, many of those signs remain unspecified and can be entirely subliminal. Such is the effort by which we enter the intimate structure of a skill or a chess game and grasp the power of the person who is concealed behind it. This is also the method by which a historian explores a historical personality. (Polanyi, 1966b: 31)

In the organization numerous messages circulate tacitly and create in this way a sort of 'underground layer' of tacit knowledge that fashions relationships between actors. We are influenced by what we know tacitly and we can influence others, consciously or unconsciously, by the tacit knowledge that circulates of our intentions. Reputations are elements of tacit knowledge that precede and follow actors; their circulation is sometimes voluntary, but is often automatic. There are therefore two readings of a flow chart, as we all know: that which traces hierarchical links and gives titles, and that which is *tacitly known* by all members of the organization. The power structures within an organization also have many tacit aspects. Titles can conceal people with no power and no real duties, a token position, or with the 'power to make it rain or shine'. Nothing of what is explicitly circulated can mark the difference between two people holding the same title. As Moullet (1992) suggested, in the underlying structures of an organization, lasting relationships between actors can lay the foundations for 'clandestine management'.

As Polanyi stresses (1966b: 61), the transmission of knowledge from one generation to another is predominantly tacit – young children learn to interact with the world by trying to understand 'the hidden meanings of words and of adult behaviour'. Most of our knowledge is acquired in the course of our socialization. We note for example the reticence of organizations to hire young managers without experience. They generally feel they will have to teach them everything, and that the first year will cost the organization a great deal. This does not represent any distrust of the teaching that these young managers have received but is a simple observation that their type of knowledge is not directly exploitable in the firm, because what the young managers do know is the aggregate of the explanations society has produced about organizations: scholarly writings and theorization. They lack what Riveline (1986) referred to as 'soft knowledge' – the opposite of hard knowledge – that which they will acquire through socialization: a rich and tacit understanding of the functioning of an organization.

So the act of discovery, of learning, 'appears personal and unspecified. It begins with a solitary familiarity with a problem, through scraps picked up here and there which seem to offer signs of something hidden. We look at the fragments of something unknown, yet coherent. This attempt at vision has to transform itself into a personal obsession, because a problem that does not worry us is not a problem' (Polanyi, 1966b: 76).

WHAT WE KNOW WITHOUT KNOWING WE KNOW IT   Discovery is not however always the product of an obsessive search. In the middle of the nineteenth century it was found that many inferences that are part of the construction of knowledge are made unconsciously. It was admitted that many unconscious and automatic codings occur in the development of knowledge. At the time automatism had recently become a subject of general interest, notably after the discovery that operations as fundamental as encoding in relation to the location of objects and the frequency of events in an environment took place automatically, and in large part with no awareness of the encoding process (Hasher and Zacks, 1984). These cognitive processes are relatively independent of age, level of development, intellectual ability or personal emotional state; all of which normally disturb cognitive phenomena. Despite considerable disagreement – notably over the frequency of events – the fact that 'automatic knowledge' answers to laws of its own, and in this is far from conscious cognitive processes (that demand great effort), was generally admitted.

We can most easily identify the existence of these unconscious and automatic learning processes in our 'procedural knowledge'. We can make a distinction between 'declarative knowledge', which we are aware of and can therefore articulate, and 'procedural knowledge', which can guide our actions and our decisions without being in our field of consciousness. Anderson (1976, 1983) proposed that the formation of knowledge begins with declarative processes, conscious and controlled, which then give way to procedural processes; the process of knowing is still 'under control', but unconsciously. This proposal went somewhat against traditional ideas about implicit learning, which held that the first phases of knowledge acquisition were largely characterized by a lack of awareness, and that conscious processes emerged – 'crystallized' – around the knowledge that had been so acquired. Both of these approaches entail one unavoidable element: the existence of implicit memory.

Both the Cartesian philosophical tradition and the Freudian psychoanalytical tradition rest partly on this notion of implicit memory. For Freud this was the suppressed memory of experiences incurred during childhood which 'unconsciously' affect the behaviour of the adult. No doubt under the ascendancy of psychoanalysis, studies carried out on implicit memory characteristically heightened the pathological study of memory. It is only during the last two decades that this research has broadened its scope of inquiry to include more everyday phenomena, with a more marked interest in generalization.

The first significant works outside the psychoanalytical field were those concerning the existence of subliminal phenomena. In one of the most typical experiments concerning subliminal cognition, subjects were exposed in rapid succession to masked images with no indication being given as to their identities. In these ambiguous and mutable conditions subjects were able to demonstrate memorization of these truncated images without being able explicitly or consciously to make any sense of them. They were able to codify them. While remaining incapable of describing what they had been exposed to, subjects retained a residual memory of the stimuli. They could not, however, select or sort these 'old stimuli' when asked to – they could not force recognition (see the discussions of Kunst-Wilson and Jazonc, 1980). The existence of implicit memory does not imply that repeated exposure to the stimuli would be ineffectual. In the sphere of the unconscious as in that of the conscious, the number of times we are exposed to a stimulus is undeniably an important factor in our memorization of it, a phenomenon that has been demonstrated in areas as different as lexical recognition and perceptual identification (Jacoby and Dallas, 1981; Scarborough et al., 1979).

WHAT ONE KNOWS THROUGH PRACTICE   In 1922, in *Nature and Human Conduct*, the American philosopher Dewey identified two forms of knowledge: *knowing how* (that gleaned through habit and intuition) and *knowing about* (which implies reflection and conscious appreciation) – practical knowledge and constructed knowledge. For a better appreciation of the agonies of interpreting practical knowledge we have to return to the nature of experience, as expressed in the tenets of Gestalt psychology. For Christian von Ehrenfels, founder of the movement in the 1890s, actions of a complex order are carried out by being divided into relatively routine tasks, each of which can be executed without recourse to thought or conscious reflection. Here we find the source of Taylorism, which turned human endeavour into a 'division of chores' (chores that become automatism) and opened the way for assembly line production. The central idea of Gestalt psychology is that our perceptual experiences do not emerge as a result of the conscious or unconscious application of rules or concepts to data received from our sensory receptors, but that these experiences come from immersion in a perceptual environment in which the information we perceive already carries meaning. Perception is then an indivisible holistic structure, uniting our lived experience and the experience we are in the process of living, and it is through continually looking back on our experience that we construct a repertory of perceptual structures.

Gestalt psychology raises the question of recognition, which is little studied in management. It explains how we can recognize a person instantaneously by their physiognomy even from some distance, and even though we may not be able to precisely make out their features. Recent research on organizations' 'cognitive maps' is not so far from this concept. This capacity for recognition would allow us to automatically take appropriate action in a given situation, without having to make an effort of analysis to decide what approach to apply. The Gestalt psychologists' argument is that our sense-making capacities are indivisible from a physiological-psychological whole, which embraces both thought and perception.

It is in our everyday learning, in the development of our practical knowledge, that these automatisms are deployed. At least this was the central argument advanced by Merleau-Ponty in 1941, in a veritable defence of practical knowledge (Merleau-Ponty, 1963). Through practice we acquire patterns of behaviour – skills such as walking, running and speech – which we can then call up spontaneously. In 1966 Polanyi continued this study of tacit knowledge by looking at similar kinetic phenomena. We learn how to swim, to coordinate our movements, to float, in the context of the experience itself, and 'we know more than we can express'. For Merleau-Ponty, these patterns become 'a part of us'. It was in the repetition of practice that Merleau-Ponty saw the true nature of human learning.

Merleau-Ponty's work was followed by that of Gilbert Ryle in 1945 in his article 'Knowing how and knowing that', which also directed attention to this dichotomy of knowledge. This pragmatic American philosophy and German Gestalt psychology were however antedated by Greek philosophy: by Aristotle and Plato. Practical knowledge and social practice were then rated very highly, as they were the road to *phronesis* (social wisdom). It was in social interaction, in the observation and imitation of others, that the Greek philosophers saw the roots of learning and education. Defenders of practical knowledge, they saw it as the essential source of all wisdom, but also of all ruse.

Conjectural patterns

This last part of my investigation of knowledge is concerned with a 'mode of knowing which it is easier to recognize than to explain – a mode of knowing that falls into the gap between those forms of knowledge we explicitly recognize and those that make up our daily social practice' (Raphals, 1992: xi). Four authors and three major contributions to the understanding of conjectural knowledge have served as the basis for this development:

- Marcel Détienne and Jean Pierre Vernant, *Cunning Intelligence in Greek Culture and Society* (1978) is still the authority on this form of knowledge.
- Lisa Raphals, *Knowing Words* (1992) is one of the rare comparisons established to this day between the forms of cunning knowledge and wisdom of Ancient Greece and China.
- Carlos Castaneda's *The Teachings of Don Juan* (1968) describes in a narrative, but convincing, style, the fundamentals of the knowledge of Native Americans.

The mètis *of the Greeks: conjectural and tacit knowledge*

AN INTUITIVE TRACK Does a form of knowledge dedicated to ambiguity exist today? Our thoughts move naturally to the world of politics, and in fact it is in the origins of our modern political ideas that we find an early conception of such a form of knowledge. Looking back again to the Ancient Greeks – Plato, Socrates and the Sophists – we realize that this knowledge, or something close to it, has existed. The Greeks called it *mètis*, the knowledge required to escape 'puzzling and ambiguous situations'. Détienne and Vernant introduce *mètis* as a 'form of wily intelligence, of effective, adaptable cunning which the Greeks brought into play in large sectors of their social and spiritual life, which they valued highly within their religious system . . . and which has never been the object of an explicit formulation, of any exposition of a theoretical nature'. *Mètis* was practised by the Greeks in various areas of life; 'it is found in the skill of the sophist, in the know-how of the artisan, in the prudence of the politician and the art of the ship's captain navigating dangerous seas'. Multiple and polymorphous, *mètis* is applied to situations that are 'transient, shifting, disconcerting and ambiguous, situations that do not lend themselves to precise measurement, exact calculation or rigorous logic'. Committed to action and its consequences, this form of intelligence has since the fifth century AD been relegated to the shadows by philosophers. In the name of a metaphysics based on Being and immutability, the conjectural and oblique knowledge of the clever and the prudent was rejected as non-knowledge.[4]

Mètis is a certain type of intelligence that is committed to practice, confronted with obstacles that must be dominated by cunning to obtain success in the most diverse areas of action: 'a hunting trap, a fishing net, the skills of a basket-maker, of a weaver, of a carpenter, the mastery of a navigator, the flair of a politician' are examples of the levels this intelligence operates on:

> Although *mètis* operates within so vast a domain, although it holds such an important position within the Greek system of values, it is never made manifest for what it is, it is never clearly revealed in a theoretical work that aims to define it. It always appears more or less below the surface, immersed as it were in practical operations which, even when they use it, show no concern to make its nature explicit or to justify its procedures. . . . There is no doubt that *mètis* is a type of intelligence and of thought, a way of knowing; it implies a complex but very coherent body of mental attitudes and intellectual behaviour which combine flair, wisdom, forethought, subtlety of mind, deception, resourcefulness, vigilance, opportunism, various skills, and experience acquired over the years. It is applied to situations that are transient, shifting, disconcerting and ambiguous. (Détienne and Vernant, 1978: 14)

Does this then represent the first recorded 'knowledge of ambiguity'? What can we make of this *mètis*? To start with, Détienne and Vernant explicitly label it 'a way of knowing', involving wisdom and flair, that is applied to 'situations that are transient, shifting, disconcerting and ambiguous'. We also find it has a coherent body of characteristics, a cohesiveness in the types of knowledge it encompasses, and an entirely specific dynamics. Research in management has always tried to explain why managers have different degrees of success in their interpretations of reality. Why do some managers consider far fewer alternatives than others when arriving at their decisions? Is it a question of flair (intuition) or expertise? In their 1972 work *Human Problem Solving*, Newell and Simon compare chess masters with good players who have yet to reach the same level of mastery of the game. They explain that the 'flair' of the grand master is nothing but the fruit of a long apprenticeship, transformed into a tacit knowledge of the chances of success of the various possible moves. So we find then, in the Greek *mètis*, the prediction and vigilant attention that are later to be evoked in the

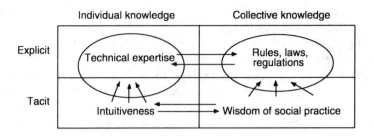

Figure 3.1   *Four inseparable types of knowledge*

literature of organizational scanning (e.g. in the writings of Aguilar, 1967; Thomas, 1980; Wilensky, 1967a).

This 'knowledge of ambiguity' which Détienne and Vernant present us with is reminiscent of more recent works concerning the invention of solutions as generated through action, and the body of work on organizational learning.[5] While this branch of the knowledge of Ancient Greece may be new to us, we find within it certain familiar elements. Firstly, we find it involves knowledge that is explicit and individual, techniques that allow us to counter nets and traps. Secondly, we can identify collective explicit knowledge; the profound knowledge of a terrain, of an environment, of rules and laws that we are to outwit. Thirdly, we can divine in it a body of knowledge that is tacit and collective; a knowledge of the unspoken, of the invisible structure of a situation, a certain wisdom (*phronesis*) that is acquired through social practice. Fourth and lastly, in *mètis* we discover a body of knowledge that is tacit and individual; this 'flair' – tacit expertise that is complemented by 'hard' technical knowledge – a sort of inimitable technical skill, without which the fisherman's net would not be effective and the sailor would not be able to confront the crossing of the Mediterranean without sophisticated navigational instruments. These four forms of knowledge are indissociable. Their astute combination, their clever implementation, *is mètis* (see Figure 3.1).

KNOWLEDGE STRATEGIES   According to my analysis, the *mètis* of the Greeks reveals four modes of knowledge; the rest is strategy. In the first phase, the individual appropriates the rules of wisdom through social practice, and so constructs 'flair'. At the same time, they develop their technical understanding (*techne*) by appropriating rules – there is a lateral transfer of knowledge, from the collective to the individual. Once this appropriation is established, the actor assimilates the various lessons: their flair will improve their technical skill as well as their social practice (see Figure 3.2).

In a second phase the actor will penetrate the rules, and infiltrate the hard knowledge that disconcerts them and prevents them from achieving

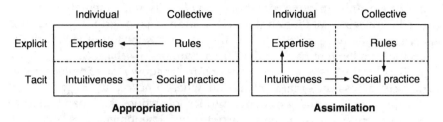

Figure 3.2 *From appropriation to assimilation*

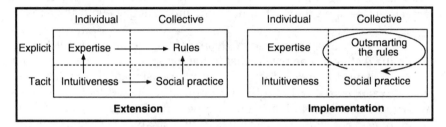

Figure 3.3 *Shifting the rules*

their goals. To do this they use 'conjectural and oblique knowledge'. Once they have successfully realized this extension of their knowledge they will be able to skilfully implement their plans to outwit these very rules, now having at their disposal knowledge that is 'polymorphous and rich' (Figure 3.3).

This is of course a literary example, but it offers us the possibility of a different reading of the confrontation of ambiguity. Neither choice nor decisions figure on these graphs. They provide us instead with a dynamics of knowledge: its movements, its transformations and its strategies.

THE SHADOWY ZONES OF HUMAN INTERACTION   To evoke *mètis* is to explore the unexplorable, to go beyond the evident and the observable. It is to measure 'the confrontation of the apparent and the underlying structures of the organization' (Moullet, 1992: 219). In defining it we have contrasted it with knowledge that is explicit and objective, in placing it in the unspoken, the personal, as belonging to small groups or collectives (for example a firm's clandestine networks). When an individual, or a group of individuals, makes recourse to *mètistic* processes, they use their knowledge obliquely – playing on its malleability, manoeuvring it, mobilizing its mutability.[6] The *mètistic* process is not necessarily the property of the educated or the erudite, as devious intelligence can just as easily be founded on a broad as on a narrow knowledge base. Such a process develops emergencies: the unpredictable, unsettling and puzzling situation provokes its implementation by the need for a rapid solution. If the *mètistic* individual or group is wary, it is because they have no choice – if they do not want to fall victim to the unpredictable, they have to develop a state of *inquietude*.

This instinctive vigilance develops in 'shadowy or turbulent zones that cut across all organization, and where uncertainty reigns . . . at the threshold of this world, repertories of actions and habitual procedures are useless. Events surprise us. Phenomena are not well understood' (Moullet, 1992: 219). Vigilance unfolds, and then develops rapidly, in the incommunicable. It plays on unconscious repertories: a knowledge that is there but that we cannot explain, or do not want to explain. It feeds on the tacit dimension, and dialogues with the explicit dimension.

We could, however, reproach Détienne and Vernant for not having made the distinction between what in the nature of cunning comes from aware behaviour, and what comes from physiological adaptation to conditions of existence in hostile surroundings. The fact that the octopus possesses tentacles, veritable moving nets for its prey, is not due to a voluntary behaviour. Similarly, we cannot say that the chameleon is a cunning animal because its colour adapts to that of the environment in which it evolves. Just because its skin becomes sand coloured when it moves on to the sand, it does not follow that it possesses a particularly wily character. If the chameleon chose a specific path in its environment, so as to profit from its automatic capacity to change colour to its advantage, we could then say that its behaviour was wily.

In my analyses I will show that it is the same for organizations and their actors. When an organization (or one of its actors), on the foundation of a rich knowledge of its environment and its own capacities, voluntarily chooses a 'path' that accentuates given advantages, then we will be able to say that it is deploying ruse. But the cunning intelligence of *mètis* often remains mythological.

A MUTABLE AND INFORMED KNOWLEDGE   'Mètis operates on a shifting terrain, in uncertain and ambiguous situations.' In the typical situation in Greek literature, two antagonistic forces confront each other, and at any moment the situation could turn in one direction or the other: 'the man of *mètis* – compared with his opponent – displays at the same time a greater grip of the present where nothing escapes him, more awareness of the future, several aspects of which he has already manipulated, and richer experience accumulated from the past'. *Mètis* is thus knowledge in the invisible, as it acts in the unseen, 'arriving at the most correct idea concerning the future, taking the widest point of view and foreseeing, as far as possible, the hidden advantages and disadvantages in what cannot be seen'. This is a dense type of knowledge, 'wily' and 'cunning' and 'full of inventive ploys'. 'Its field of application is the world of movement, of multiplicity and of ambiguity. It bears on fluid situations which are constantly changing and which at every moment combine contrary features and forces that are opposed to each other' (Détienne and Vernant, 1978: 21–8).

Mètis is above all a knowledge of the mutable: 'Victory over an unstable, wavering, reality, whose continual metamorphoses render almost elusive, can only be obtained from mobility, a even greater power of transformation.' But to be more mutable than reality itself necessitates a strong 'connivance with the real'. Here we find the principles of Chinese wisdom; to be fluid with the fluid, to oppose an open field to a surging army, as in Sun Zi's Art of War. We also find mètis in the wise council of Oppien: 'Deliver to each of your friends a different aspect of yourself. Take the example of the octopus that gives itself the appearance of the stone where it will affix itself. Attach yourself one day to one, then another day change colour. Skill is worth more than intransigence' (Détienne and Vernant, 1978: 47). In this way mètis presides over 'all those activities where man must learn to manoeuvre hostile forces, too powerful to be controlled directly, but in spite of which one can use mètis, avoiding confronting them face to face, to bring about through unforeseen means the project one has planned' (1978: 57).

The wisdom of Ancient China: moral and instrumental

In their investigation of the Greek mètis, Détienne and Vernant advanced the idea of a polarity of knowledge in the Greek world, with speculative reason on one side (Aristotle and Plato) and conjectural and cunning intelligence on the other. 'As in the Greek example, mètistic intelligence has fed tacitly on many aspects of classic Chinese culture and society, including political and social morality and military strategy' (Raphals, 1992: xiii).

Chinese thought of the millennium before our era, in the fashion of Greek thought, never formulated any explicit treatises on cunning intelligence. Nonetheless, wisdom and practical intelligence are omnipresent in the writings attributed to Confucius, Laozi, Zhuangzi, Sun Zi and Mencius, and 'haunt their peripheries as a sort of after-image'. Normative Confucianism has haunted China in the same way that the ethics and the rationalism of Plato have haunted the Western world. Throughout China's history, alongside their normative and moralistic counterparts, there have always been those philosophers who recognized the importance of conjectural knowledge. The military tradition (Bing jia), in strong opposition to Confucianism, presents a martial (and in certain ways amoral) view of the utilization of the intellect, as Sun Zi's The Art of War testifies. The Taoist tradition (Dao jia) also opposes Confucianism by seeking roads to wisdom in aphorisms of action that are close to conjectural intelligence.

It is in the elaboration of castes, the categorization of people into a typology, that we find the first traces of conjectural intelligence. Confucius classifies individuals into four categories: 'the highest is the man born with knowledge. The second is he who must acquire knowledge by study. The third is he who, despite limited skill, will however be able to learn. The fourth is he who will not be able to learn.' There is no place in this classification for a knowledge defined outside norms of morality. Confucianism's preference for moral virtue rather than intellectual acuity draws a clear and uncompromising line between a virtuous conception of wisdom, which alone is allowed, and all other forms of wisdom, such as cunning wisdom.[7]

THE EMERGENCE OF AN INSTRUMENTAL WISDOM   It was with the arrival of Taoist thought that a more instrumental wisdom emerged in China, with the rupture in the continuum of Confucianism. The rejection of 'Confucian ethics as artifacts of language became a consequence of the view expressed in these works that knowledge is not, by nature, discursory. The intelligence that develops outside the language used to describe it is a *mètistic* intelligence' (Raphals, 1992: 70). Writings on Taoist thought, notably the *Laozi*, 'replace Confucian vision with a humanism that has a vision of nature, and reject textual and ritual Confucian knowledge in favour of a form of knowledge that one cannot express within the arbitrary constraints and restrictive divisions of language'.

The emergence of this idea was contemporary with the emergence of a desire for 'strategy and political control' (1992: 71). It was the beginning of an attack by Taoism on the conventional view of Confucianism: 'Confucian wisdom lies in the mastery of linguistic practice. The distinctions implicit in language are the cause of this, and correspond to modes of conventional action that make up Confucian virtue. To escape this mentality and this mode of action, the Taoist has to modify or abandon Confucian linguistics and the "knowledge" that goes with it' (1992: 73). Confucian knowledge is rejected as incapable of maintaining social order. It is not close enough to reality, it is nothing but language, it is not instrumental enough, it has to become more conjectural. Soon wisdom and conventional knowledge were accused of being the real hypocrisies, and the real stupidities. *Laozi* accentuates this inversion of conventional knowledge and unconventional stupidity: 'My mind is that of a simpleton – how puzzled I am! Vulgar people possess clarity. I alone am drowsy. Vulgar people are alert. I alone am disturbed. Calm as the sea; as a wind that never ceases. The multitude has all the purpose. I alone am stupid and coarse' (Lao, cited in Raphals, 1992: 20). People became aware that linguistic skilfulness is not illuminating, that conjectural wisdom exists, that of 'vulgar folk', and that it is Laozi, who is aware of possessing knowledge, who feels stupid.

Contradiction had begun to be cultivated, as taking some of the moral distance from the vision of the world, bringing us closer to a reality intermixed with truth and falsehood. Action through the practice of contraries, through the practice of the mutable, that which defines the Greeks' *mètis*, made its entry with Taoist thought: 'If you want to narrow it, be sure to widen it. If you want to weaken it, be sure to strengthen it. If you want to supplant it, be sure to promote it. If you want to profit from it, be sure to give it. This is called "subtle illumination"' (Lao, 26, cited in Graham, 1989: 229). By cultivating contradiction as a system of thought, the wise Taoist naturally develops a cunning wisdom: 'To see that which is small is called discernment, to protect that which is weak is called force', or again: 'The further you go the less you know. Consequently, the sage does not stir but he knows, he does not see but he distinguishes, he does not act but he accomplishes' (Lao, op. cit.: 47). The wisdom that tells us the state of things knows a profoundly modified perception: 'in fact, the sage who conducts the affairs of the state does not count on the disposition of its people to treat him well, but uses their incapacity to hurt him. If he relied on people to treat him well, there would never be enough of these people even if he were to count them by tens. But if he uses the incapacity of the people to hurt him, then a whole state can be enlisted' (Han Fei, op. cit.: 19.50.IIb).

RUSE AS AN ELEMENT OF WISDOM By becoming conjectural and closer to reality, the Taoist conception of knowledge rests not on explicit universal laws – as the wisdom of the Confucians had – but on a rich, intentional and tacit comprehension of reality. Little by little there emerges 'a point of view for which ruse is not only acceptable but necessary for wisdom; this attitude . . . is associated with the martial sphere. This point of view appears in two representative texts, of two genres that admit and admire conjectural wisdom: military strategy manuals (*bingfa*) and works concerned with persuasion and rhetoric (*zong heng*)' (Han Fei, op. cit.: 101). The approach to knowledge becomes resolutely instrumental. Sun Zi proposes the manipulation of it to create false impressions within the enemy camp: 'In this philosophy of war, victory depends on the skill of the commander, or the strategist General. This includes the comprehension of the order that hides behind apparent chaos (be this by anticipation or by presence on the battlefield)' (Han Fei, op. cit.: 103). For universal and explicit rules of wisdom was substituted the need for an underlying comprehension of 'hidden reality', that which we cannot express in words, that of which 'we know more than we can say'. Cunning wisdom develops in the sphere of the unspoken, 'the inaudible'. Thus, 'subtle and insubstantial, the expert leaves no traces; divinely mysterious, he is inaudible' (Sun Zi, op. cit.: 6). The cunning and wise strategists make themselves discreet, 'insubstantial'; they base their knowledge on that which cannot be seen, but may be perceived. The strategist embraces, reduces and condenses the two dimensions of knowledge: tacit and explicit.

Anticipatory knowledge

A DIFFERENT CONCEPTION OF SPACE, TIME AND PURPOSE Knowledge possesses another intangible dimension that belongs neither to automatisms (procedural knowledge, repetition of procedures of action becoming unconscious), nor to the area of the unconscious assimilation of external elements, but to imagination and elaboration. It is interesting to look at this form of knowledge for two reasons. The first is simply its existence, and the part we can suppose it plays in managers' actions. What we call the irrational could simply follow a dreamlike rationality, imagined in a fantastic universe that a manager projects on to a reality which he or she no longer takes account of. The second reason is the power of this form of knowledge which, if not explanatory, at least throws a little light on tacit knowledge. If, according to Polanyi, tacit knowledge is a vast area 'where we know more than we can express', then it is there that we can question the possible nature of this inexpressible knowledge. The area of the fantastic is certainly not to be neglected in such an investigation.

What I call a 'fantastic knowledge' is the knowledge derived from images that come from dreams, hallucinations or fantasies. It is not impossible to think that we sometimes know more than we can express, precisely because *we feel we know* – we feel we recognize a situation with a sentiment of *déjà vu* – a reality, or its continuation, that we have already dreamt of or strongly desired. Castaneda's works speak of this knowledge within Native American communities.

On the first page of *Tales of Power*, we read the following passage from Saint Jean de la Croix's *Dichos de Luz y Amor*: 'The conditions for a solitary bird number five: the first, that it can fly to the highest point; the second, that it does not miss the company of others, even of those of its own kind; the third, that it points its beak to the sky; the fourth, that it is of no defined colour; the fifth, that it sings very gently.' Here we find *mètis*'s polymorphism. To take the colour of the sky, to sing very gently – we have come back to a knowledge of the invisible.

In his fictionalized accounts of his encounters with a sorcerer by the name of Genaro, Castaneda opens a window for us on to Native American knowledge. The Yaqui path to knowledge depends 'on a double vision'. This power of splitting knowledge is a reading similar to those, of different levels of depth and horizon, in which 'the warrior is capable of conquering *vision* and *dream*, and is aware of his *luminosity*' (Castaneda, 1974: 63). To return to my matrix, the man of knowledge – for to the Yaqui this knowledge was the preserve of men – has developed a capacity to penetrate deeply into the tacit, individual, introspective and collective dimension of knowledge. Unlike *mètis*, Yaqui knowledge is based on automatisms: 'A man of knowledge is a master of self without having to control himself in any way' (1974: 64).

It depends on a different understanding of the world, 'a world in which metaphysical presuppositions differ from ours: space does not conform to Euclidean geometry, time does not form a continuous unidirectional flow, causality does not consult Aristotelian logic, man is not differentiated from non-man, or life from death, as in our world' (Goldschmidt in Castaneda, 1968: vii).

Yaqui knowledge permeates the world, it detaches itself from the person to 'fly' above the world that it tries to know. Hallucinatory practices are incorporated into this. This world conception, so fundamentally different from our Copernican or Cartesian view, rests on a spirituality – a *purpose* – very different from ours. Access to Yaqui knowledge demands a preparation, a spiritual and physiological commitment, and necessitates the usage of hallucinatory mushrooms. It is always the power to see the hidden dimension, that of dreams, that of invisible and tacit knowledge, that is sought.

A LEARNING PROCESS 'It was implicit that learning was the only means of becoming a man of knowledge . . . the result of a *process*, the opposite of an immediate acquisition by an act of grace' (Castaneda, 1968: 145). It involves conjectural learning, registered in practice, which necessitates 'an unalterable will to remain at the frontiers of acquired knowledge . . . made of frugality, of veracity of judgement . . . because most of the acts used to establish it were connected to proceedings or to elements outside the limits of ordinary life'. For the Yaqui this learning was established in experience, in natural surroundings, through deep immersion in events. It is based on clarity of the mind, continually reaffirming the validity of the path taken, while maintaining a specific purpose and the freedom to choose this path, and by remaining fluid. 'Fluidity created a sense of direction by giving a sensation of being malleable and full of resources' (1968: 146–7). To attain Yaqui knowledge demands considerable effort, it is expensive, it takes time. As it is not based on anything explicit, apprentices have to accustom themselves to the unspoken, to reading hallucinations, to the instability of perceived reality. The process is unceasing and demands permanent wakefulness, an assiduous and fluid reading of everything brought to one's awareness. It was never certain that by following assiduously the steps to becoming a man of knowledge, one could become this. Thus, it involved a task which one knew one could never completely finish; it was more an unceasing quest based on the idea that its purpose was to renew itself unceasingly, that it was unachieved, and that it had to be followed with the heart, rather than with reason. To undertake this voyage into knowledge was enough in itself; it was not necessary to have any point of destination. The accent was put on mobility in tacit spheres of knowledge, a refusal of rigidity, a refusal of a stilted reality, a refusal of finitude. This is a humble attitude, as 'nothing more can be attempted than to try to establish the beginning and the direction of an infinitely long road. For the Yaqui, the pretension of any kind of systematization or completion would be at the very most an illusion. Perfection cannot be contained by the individual who studies it only in the subjective sense that he communicates nothing but what he has been able to see' (Simmel, 1906: 1).

INGESTION-ABSORPTION   All the philosophy of Yaqui knowledge is founded on faith in the existence of an out-of-the-ordinary reality that contains the resources and responses of ordinary reality: a hidden dimension accessed through phantasmagoria, intimacy, projection or allegory. One does not discover this second reality, one voyages there, one 'drinks of it'. The learning involved is implicit, tending towards the 'ingestion-absorption' of this non-ordinary reality. It is the equivalent of what we in our Aristotelian world call 'intuition', yet at the same time it differs from it fundamentally as, if intuition is inexplicable in our social construction, 'ingestion-absorption' is the object of a precise, stable, permanent process. The daily world is a dream, a construction, and the dream is itself the only way out, to the non-ordinary reality which is constant and singular. The ingestion of this second reality is both spiritual and physical. It is represented by the datura, a hallucinatory potion 'that produces a state of non-reality . . . an unspecified sensation of well-being, and a feeling of discomfort; according to whether the affinity with this second reality is present or absent' (Castaneda, 1968: 160). The potion made from the root of the datura plant is absorbed, and an ointment made from its seeds is smoothed on the forehead and temples. By this process of ingestion-absorption, 'the sorcerer was able to fly incredible distances; this flight of his body demonstrated the sorcerer's ability to move in non-regular reality, and then to return at will to ordinary reality' (1968: 163).

THE QUEST FOR CONSENSUS WITH OUT-OF-THE-ORDINARY REALITY This ingestion-absorption constitutes the preparatory step towards the establishment of a consensus with out-of-the-ordinary reality. 'Consensus signified an implicit and tacit agreement on the elements of the out-of-the-ordinary reality. . . . This consensus was in no way fraudulent or counterfeit, as elements of dreams that two persons recount may be. It was systematic; to produce it necessitated the mobilization of all available knowledge. With the establishment of a systematic consensus, actions and elements perceived in out-of-the-ordinary reality became consensually real.' The transition into non-reality, or out-of-the-ordinary reality, is the fruit of a consensual commitment. 'The acceptance of a consensus with regard to all the states of out-of-the-ordinary reality, as well as all the states of ordinary reality, was intended to consolidate the awareness of a necessity for consensus in everyday life' (Castaneda, 1968: 176).

Conclusion

In the first part of this chapter we discovered that behind the apparent in what we learn and perceive, and in how we explain our decisions, and behind what we know, lies an invisible body of mechanisms. Drawing on a range of writings, I analysed different examples of this 'invisible cognition', of which the more characteristic traits are summarized in Table 3.2. We have observed that tacit knowledge plays a central role in our learning processes, although we are not conscious of it, and that it comes into the scope of practice, where it is properly abstracted. It is continually present in all of our activities. We recall the impossibility of dissociating our acting body (practice) from our thinking subject (learning). Two characteristics emerge from this analysis: the conjectural character of the construction of tacit knowledge, and its automatic character.

In the second part of this chapter I attempted to contrast intentional tacit knowledge with automatic tacit knowledge. I identified 'conjectural wisdom' as knowledge marked by intention, whose foundations are tacit. It is marked by intention because its purpose is to confer, on whoever uses it, an advantage over their contemporaries. It is founded on tacit knowledge because we learn it through practice.

I draw particularly on three examples of tacit knowledge: the *mètis* of the Ancient Greeks, wisdom in Ancient China, and the anticipatory knowledge of Native Americans. Individuals gifted with *mètis* use their underlying and tacit knowledge of a puzzling situation to impose their decision and to clear themselves a path. Conversely, Confucian China repels this form of knowledge – revering morality and study as the only roads to wisdom. This is in turn rejected by Taoism as being incapable of maintaining social order. Starting from the observation that 'vulgar people are alert', *Laozi* rehabilitates conjectural knowledge – no longer founded on moral principles, but on a rich, intentional and tacit perception of reality: 'Subtle and insubstantial, the expert leaves no traces; divinely mysterious, he is inaudible.'

The anticipatory knowledge of Native Americans provided another example of the deliberate utilization of tacit knowledge: apprentices try to detach themselves from explicit reality (ordinary reality) so as to penetrate unconscious reality (out-of-the-ordinary reality). Going to the extreme of a probable continuum of uses of tacit knowledge, anticipatory knowledge places the individual completely in the hold of a knowledge which is phantasmagoric. The explicit world is rejected *en bloc* (by refusing Euclidean geometry and Aristotelian logic, only to replace them with intuition and ingestion of reality).

IMPLICATIONS FOR MANAGEMENT AND ORGANIZATIONAL LEARNING   As Table 3.2 suggests, unconscious and automatic tacit knowledge is present in each of our repertories of action and thought. Used

Table 3.2 *Knowledge: visible and invisible*

	What we can see	What we cannot see
Learning	We know a lot of things which we have no recollection of having learnt. The complexity of that which we can learn is great.	Learning without being aware of what is learnt (Thorndike and Rock, 1934) Complex information processed unconsciously (Reber, 1967)
Perceiving	We cannot explain after the fact the rules that have dictated our behaviour or led to our decisions. We suddenly recall details that had seemed insignificant. We are subject to reminiscences. We have feelings of *déjà-vu*, we act on the basis of things we cannot explain. Some things we perceive directly, and others we do not perceive at all. We adopt rules that are not our own, improvising or borrowing our interpretations, yet going along with them.	Implicit unconscious rules within patterns of perception (Gibson, 1969, 1979) Weak signals are perceived without us being aware of it (Gordon and Holoyak, 1983) We perceive more than we think we perceive, and this knowledge is unknown to us (Uleman and Bargh, 1989) Filters hamper our perception (Starbuck and Milliken, 1988a) Contingency and inherence of our perception: 'that which our brain is' (Mace, 1974)
Explaining our decisions	We invent problems to fit our solutions, we rationalize after observations to explain our behaviour and our decisions. We sometimes act mindlessly.	There is a gap between the explicit knowledge that we think we have used and the implicit knowledge that we have really used (Nisbett and Ross, 1980) We use placebo-information (Langer, 1978)
Knowing	We know things before they happen. We are surprised that everybody else knows what we put forward. We know how to accomplish tasks without being able to explain how we perform them.	We use tacit foreknowledge (Polanyi, 1966b). An underground layer of tacit knowledge exists which we are unaware of (Polanyi, 1966b) Practical knowledge (Dewey, 1922; Ryle, 1945) Submerged knowledge (Gestalt psychology)

deliberately, it can be instrumental (*mètis*), become a governing principle (Taoism), perhaps assert its primacy over explicit knowledge (as anticipatory knowledge). While revealing the indispensable role of the 'non-expressed', this chapter raises a series of singular questions: how can organizations exploit tacit knowledge? Is there some understanding of how to systematize tacit knowing? What could be prescribed to organizations in order to protect, enrich and use tacit knowledge when faced with crises and puzzling situations? Organizations may well be the most inappropriate settings for preserving and improving individual tacit knowledge; yet organizations do maintain large bodies of collective tacit knowledge through ceremonies, rites, traditions and communities of practice. Most importantly, organizations value knowledge they cannot codify, i.e. skills, while making enormous investments in codifying and rationalizing both cognitive processes and knowledge within their walls. Similarly, Ancient Greek society was founded on extensive ruling and codification of socialization, while its mythologies and religion emphasized heroes with uncodifiable and inimitable skills, rooted in tacit knowledge. A similar contradiction is found in Ancient China where the art of warfare was described as an extensive code of contingent and codified learning, while artful generals are depicted as insubstantial and inaudible.

Notes

1 Hume (1955); Locke (1894: Book II, ch. XXVII).

2 This distinction on the part of the Greek philosophers has been discussed in a number of recent works, notably Spender's analysis of 1993; and that of Détienne and Vernant (1978).

3 A mythological temptation – Roland Barthes writes about this in 'Einstein's Brain' (Barthes, 1972: 91–7).

4 All of the quotes in this paragraph are from Détienne and Vernant (1978: 9).

5 Starbuck (1983) discusses the generation of solutions through action. Writings on organizational learning include: Argyris and Schön (1978) and Hedberg et al. (1976).

6 This notion of 'oblique knowledge' is returned to in Baumard (1994a), in which the use of oblique knowledge to resolve ambiguous situations is updated in a current – and not mythological – context.

7 This discussion of Confucian thought draws upon Raphals (1992). The quoted passage is taken from page 23 of this work.

4

Investigating the Non-Expressed

Man can do nothing about gravity, but he knows how to
use a waterfall.

Elsa Triolet

Tacit knowledge definitely escapes observation and measurement. To develop an adequate methodology to study the non-expressed is hence a preliminary condition to its study. As early as 1906, in the introduction to his *Sociology*, Georg Simmel suggested that the non-expressed was not only present but probably a universal keystone in human relationships, whether they are of a superficial or a profound order, of a disinterested or transactional nature. Not only do we know more than we really *want* to express, we know more than we *can* express, and this body of unspoken knowledge complements that which is made explicit in our relations with those around us, even to the point of supplanting it.[1] Before Simmel, Helmholtz too had been interested in the less evident aspects of human behaviour, and had precociously (in 1867) volunteered that cognition encompassed numerous unconscious inferences. Helmholtz argued that, just as we are not always aware of what we see, neither are we aware of the inferences our brain makes from what we are unaware of having seen (see Helmholtz, 1962).

In our never-ending quest for comprehension, explanation and prediction, data is the staple diet of the management sciences: detailed discussion, direct observation (whether participant or dormant), archival studies, analyses of internal documents, actors' statements and so on. We work within the observable, and are afraid to stray from it for fear of threatening the internal validity of our research. We measure the degree to which our theories may be generalized by proposing that our peers replicate our experiments 'under the same conditions' – that they reproduce our results using another experimental set, in another 'natural environment'. In short, we all tolerate the same imprecision: we accept as a priori that the replication of the visible is a necessary and sufficient condition for the replication of the real.

But 'reality' always camouflages other explanations, other ways of understanding which can frustrate our attempts to predict it – the realm of the non-expressed. In this chapter I will discuss how the non-expressed has been included in my research design.

Realities that shirk the question

Criticism of 'ungrounded theory' is never severe enough. In 1938, writing at the behest of the Social Science Research Council, Blumer denounced Thomas and Znaniecki's *The Polish Peasant in Poland and America*, claiming it was unnecessarily repetitive – that 'the major outlines [were] foreshadowed in the previous writings of Thomas'. But worse than this, Blumer insisted that 'their *particular* interpretations of Polish peasant life were not formed solely from the materials they present; we have to assume that the familiarity with the Polish peasant life which enabled their interpretations was made in a wide variety of ways.' Blumer reasoned that 'the important question is whether the materials adequately test the generalizations (regardless of their source) which are being applied to them . . . [but] the answer is very inconclusive . . . the interpretation is either true or not, even though it is distinctly plausible' (Blumer, 1939: 74–5, cited in Glaser and Strauss, 1967).

Historians are well acquainted with the dilemma posed by the possibility of verifying findings which support the generation of their theories. Foucault is often reproached for having based *Discipline and Punish* on regulations which were never applied. In 1983, in *Colonial Empire and French Capitalism*, Jacques Marseille applied a reading of decolonization based on economic data, and so overturned his peers' earlier conclusions. The datum is central to the construction of an interpretation, and the weakness of Thomas and Znaniecki's (1974) work no doubt lies in what they called '"human documents": letters, agency records, life histories and court records' – data that is only the explanation made by others of a phenomenon they have not themselves observed.

Glaser and Strauss were to write that Blumer had here 'raised the issue of how to theorize from data rather than from the armchair' (Glaser and Strauss, 1967: 14). This intimacy with the data that was lacking in Thomas and Znaniecki thus encouraged Blumer to publish a year later an article in which he wrote that 'to develop a rich and personal familiarity with the type of conduct being studied and to employ all relevant imagination that observers can happily possess' should compensate for this type of weakness 'by an improvement in judgement, in observation and in concept . . . in a long process of maturation' (Blumer, 1940: 718–19).

In truth, all models are a lie; they cannot help but reduce reality to 'schemata' that distort and maltreat it. In his work *Vital Lies, Simple Truths*, Goleman defines a schema as 'a sort of mental code for representing experience':

> Schema operate in the unconscious, out of awareness. They direct attention toward what is salient and ignore the rest of experience. . . . Shared schema are at work in the social realm, creating a consensual reality. (1985: 22–3)

Researchers are not a species protected from the ills they know how to detect in others. Just as Cyert and March recognized with regard to 'actors' in the organization, savants too are subject to a bounded rationality; they too look for solutions in the vicinity of the problems they detect. And they too can be tempted to favour a measure because it is available, and not because it has received theoretical support or because it is the 'the most faithful' measure for the problem at hand.[2]

There exists in the United States today an abundance of statistical data on organizations, notably in sector-based databases. The validity of these databases is so generally accepted that the 'data question' often boils down to their citation. The statistical datum is nevertheless fickle. Significant correlation can be made between series which have absolutely nothing to do with each other, if one masters, just a little, their shared 'time' variable. The labelling of boxes of archives is sometimes vague; however, these 'imprecisions' do not lack sense. The datum, in other words, is a human production and, like all human productions, it has to be approached with prudence: in what historical, social and political conditions has it been produced? What are the risks associated with it? Who can, or could, have had an interest in shaping this datum, and why – for what reason or end? Finally, without the 'live memory' of archival custodians – if they have been a witness to events – we cannot orient ourselves within the contents of the archives in order to discover . . . what we do not look for: discoveries.

Data are signatures. Archives sign an organization's history, a history over which the firm wants to have a certain degree of control; be this by omitting directorate memos from historical collections or by organizing records to favour one reading rather than another. As for annual reports, they are destined to be read by the public, the competition and shareholders, and the data they contain are correspondingly subject to a threefold constraint: to win over the public; not to inform the competition; and to reassure shareholders. Memos, although written traces of decisions taken in the organization, are drafted by actors who are strongly aware that they may later constitute 'written proof' of the value of their analyses and their decisions. They too are subject to a constraint of prudence. The behaviour of an actor who is knowingly observed – by a researcher as well as by an internal listener

– is very likely to be different from the behaviour of the actor liberated from all external observation.

The obstacle of singularity

Beyond the datum understood as 'human production' there still remains a limit, which I will call *philosophical*, to the study of organizations in general, and to the generalization of observed phenomena, in predictive capacities especially. This limit is raised by Spender (1989), who contends that industries are idiosyncratic because the tacit knowledge they convey is not accessible from without, and there is a danger in wanting to transpose to all industry what one has been able to observe in one. Spender speaks of industrial 'recipes' that are difficult to imitate because of their strongly tacit content. Less categorically, Morin simply notes that any given world has certain behaviours and knowledge that are inherent to it, and he remarks on the difficulty of understanding a world of which we know very little as we do not belong to it: thus 'the knowledge of physical things presupposes belonging to the physical world, knowledge of living phenomena presupposes belonging to the biological, knowledge of cultural phenomena presupposes belonging to a culture'. I do not mean to imply here an insurmountable idiosyncrasy, simply that 'the subject who wants to know must, in some way, distance himself to become his own object of knowledge' (1986: 205).

Non-expressed for fear of self

To become one's own object of knowledge is no easy task. Actors 'are ignorant of their own mental states and reticent to recognize them, and so deceive themselves about their own desires, motivations and emotions' (Dilman, 1971). This phenomenon, studied more in psychology or philosophy than in management, is commonly called self-deception – and the easiest person to deceive is still oneself, because we are not aware of the mental frameworks that prevail over our perception, and because we rationalize lived experience beside unfolding experience (see Demos, 1960; Kottkamp, 1990; Starbuck and Milliken, 1988a).

Although actors could become at least to some extent aware of these frameworks, notably through reflexive practice, the revelation of one cognitive framework can beget its successor. Fingarette notes that actors have a capacity to become 'ex-self-deceivers', who have finally 'acknowledged their egotistic nature – and whose self-reproaches, far from leading to self-reformation, become by a brilliant volte-face, the supreme medium of expression for their now fully conscious egoism' (Fingarette, 1969: 61). The versatile nature of human knowledge, its ability to turn back on itself, has a parallel in what Montaigne in his *Essays* called 'pulling the skin of the beast over one's head'; that is, the formidable capacity of human cowardice to find even in flight the reassuring texture of humanity.[3] This leads us to question the feasibility of recommendations such as those that encourage organizations to operate to a 'third order change' by teaching organizational members to be 'aware of their own cognitive structures' (Bartunek and Moch, 1987, for example).

Non-expressed for fear of others

'The true hypocrite is he who ceases to perceive his deception, he who lies with sincerity' (Gide, 1955: 393). The genesis of personality is a game of hide-and-seek between the private self and the social self; the one watching the other, both learning and unlearning lessons from this duality. All social systems must then possess some kind of interior life, even if this is nothing but the sum of individual private realities, for all that masking the organizational reality. But actors do not readily disclose themselves to others: to do so would be to show their hand and would be an obstacle in the relationship of seduction that they establish amongst themselves (Doi, 1985). More particularly, the public arena – that which a prying researcher represents – does not present much natural appeal for actors, for when individuals give themselves over entirely to a researcher they unveil their strategies and they divulge their intentions and motivations, their reasons for being abstruse.

Actors base their relationships on reciprocal faith. This principle can be extended even to a transactional reading of the organization: amongst the solid 'knot of contracts' (Coase, 1937/1987) each explicit contract is accompanied by a moral contract that aims to respect the formal integration of actors. Under French law, a senior manager can be dismissed for defiance, provided that this defiance is 'real and serious': the faith actors have in decision-making structures is thus recognized as an essential factor in the preservation of an organization, which is understood as a group of actors linked by the same purpose. Relationships based on mutual faith are also found in strategic alliances between organizations. Opportunism occasions a 'moral risk' on the part of the partners in a transaction (or a cooperation), to the extent that personal goals can be pursued to the detriment of the collective interest. Cooperation is based on the mutual respect, faith and tolerance of both partners. The knowledge that each party in a transaction possesses about the other is no more than a representation of their relationship, whose actual nature cannot possibly be reduced to its explicit expression: what is known explicitly is truly only 'the tip of the iceberg of the whole body of knowledge' (Nonaka, 1994). Accordingly, the tacit, that which an actor knows without being able to express or without wanting to express, is central to all agreement as much as it is to all conflict, central to cognition as much as to conceptualization.

This faith – this common acceptance of a reality that may be either indicated overtly or understood without having to be voiced – lies in our ability to create intimacy with others while respecting their mystery. Once unmasked, reality becomes harmless; it becomes schematic and reproducible. We return to the idea of reality as a pretence, insignificant because it is 'seized upon simultaneously as necessity and fate' (Rosset, 1977: 32). In such a duality, the actor projects an imaginary significance and 'superimposes it on the thing perceived without feeling the need to establish even a mediocre causal link between the thing perceived and the meaning deduced from it' (1977: 35). The unguarded way in which knowledge is passed from one person to the next encourages the employment of the schematic, the ritual, the placebo-signifier: 'The more two people in a relationship learn about each other, the more their mutual secrets are divulged, and the more the relationship risks becoming something cold and insipid' (Doi, 1985: 125). This fear of others is manifested in the interviews a researcher conducts. The researcher's 'intrusion' into the domain of the interviewee (emotional, cognitive, connotative, sensory and imaginary) can constrain the inter- viewee to express only that which they feel is 'expressible' in accordance with their belief in who the interviewer is, and what the interviewer wants.

Non-expressed for fear of authority

'While the complexity of social organization, in all systems one can think of, continually increases, its components – even in the most totalitarian of systems – have a tendency to develop what I would call *social slack*, by which I mean a certain degree of liberty to act by themselves' (Dedijer, 1975). This incompressible 'freedom zone' finds expression in 'a reality hidden by its measures'. In fact, actors act and express themselves according to criteria on which they feel they are judged, and so are thrown into what Milgram refers to as an *agentic* state:

> By this we designate the condition of the individual who considers himself as the executive agent of a foreign will, as opposed to the autonomous state in which he considers himself to be the author of his acts. (1974: 167)

This obedience on the part of the actor is not inevitable, as it 'responds to an internalized motivation and not to an external cause' (1974: 176). It accompanies the formation of the actor's identity within the social organization, in which 'the institution . . . necessarily presupposes a potentiality of obedience from these who want to benefit from it' (Milgram, 1974: 167).

NON-EXPRESSED BECAUSE NOT PERCEIVED   Because actors need a stable representation of their environment, they tend to include a large number of complex and connected functions in a single representative image (Donovan, 1986: 22). As they attempt to make sense of the perceived – the body of stimuli that has been able, somehow, to reach them – actors notice what they wish to notice, and may distort, or simply fail to perceive, the essential nature of a situation.[4]

To speak of what is not expressed because not perceived is not tautological. Actors are subject to what Goleman terms 'dormitive frames' – 'the forces that make for a waking sleep at the margins of awareness' – and the question for the researcher then becomes: 'If we so easily lull ourselves into subtle sleep, how can we awaken?'[5] The full paradox of the unequal and complex system that is human consciousness is summarized in one of R.D. Laing's *Knots*:

> The range of what we think and do
> is limited by what we fail to notice
> and because we fail to notice
> *that* we fail to notice
> there is little we can do
> to change
> until we notice
> how failing to notice
> shapes our thought and deeds
> (Laing cited in Goleman, 1985: 24 and Starbuck and Milliken, 1988a)

Is this problem, finally, unresolvable? The non-expressed because non-perceived is actually a two-tiered obstacle. It includes both that which the actor has not perceived, and so cannot express, and that which, although able to be expressed by the actor, the researcher has not perceived, and so cannot express.

THE INSTRUMENTAL NON-EXPRESSED   Nor can one lay the blame on the unconscious in order to clear the actor, or go to the other extreme and condemn the actor by ignoring the unconscious. At times there are things actors cannot express because they are what Goleman, here taking his term from Ibsen, refers to as 'vital lies' (1985: 16).

Actors are half aware, half unaware of these vital lies. Goleman explains that, 'If the force of facts is too brutal to ignore, then their meaning can be altered . . . the vital lie continues unrevealed, sheltered by . . . silence, alibis, stark denial' (1985: 17). And thus may the non-expressed assume a certain instrumentality. It can reduce the psychic discomfort of past or present situations whose true nature would otherwise be unbearable; by belittling, mocking or avoiding evidence, or by giving it another name. As Goleman continues, 'Semantics plays a big part in minimizing what is actually occurring; euphemisms are employed to hide what is really going on'. This is why organizations are often inaccessible to the research, imbedded in an inherence that can just as easily be characterized as biological as spiritual: the fact of belonging totally to a world, whether this be a social construction or born of individual commitment.

As the barriers between them – the lies that disguise the inexpressible – have already been lowered, a conflict between two people who know each other takes on much greater significance than a conflict between strangers. Hence, as Simmel insists, two people in conflict have no way out other than to construct a more heightened moral or spiritual reality than had existed prior to the conflict. The instrumentality of the non-expressed takes the form of a tolerance formulated in the renewal of commitment, in the tacit agreement between two beings whose future together has been torn apart. We have all known at the beginning, the middle or the end of our lives dilemmas of this dimension. Why, as researchers, would we make of the organization some sort of shell devoid of emotion?

Actors in organizations guard their own personal 'vital lies'; things they cannot divulge even to their spouses or closest friends, let alone to the researcher who shows up – and they generally are not sure why – to question their motivations, their behaviour and their decisions. 'People seem to anaesthetize themselves . . . they avoid acquiring information that could make vague fears specific enough to require decisive action . . . they contrive to ignore the implication of the information they do allow to get through' (Goleman, quoting Greenspoon, 1985: 19). Consequently, actors questioned by a researcher cannot secure a piece of information that they themselves have placed in the blind spot of their attention: 'What enters our attention is within the frame of awareness, what we crop out vanishes' (1985: 20).

THE NON-EXPRESSED AS A SOCIAL CONSTRUCTION   When 'deception is mutual, and its methods collective . . . nobody acting in concert with others has an interest in speaking, or in producing a proof against the false belief or the questionable desire that each wants to maintain' (Ruddick, 1988: 380). Thus, collective deception becomes the best means to avoid bitterness and regret. Social pressure and mimicry – the unavoidable adherence to a collective intention under threat of exclusion from a group – influences actors, both consciously and unconsciously, in their representation of reality.

For the researcher, interviewing several actors can result in data that is not representative of a phenomenon, but rather of a collective fear of expressing a felt reality. Each of us is socially linked to a particular environment: 'We tacitly encourage one another's lies by virtue of an unwritten social code that says we will see only what we are supposed to see; the unseeable stays out of the frame' (Goleman, 1985: 20). As researchers, we sometimes believe we are questioning people when we are really only questioning representatives of a social mind-set, a particular schema. Sometimes we obstinately seek to pierce this schema, because we have learnt another schema that says that a counter-intuitive result is always more attractive than a null hypothesis, and we throw ourselves body and soul into the 'anti-schema' (the argumentative schema) – into its ideology – because it is more seductive, because it furnishes us with a greater explanatory power. In a retrospective look at his life as a researcher, Starbuck writes: 'Over time, I concluded that normal experiments are not useful. Because people are so flexible and versatile, it is rarely worthwhile to show that they are capable of certain behaviors. One has to show that certain behaviors occur under realistic conditions. Yet, one cannot approximate in a laboratory the rewards and socialization experiences that occur in real-life organizations' (1993b: 76). Starbuck invites us to 'surmount our human limitations', to consider with humility the possibility of treating the null hypothesis – that of non-change – as an honest hypothesis; to accept, without complacency, the paradox within which the researcher lives (Starbuck, 1988).

The language in which we communicate our research is itself a social construction, itself an assemblage of frameworks that signify our membership in a given social environment.[6] As Foucault recognized, the formulation of our discoveries organizes itself into a discourse, into a statement the paternity of which we acknowledge as one delimits a territory:

> Because in our societies the property of speech – understood as the right to speak, the competence to understand, the immediate and lawful access to the corpus of statements already formulated, and the capacity to invest this speech in decisions, institutions or practices – is in fact reserved (sometimes even statutorily) to a defined group of individuals. (1972: 90)

This membership of a defined group cannot be signalled explicitly. We do not generally proclaim ourselves to be Judaeo-Christian or Neo-Marxist or constructivist. We employ and adhere to language that, without openly declaring itself as such, signifies our membership of a group.

NON-EXPRESSED BECAUSE FORGOTTEN   Finally, actors cannot express what they have forgotten, and they 'forget' by retaining what pleases them, by rationalizing the rest, by distorting the facts, and by editing their past according to the editorial line of the awareness they have here and now (see, e.g., Bartlett, 1954; Fischhoff, 1982).

Then are we not in effect insincere? If we all look at history through distorting glasses, its outlines perpetually blurred, then how can we justifiably describe what an actor says today as 'fact'? Our memory of past actions is not always faithful, and if we try to retrace the steps of our decisions they seem to elude our memory (because what is implicit and non-rational will probably never pierce the immediate level of our awareness), so we end up justifying our actions as something far from what they really were, even though we can give no reasons for wanting to disguise the facts. We are quite simply unaware of them. They escape our conscious rationality, which is not to imply that they systematically follow an unconscious rationality. We seem to follow instead a psychology whose thought is implicit and non-intentional, and our cognition is often independent of what we think to be rational and of what we are aware. In other words, we perceive more than we believe we perceive and, once perceived and assimilated, this knowledge that is ours is often not known to us.

When working within such a chimerical framework, can we even be sure of the present–past dichotomy?

> It is the lot of deep-seated acts to become perceptible only when an amount of time has passed since they were committed . . . the representation of reality is generally belated, but this is not to suggest that reality is only perceptible by means of memory. Reality's access to our consciousness, although it intervenes after the fact, does not for that constitute a memory; rather than returning to our awareness, reality is entering it. (Rosset, 1977: 130)

Just as 'nobody makes history, we do not see it, any more than we see grass grow', we cannot isolate and encapsulate an organization's past in a compact and coherent body while its present lives on, stretching forth into the future. The argument does not hold epistemologically – the past and the present are two symbiotic components of the one reality, and to say that actors rationalize the past is to say that they construct reality anew.

How can we take the non-expressed into account?

Whether we are talking about what is intentionally non-expressed (lies, omission, concealment) or what is unconsciously non-expressed (delusions, placebo-actions, perceptual frameworks, automatisms, tacit knowledge), the problem we find ourselves faced with is how to take account of the non-expressed analytically, and how to gauge to what extent this can actually be done.

There is a traditional approach to cognitive research into the non-expressed, a tradition found in two different academic paradigms. The first involves the cognitive sciences in general, which like to ponder the 'unconscious inferences' of our cognition. Strange as it may seem, grammarians take a particular interest in the non-expressed; to give just one example, they are interested in understanding the process that takes place in lexical recognition – a process subjects are unaware of. As Figure 4.1 illustrates, both of these research traditions, the linguistic and that of the general cognitive sciences, operate within the context of the

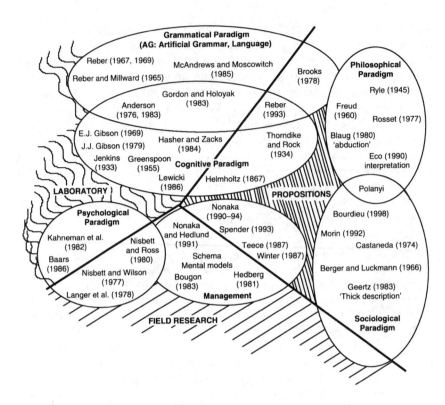

Figure 4.1   *The fragmented paradigm of the study of the 'non-expressed'*

laboratory; their experimentation usually hinges on recognition and/or visual or audio-visual restoration, in conditions more or less constraining for the subjects, who have willingly lent themselves to the game.[7]

The second great tradition of research into the unconscious and the non-expressed is that which we have qualified as 'philosophical', partly because it is here we find those philosophers who have wondered about representations of reality (including Rosset as well as Freud, that incessant questioner of our relationship with the unconscious), but equally because this tradition rests on a determination to generate critical propositions which do not rest fundamentally on an empirical base. This is the case with both Polanyi's studies of personal knowledge and Umberto Eco's evocation of *The Limits of Interpretation* (Eco develops a number of analyses through literary examples, such as using a fictional character along the lines of Sherlock Holmes to illustrate the process of adduction). These critical propositions have had a fair amount of influence on other works and other streams of research; Polanyi in particular is abundantly quoted, by 'cognitivists' as well as by Nonaka and Spender in the management sciences. Distinctions introduced in the framework of critical propositions, such as Ryle's

(1945) 'knowing how and knowing that', are found tested in research designs or discussed by other cognitivists.

The third research tradition – if we can speak of a 'tradition' or a 'paradigm' for such a discontinuous and scattered fraternity – concerns the study of unconscious phenomena, or the presumption of such phenomena, in a natural milieu. Nonetheless, those authors engaged in such work have not truly backed up their 'inductions' with empirical verifications. For example, the dynamics of knowledge creation in Western and Japanese organizations have often been compared, but generally by inducing conclusions from personal experience. To sum up, there are very few antecedent methodological attempts dedicated to the study of tacit or non-expressed phenomena. To try to establish the premises of such a methodology, I will now move on to look at two of its Gordian knots: detection and validation.

Detection strategies

The first question to consider is the following: why is this datum unspoken, or why can it not be expressed? To answer this must we know what we are looking for? In fact, a successful strategy for detecting the non-expressed must necessarily dissociate itself from such a need to specify, as actors are not aware of their tacit knowledge. This poses another problem: if we do not know precisely what it is we are looking for, then how can we induce or deduce its existence? But the fact that we have no precise image of what we hope to find should not deter us; in any event, 'from the moment when we have chosen certain observations among the infinite number of those that were possible, we have already formed a viewpoint and this viewpoint itself is a theory, as coarse as it may be' (Blaug, 1980: 14). Yet, for all this, the study of the non-expressed is far from being irreconcilable with a rigorous process. If we cannot use formal induction, because we have no 'facts' or 'data' from which to begin such a process, we do have the possibility of employing an adductive process. 'This involves an entirely different mental orientation; adduction is the operation that does not belong to logic, it allows us to leap from the chaos that constitutes the real world to a conjectural test of the actual relationship that the body of relevant variables bears out' (Blaug, 1980: 16).

The only difficulty is that this approach more or less inverts the research process, or at least demands a great flexibility of conceptualization as well as intentional and frequent returns to the field. The procedure is inverted because the empirical base is to be 'provoked' until it offers a 'salient' combination of relevant variables which will allow the adduction.

CONFRONTATION STRATEGIES   For example, and to reply in advance to a question concerning the study of the tacit in historical research, a cross-validation of different archives can lead to the first inkling that there is something non-expressed in an organization's history (of course, if we were to follow a strategy of suspicion we would consider that there is always an element of non-expressed knowledge in the history of an organization). From this point the detection of the tacit can be realized through one of two means: (a) the existence of several 'histories' of the organization; or (b) the possibility of accessing a number of witnesses of the period studied. The research strategy consists of comparing two or more (n) explicit versions of the organization's history and listing the differences in their explanations of past phenomena.

We must then confront any differences we may notice between the witnesses' explanations of phenomena. We clearly cannot annul the effects of actors' rationalizations of events, nor the body of biases linked to the solicitation of the actors' memories long after the period in question, but people have a tremendous capacity to differentiate between the 'official' and the 'unofficial' story, as well as a good capacity to recall the informal ties and commitments which bound actors in the past (these include moral, financial and subjective debts). Actors may also be influenced by earlier explanations of the organization's history; this was the case with the Pechiney group, in which two historical studies of the company, referred to as 'the Messud' and 'the Gignoux' (the names of the respective authors) repeatedly cropped up as the actors were interviewed – even though one of these works had never actually been published. The simplest strategy to take in such a situation is the most direct – that is, to confront the explanation that has been given of the work to the witness being questioned, and then to ask them whether 'it really happened like that' (one should here hold in mind that people do have a tendency to embellish their own role in events and to diminish that of their colleagues). Of course, their reply will be: 'No, it didn't happen like that. . . .' Such is the process of adduction. We do not look for proof, but for an exhibition of a sufficient amount of evidence of a phenomenon still unknown to us, which we will discover – perhaps – by undertaking a leap from chaos to a conjectural test.

Happily, the tacit sometimes presents itself in explicit forms: through suggestion or through differences between two texts. This too was the case with Pechiney where the discovery of the $3C^3$ process, which Barrand, Gadeau et al. (1964) had ascribed to the company's engineers, claiming it was the result of a long maturation, was later described as the individual achievement of a manager who had successfully captured adequate knowledge from Pechiney's American partners (Lamourde-dieu, 1990). This discovery was made by chance, which is to say without even seeking to explain the birth of the $3C^3$ process, nor having any particular need for the explanation. The search for the non-expressed (in this example non-expressed because the engineers knew more than they wanted to express) may well be tinged with systematization, in the absorption of a maximum number of signals and stimuli, but it is always subject to the good fortune of obtaining 'the' combination that will provoke the adduction.

STRATEGIES OF USURY, OF THE NULL HYPOTHESIS, AND POLITICAL STRATEGY Confrontation strategies can take on another aspect: they can become strategies of usury. By this I mean we can return charges to the interviewee – but here by failing to modify our questions, or by including only minor modifications – in order to measure any gaps in responses. In such a strategy innocence pays more than intelligence, for a reason touched on above: the fear that the intruder (here the researcher) can inspire.

Because actors have a propensity to believe in evolution and change, any strategy that seems to defend a null hypothesis can provoke in interviewees a desire to demonstrate change, and so to express what they have not wanted to express, or what they have not been able to express (through inhibition or because vital lies were involved). The present and the past are interwoven in reality, and they represent political risks as much at the individual level as they do collectively, where a past or a present may be defended so as not to betray it or distance it from collective beliefs. The opposite of the strategy of the null hypothesis is therefore the political strategy, which pleads multiple changes so as to provoke the revelation of political meaning. Both strategies are far from the hypothetical-deductive method. Adduction is an open and flexible approach, it entails neither the principle of *tabula rasa*, of starting from a 'clean theoretical slate', nor the adherence to pre-existent models.

THE 'SECOND ASSESSMENT' STRATEGY The strategy of exacting a second assessment consists of confronting the interviewee with another set of data aimed at showing signs of the existence of processes or knowledge which they have been unable or have not wanted to express. The researcher does this not from a position of exposing truth, but of presenting a second hypothesis and encouraging reflexive practice and discussion of a reality which differs from the actor's own (Osterman, 1990). This method can encourage actors to confront three of their apprehensions: the non-expressed for fear of self, the constructed non-expressed, and the instrumental non-expressed – by allowing them to, respectively, be released from the framework of 'subject of knowledge'; to distance themselves from the framework in which they normally operate; and to move the discussion to neutral terrain, where the instrumentality of a vital lie loses its meaning (as they discuss a representation that is not their own). In presenting the second representation the researcher will take care not to identify it – not to declare: 'X told me that . . .' (a strategy reserved for a political approach) – and will avoid provoking in the actor a fear of the 'other' (the researcher) or a fear of authority, either of which could lead them to stifle their expression.

Tracking the tacit

A challenge for the observant

The phenomena we perceive, for the most part, reflect only ourselves. In research, phenomena that we believe we have identified most often reflect our observation tools, and our results tell us far more about our method than they do of the phenomenon which has solicited the observation. Such is the difficulty we must try to circumvent: we must steer clear of the tool that takes the place of observation, the analysis that carries within it a mythology of phenomena that exist only in the imagination of the researcher.

The non-observable character of a phenomenon is generally a result of the misleading or narrow perspective adopted by the observer. Leibniz recognized the propensity for this in 1697:

> Consider a very beautiful painting. If we were to cover it, hiding all but an infinitely small part, what would we see that is singular in it, or exceptional, however close we were to examine it, other than a confused heap of colours with no sense, and no art? Yet if, once the cloth had been lifted from it, were we to consider the entire painting from a suitable perspective, we would understand that what had appeared to be randomly applied was for its creator a work of supreme art. (Leibniz, 1697: 338–45)

The choice of perspective – that is to say, of the tool to be employed in the observation – necessitates the consideration of a number of questions. The phenomena I propose to study are complex and will bring tacit and explicit forms of knowledge into play; it would be presumptuous to assume that they will lend themselves to a hypothetical-deductive approach. Who can guarantee, in the context of such exploratory research, that there will be a priori a definite causal link between the 'knowing modes' that actors employ and their firms' successful resolution of ambiguous situations? This is the first point.

Secondly, in such an exploration we must reconcile our desire to go beyond the deceptive stage of the interpretation with our desire to enter into the reality of the phenomena. But how is this to be achieved? And if we are mistaken in our conjectures? If, finally, the tacit dimension of knowledge is nothing but an incoherent vapour of dreams, emotions and phantasmagorias that has no great role in the organization? The only way to find this out is to study what happens in 'real life' – 'through experience and not through some type of reflection or abstract reasoning' (Hume, 1955). We must admit that 'there is no object of which we can determine from a single examination, without consulting experience, that it is the cause of another, nor any object of which we can determine in the same manner with certitude that it is not the cause of another' (Hume, 1955).

Because they do not readily lend themselves to measurement, the nature of the studied phenomena – knowledge transformations – requires the choice of a method that is as empirical and inductive as possible, and as close as possible to the organizational terrain. The study of modes of knowledge within the organization is a nascent field; introduced by Nonaka in 1987, the idea of a dynamics between different knowledge bases has not yet given rise to much empirical research, and except for Spender and Bird few authors have followed Nonaka into this no man's land. Nonaka himself has not yet developed his discovery empirically; the work he and Hedlund have carried out at the University of Stockholm is based on a narrative tradition in its comparison of knowledge management in Western and Japanese organizations (Nonaka and Hedlund, 1991). All the same, studies of organizational knowledge creation within epistemological and ontological perspectives do follow an adductive process. Other works in the field are, for the most part, also written within an epistemological perspective, close to that of the sociology of knowledge.

Faced with the small number of existing empirical works, I am constrained to play my part in rectifying this, in carrying out research on phenomena now seldom approached in the management sciences. The body of work on 'knowledge' that does exist has for the most part been developed in the fields of sociology, psychology or philosophy.[8] Although quite a large amount was written on 'knowledge-intensive firms' during the 1980s, this did not concern itself with transitions between the tacit and the explicit (with the possible exceptions of the work of Teece, 1987 and Winter, 1987).

In a relatively new field it is recommended that a 'naturalistic' investigation and, more precisely, case method should be adopted (Lincoln and Guba, 1985; Yin, 1984). To perfect this strategy, it is necessary first to define what types of event are going to be studied: contemporary or past? My reply to this question was twofold: to devote myself only to contemporary phenomena would be to deny myself the consideration of long-term perspectives on comprehension. If we undertake an exploratory study, it does not mean that we have to isolate ourselves from current phenomena. The opposite is in fact the case. To revisit situations, cases and companies whose decisions and events have already been illuminated by other researchers can provide a rich base for comparison. The second aspect which supports this strategy is that a retrospective case study permits the testing of the theoretical construction against a long temporal horizon. In a study of the dynamics of organizational knowledge, this option can only be enticing: does the dynamic movement of knowledge in ambiguous situations leave traces in the organization? I therefore retained this option, despite the risk of bias which accompanies all retrospective research.[9] But what is truly interesting, beyond allowing sufficient distance to reach a more profound understanding of the phenomena, is to be able to compare past and contemporary situations, including those that are current and unfolding.

HOW CAN WE ENSURE THAT OUR OBSERVATIONS ARE WELL FOUNDED?   The adoption of an interpretative approach to the detection of the non-expressed does not disallow the possibility of testing our discoveries. The only test I have been able to substantiate is a return to the field with those conjectures that have been established, so as to confront the interviewees with them. Although it is certainly no absolute guarantee of the validity of the results when actors then say 'yes, it happened just like that', what I have found is that actors respond with a variety of attitudes when confronted with a body of non-expressed knowledge. Some do not want to hear any reality but the official reality, that of the 'Messud' or the 'Gignoux', while others will validate the results but in doing so will modify their own representation of reality (reality as understood by Rosset: as an ever-renewing conglomerate of the past and the present) this time taking into account the now unveiled but previously non-expressed knowledge, yet still retaining an indecipherable non-expressed element.

Because of its tacit nature, researchers of the non-expressed cannot research the 'truth'. As we can only dip into the barrel of the unconscious without ever draining it, our object can only be to reduce the inexpressible residue to a minimum. Redundant questions can be used to test the research process: have I been observant enough? Have I understood correctly? Have I reconstructed events scrupulously? These questions, which we traditionally pose to our colleagues, to other researchers, should also be posed to the interviewees themselves in order to reduce the role chance plays in the attribution of data to categories of observations that are all the more fragile as they concern phenomena or knowledge that the actors cannot or do not want to express.

WHY WE MUST TAKE RISKS   The study of the non-expressed can justifiably be described as 'adventurous research'. Like any explorer, the researcher who is determined to delve into the non-expressed must follow uncharted and potentially hazardous paths, and implicitly surrender themselves to severe criticism from their peers. The limits of their research will be decided as much by the 'sturdiness' of the categories to which they attribute their data as by the work's internal and external validity. Perhaps here we should question the notion of 'validity', and the *raison d'être* of research itself? Is there anything to be gained by moving within the finite space of existing paradigms?

> His imagination is hindered, and even his language ceases to belong to him. And this is reflected even more in the nature of scientific facts, which are lived as if they are independent of opinions, beliefs and cultural

memberships. It is therefore possible to create a tradition and to maintain it by strict rules; this, to a certain extent, enables success. But is it desirable to sustain such a tradition by rejecting all other possibilities? Should one give it exclusive rights over knowledge, with the consequence that all results obtained by other methods are eliminated without appeal? (Feyerabend, 1979: 16)

Research into tacit knowledge is today embryonic. It is mainly supported by critical propositions and laboratory experimentation which reduce reality to tests of visual stimuli, or to adventurous manipulations of clichés on the knowledge of some and the knowledge of others. But such research calls for 'an entirely new conception of the world, including a new conception of man and his capacity for knowing' (Feyerabend, 1979: 164). It calls for the development of our personality and attentiveness – to safeguard the 'necessity to wait and to ignore enormous masses of observations and critical measures, [which] is almost never discussed in our methodologies' (1979: 164). We cannot continue to understand, explain and predict from 'data' which is itself no more than particular understandings and explanations. On the other hand, to deny *en bloc* the validity of the existent would be to refuse the idea of progress, to deny scientific research itself.

Research, and the researcher at the heart of it, poses a problem of 'faith'. Faith in both the concept of progress and change and in 'the law of nature' – as the principle of generalization hides a belief in the existence of universal laws that preside over the behaviour of people or organizations under a given set of conditions ('Pranks and human stupidity are such common phenomena that I would believe the most extraordinary events are born from their contests rather than admit such a remarkable violation of the laws of nature': Hume, 1983 edn: 205). The idea of difference, of contrast, is essential not only to the researcher but to all of us: 'for a social group, the loss of diversity announces an escalation of violence, as if all men have the same desires they become mimetic rivals, devoted to symmetrical revenges, locked in conflict without end'[10]; the only way to escape the hell of such a chain of reprisals is to ask who started it. So the null hypothesis, that of non-change, is rarely envisaged as a research proposition, because we must continually underline the idea of progress, continually illuminate a difference in our results and discoveries.

There is no reason to be a researcher, although one must have a desire to understand and explain. We do not undertake research just to conclude that 'all is both true and false', but this does not mean we should pursue dogma by placing the researcher above human fallibility, protected from deception, exempt from schemas, absolved from all error. Modern science has got rid of the philosophy it had received in literary form, filing it away as a formal exercise; yet it was philosophy that once fulfilled just this function of soul-searching, of questioning one's own fallibility. 'Sometimes I think, sometimes I am': the duality which Hume rose up against, although remaining its humble representative, is today more apt than ever. By separating a researcher's thought from the totality of their experience we risk making of research a cold logic that feeds on itself; and making of us researchers, in the most painful of paradoxes, the beings the most resistant to change.

Engaging actors in reflexive practice

Although 'operationalization' does not present major problems as far as explicit knowledge is concerned, 'tracking' tacit knowledge is more problematic. To make up for an absence or a paucity of awareness, whether individual or collective, vis-à-vis knowledge which actors cannot perceive nor transform, we must turn to techniques of cross-referencing. This is a process of the *revelation* of tacit knowledge on the field. That is to say, of engaging actors in reflexive practice.

Reflexive practice is the activity of thinking *about* one's own actions and analysing them in a critical manner, with the purpose of improving a professional practice. It requires of actors a capacity to place themselves as external observers of their own presuppositions, attitudes and sentiments, and of how these influence their practice, and from there to speculate on these once the action is past (see Imel, 1992; Kottkamp, 1990; Osterman, 1990; Peters, 1991). We should also recall Schön's work on 'reflexive practitioners' (1983, 1988), which was inspired by Dewey, Lewin and Piaget; all of whom would no doubt have agreed with him that 'learning is dependent on the integration of experience with thought, and of theory with practice' (Imel, 1992: 1). Reflexive practice is attractive as it encourages actors to freely develop their ideas of or sentiments towards the knowledge *they think they have used*. The trap to avoid is believing, just because an actor successfully expresses what up until now had been tacit, that this is the end of the matter. As has often been demonstrated, actors are capable of behaving in an entirely accidental or unconscious fashion and then later inventing a perfectly fluid rationale for their behaviour. We should also bear in mind that thought is often generated in action, compelling actors to invent problems to fit solutions that have already been established (Starbuck, 1983).

The second hurdle to cross in the data collection process is that the researcher risks 'revealing' in an interviewee knowledge that the actor could not have hitherto expressed as it simply had not been theirs. Actors may 'borrow' explanations from the researcher. To counter this obstacle, incessant returns between material and analysis and between reflection and observation are essential. Actors were invited not only to go back over their declarations, but equally to discuss, without knowing their exact source, declarations others had made.[11] But while this method proved relevant in the initial tests for individual actors, we nevertheless encountered a number of difficulties with it when it came to the mobilization of knowledge that is both tacit and collective. When we tackle the collective reference, we run into actors' sensitivity about any examination of their own beliefs or values, which leads us to a major weakness of reflexive practice: it requires both a knowledge of the practice discussed, and an awareness of a professional and personal philosophy.

OBSERVING THE FIRM'S KNOWLEDGE   Observations of organizational knowledge are finally made through simple questions, to which actors reply rather easily: how do they manage their knowledge? How do they interact with their environment? From where do they draw their knowledge? What knowledge gives them or has given them a major advantage? How did this happen? Did they know things that others did not know? Have they been more astute or more intelligent than others? In obtaining this knowledge? In distributing the rights to it? If necessary, in imposing it?

The employment of direct questions allows us to analyse all the media and modes of the actor's knowledge, to obtain a description of the actor's role such as they perceive it, and of the role of those around them, and to invite the interviewee to recount one or more anecdotes concerning experiences that have enabled them to use knowledge that was particular to them and to so gain a significant advantage. This type of questioning encourages them to identify the preferences they give to different forms of knowledge. The interview strategy consists of an initial phase in which the researcher attempts to gain the interviewee's confidence. The subject broached in this phase is harmless, allowing the interviewee to situate themselves, and it should provoke an effort on the actor's part to remember, in their particular anecdote, any knowledge which had been specific to them and which they had used to gain a major advantage. When the question of crisis arrives, the atmosphere is 'de-dramatized': an in-depth discussion can then take place of the knowledge the actor used at the moment of the crisis. This interview is followed by a thorough analysis of the secondary data relative to the anecdote (or anecdotes), so as to be able to estimate its veracity, and to return, if need be, 'for a few more details'. The second interview, when necessary, is an open interview, where the researcher returns to the actor and exposes what they believe they have discovered or understood.

When the interviewees have established what they believe to have been the motives behind their attitudes, their behaviour or the knowledge they have mobilized, they are in a situation in which 'facts' (which despite everything may be misleading) are restored. Used in psychology, reflexive analysis consists of leading the subject to engage in a reflection whose foundation is introspective; they direct their attention back at themselves. 'To engage oneself in a reflexive practice requires that an individual adopts the position of an external observer, so as to identify the presuppositions and sentiments that underlie their practice, then speculates in order to understand how these presuppositions and sentiments affect their practice' (Imel, 1992: 6).

INTEREST AND LIMITS OF REFLEXIVE PRACTICE   Reflexive practice is therefore a process that allows an actor to attribute sense to his or her own practices, either while the action takes place or afterwards. Used as an observation tool, it allows this actor then to share this reflexive activity of understanding with the researcher. On the other hand, reflexive practice is a person's own investigation of their 'system of knowledge' – the term is perhaps a little excessive – our object being to identify the knowledge dynamics involved. The reflexive method is entirely versatile: it can be used during or after actions and can be adapted to different experimental designs. It may accompany non-participant observation or be evoked to conclude a situation by demanding that actors themselves recount its development, so as to compare their accounts with what has been observed. It can be integrated just as well into research designs that anticipate an analysis 'in process' as in those that relate to ad hoc analyses. Using this method, the researcher plays the role of 'catalyst', accompanying the actors in their reflection while according the necessary attention to their profound sensitivity when asked to examine their own beliefs, values or emotions (Miles and Huberman, 1984; Peters, 1991; Rose, 1992).

Nothing should escape our attention

We cannot rely entirely on what managers have to say about their own practices, however. 'The most expert actions most often reveal that actors know more than they can express' (Schön, 1983: 51). It can happen that they do not know that they know or, more bluntly, that they just do not know . . . and so they invent.

For this reason it is good to follow the aforesaid approach of engaging in a long immersion in the organizations being studied, of at least four to ten months. This does not mean merely turning up to conduct interviews or observations, but actually 'living' in the organization, yet without taking part in the processes observed. Experience shows that direct observation is the most successful way to delimit the mobilization of collective knowledge, mainly because a good part of such knowledge is procedural – involving communities of practice or automatisms linked to the carrying out of complex tasks, often little evident to practitioners themselves, but visible to the external observer.

POSING THE CORRECT PROBLEM   The quality of an interpretation will also be strongly dependent on the attention paid to precision and detail in the initial problem definition, on the number and independence of the procedures used to solve the problem, and on the number and the diversity of criteria used to test these procedures.[12] The repetition of these procedures in a number of different organizations also enables them to be more readily controlled. Theory construction implies a simultaneous and parallel process, and not a sequential line of thought. Theorization should also distance itself from the linear resolution of a problem, for fear of being dominated by the initial research question (Ziman, 1987). Rather than adopting a general pattern of problem resolution, the researcher should see theory construction as a sense-making activity. This problem of sense-allocation is particularly critical when, as with the study of organizational knowledge, the correspondence between concepts and the observable is strained, or when the studied system is open rather than closed (Gergen, 1986; Henschel, 1971). As Starbuck has suggested (1988), the dynamic of any social system is based on the heterogeneity and the multiplicity of our frames of awareness: consequently these must be included in any research design.

According to Miles and Huberman (1984: 21) there are three aspects to the qualitative analysis of data: reduction, display and interpretation. 'Data reduction refers to the process of selecting, focusing, simplifying, abstracting, and transforming the "raw" data that appear in written-up field notes' – in this case, transcriptions of interviews, reports of direct observations, and 'secondary data' gleaned from archival readings (of memos, internal notes, etc.). 'Data reduction is not something separate from analysis. It is *part* of analysis. The researcher's choices of which data chunks to code, which to pull out, which patterns summarize a number of chunks, what the evolving story is, *are all analytic choices.*' The second major element of analysis is data display. Data display is the organized assemblage of data to allow conclusions to be drawn from it. Miles and Huberman propose an original and varied inventory of appropriate forms of data display – these include matrices, graphs, networks and charts. They explain that all of these are 'designed to assemble organized information in an immediately accessible, compact form, so that the analyst can see what is happening and either draw justified conclusions or move on to the next-step analysis the display suggests may be useful' (1984: 21–2). The final aspect of the analysis consists of drawing conclusions and establishing verifications. 'In short, the meanings emerging from the data have to be *tested* for their plausibility, their sturdiness, their *validity*' (1984: 22).

Weick argues that 'researchers cannot make deductions from concepts alone'; that the reliability of an interpretation rests on a process that 'must be designed to highlight relationships, connections, and interdependencies in the phenomenon of interest' (1989: 517). Unlike deterministic research, inductive research 'generally lacks an accepted model for its central creative process' (Eisenhardt and Bourgeois, 1988). That said, numerous modes of encoding events, actors, actions, and results of actions exist, and this has inspired the establishment of a specific category for each potentially used form of knowing. As an initial precaution, I have purposefully avoided instituting any exclusive relationship between data and categories, perhaps weakening the internal validity of the results, but avoiding the major bias that would arise from 'forcing the data' into exclusive categories (which could lead to the apparent monopoly of one form over another, when nothing of the sort has really occurred).[13] On the contrary, data related to events – to the results of firms' actions or the widening or shrinkage of the perimeter of action – have been made the object of exclusive categories.

The analyses carried out on the data should enable us to answer our four related questions. This involves identifying which modes of knowing are privileged in relation to other modes at different points during the ambiguous situation, and 'grasping' knowledge's dynamics. A two-part process was adopted. In fact, analyses were carried out during the observation stage, but no analyses undertaken in a subsequent case drew on, nor expanded on, these earlier findings. This was so as to avoid the construction of mental models.

The generation of preliminary theories can forge in the researcher a belief in these early fruits of the research process, and so influence data collection in the next case. The final case investigated could, in this way, prove to be little more than a pure translation of the researcher's desire. To avoid this trap one must avoid pre-empting theory formulation in the first cases or the first months, and must not hesitate to return to the field whenever this appears necessary. Notwithstanding, as my case studies were carried out in three different countries (France, the United States and Australia), where the distances did not encourage repeated returns, these had to be duly justified. Three returns to the source were finally necessary, including one to Australia.

An inductive approach to theory-building does not necessarily imply an initial abstraction from the knowledge one has. It is often suggested, on the contrary, that 'a priori specification of constructs' can facilitate measurement and validation (Eisenhardt, 1989). In any case, the idea of beginning research from a 'clean theoretical slate' is at most wishful thinking: nobody can abstract themselves from their own knowledge to access that of others. But the existence of a theoretical construct does not mean that one systematically researches relationships between it and the studied variables. It simply allows one to orientate the investigation in a conceptual framework which attracts attention to the critical variables (Berry, 1983; Crozier and Friedberg, 1980).

For example, for the collection of data it is critical to understand how actors succeed in making deductions and inductions on the basis of minimal and ambiguous knowledge, after the fashion of Sherlock Holmes inducing or deducing possibilities of culpability from a very limited number of clues. Umberto Eco too uses this kind of reasoning in his novels, and discusses it in *The Limits of Interpretation* (1990). My

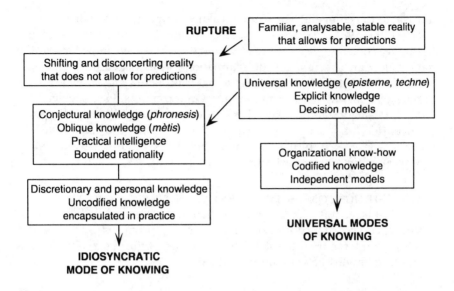

Figure 4.2   *An intuitive construct following Détienne and Vernant*

intuition is that the emergence of an ambiguous situation represents a transition from one knowledge base to another. This intuition is based on a number of different examples, including Nonaka's (1991b) account of the learning of bread-making skills at the International Hotel of Osaka, and several examples given by Détienne and Vernant (1978) of the management of ambiguous and puzzling situations in the Greek world.

In the numerous cases presented by Détienne and Vernant, actors are submitted to a rupture of their known, stable and analysable world, which suddenly becomes unsettled and disconcerting, and no longer open to measurement. From then on, their science (*episteme*) and the decision-making and behavioural models (*techne*) that they had habitually applied in ordinary situations no longer has any connection to the situation. The actors have to employ another way of knowing (*metis*), which they derive from social practice (*phronesis*), as they use ruse and cunning to get themselves out of a difficult situation. Their universal laws, their rules of wisdom are now useless to them, and they forcefully integrate themselves into the new limitations of rationality. From there a transition is established, and discretionary knowledge emerges whose nature is tacit, immersed in practice. They have changed their mode of knowing (Figure 4.2).

The transition between modes of knowing is given empirical support in Détienne and Vernant's analyses of Greek texts. However, they do not explain how this transition has occurred; whether it has been diffi-cult, tedious or expensive; or whether individuals have had to 'unlearn' to be able to achieve it. The same weakness appears in Nonaka's works (1987, 1990, 1991a, 1991b, 1994). And so, finally, the existence of my 'intuitive' construct attracts my attention to two aspects important to the data collection process: my determination (1) to penetrate the 'mechanisms' of such transitions, and (2) to describe as fully as possible all the 'modes of knowing' that I can identify. On top of this, I see the need for a precise categorization of the elements of knowledge in order to group them under the labels 'tacit', 'explicit', 'individual' and 'collective'. In other words, this intuitive construct underlines the necessity of establishing an intimate connection that goes beyond observable reality.

ESTABLISHING CONNECTIONS BETWEEN THE OBSERVABLE AND MODES OF KNOWING   Adopting a display of the data in the form of matrices, in accordance with the methodology proposed by Miles and Huberman, I have tried to establish repertories of the observable actions of the four modes of knowing identified:

A chronic problem of qualitative research is that it is done chiefly with words, not with numbers. Words are fatter than numbers, and usually have multiple meanings. . . . Numbers, by contrast, are usually less ambiguous and may be processed with more economy. Small wonder, then, that most researchers prefer working with numbers only, or getting the words they collect translated into numbers as rapidly as possible. Despite all this . . . although words may be more unwieldy than numbers, they also enable 'thick description', as Geertz (1973) suggests. That is, they render more meaning than numbers alone, and should be hung onto throughout data analysis. (Miles and Huberman, 1984: 54)

Thus, qualitative research depends fundamentally on 'watching people in their own territory and interacting with them in their own language, on their own terms. As identified with sociology, cultural anthropology, and political science, among other disciplines, qualitative research has been seen to be "naturalistic, ethnographic, and participatory"' (Kirk and Miller, 1986: 9). This research is in keeping with such an empirical approach, with the aim of leading to 'grounded theory'. Its purpose is not to test existing theories, but to generate theory from data.[14]

To 'ground' an interpretation is to observe the phenomena in process, and in detail. In this study, three criteria are relevant: the human perimeter, the decisional horizon and the structural perimeter:

The *human perimeter* can be defined as the number of actors implicated in the studied process. A process may involve a single actor or several actors. In a study of organization knowledge we want to measure whether this perimeter shrinks or enlarges according to the knowledge used. One of the underlying questions would be, for example: does the creation of objective knowledge systematically imply a widening of this perimeter?

Human perimeter
The process is individual
The process spreads to a larger number of actors
The process is collective
The process contracts to a more limited number of individuals

Decisional horizon
The action is limited (very short term)
The action is inscribed within a short-term horizon
The action is inscribed within a medium-term horizon
The action is inscribed within a long-term horizon
The action challenges the organization's identity, its *raison d'être*

Structural perimeter
The action concerns only the immediate environment
The action concerns an organizational unit
The action concerns the whole organization
The action extends to an inter-organizational context

Figure 4.3   *Action perimeters*

The *decisional horizon* is the duration of the action, its time span. This could be as short as the instant (immediate action), in which case we would speak of a limited horizon. In this study I am interested in exploring the relationship between time and the mobilization of knowledge. Does tacit knowledge need more time to articulate itself than explicit knowledge?

The *structural perimeter* refers to the environment in which the action unfolds. This may concern only the actor's immediate environment or its consequences may be much broader. Here I hope to determine whether actors mobilize different knowledge according to whether they envisage actions as being of short or long term, or as having a local or a more global reach (see Figure 4.3).

For each time that an event unfolds I have analysed what knowledge is mobilized by actors and in what perimeters it is used. In this way knowledge familiar to management research was identified: communities of practice, instinctive knowledge, scientific expertise, procedural knowledge. Each belongs to one of the matrix's four categories. We can then establish which modes of knowing are most frequently mobilized at the moment of observation (see Figure 4.4).

The same classification operation has been realized for actors' behaviours while events are occurring. Sometimes they demonstrate a common anxiety, making the figuration collective, while sometimes their behaviour is more confident, even cocky – they may seek contact, showing their openness about the situation. These different behaviours can be grouped according to the same matrix (see Figure 4.5). Classifying behaviours allows us to define potential relationships between a

Explicit individual knowledge	Explicit collective knowledge
Reference to written notes, a personal dossier	Use of databases, reference works, other texts and publications, plans, organizational agendas, norms and standards (Spender, 1993)
Positional knowledge (Hirsch, 1977)	
Reference to statutory expertise: the quality of an engineer; a geometrist, an expert, etc. (Foucault, 1972)	Recourse to a hierarchy (hierarchical circuit)
Technical knowledge, declarative knowledge, skilfulness or method (Polanyi, 1966a)	Reference to an institutionalized rule (DiMaggio and Powell, 1983)
	Methods employed to delimit the situation
	Reference to performances (Berry, 1983)
Tacit individual knowledge	**Tacit collective knowledge**
'Animal' knowledge – instinctive incrementalism, impulsion, reflex, intuition (Griffin, 1982, 1984; Morin, 1986: 53–67)	Reference to common sense (Isaacs, 1950)
	Reference to local collective knowledge (Berry, 1983; Spender, 1993)
Automatic knowledge (Polanyi, 1966b; Spender, 1993)	Reference to a form of collective thought particular to the organization (Weick and Roberts, 1993)
Adduction, creating form from chaos, serendipity, accidental discovery (Blaug, 1980; Eco, 1990)	
Imagination (Castaneda, 1968, 1974)	Employment of a repertory of actions used in the organization, or derived from a social role (Barton, 1969: 126; Starbuck, 1983)
Practical knowledge (Nyíri and Smith, 1988)	
Procedural knowledge (Anderson, 1976; Scribner, 1986)	Reference to tradition, to the organizational culture (Nyíri and Smith, 1988)

Figure 4.4   *Potentially mobilizable knowledge*

form of knowledge, the condition of its unfolding (the characteristics of its environment: is it more or less turbulent, more or less fragmented?) and the behaviours adopted by actors at the time.

The third analysis that must be carried out if we are to delimit the employment of knowledge in firms is of those actions through which knowledge is principally generated. For example, it has been shown that tacit knowledge is acquired through socialization. But what type of socialization is involved? Here we must categorize the actions observed during the course of the events under scrutiny (Figure 4.6).

Following this we need to articulate all of our observations surrounding the event. For example: a crisis occurs, and actors react. How many of them react? Do they undertake short-term action or do they instead approach the situation with the long-term perspective in mind? What does their action involve? Does it concern the firm as a whole,

Explicit and individual Lying in wait Explicit avoidance of a situation Attempting to verbalize situation Conflict seeking Showing awareness of the situation Focusing efforts on problem-solving	**Explicit and collective** Collective implication in the process Collective avoidance of the process Deliberate sharing of knowledge Formation of a team or a task force Constant striving for collective explicitation
Tacit and individual 'Floating' attention Infiltration, impregnation Automatic behaviours Reflexes, 'animal instincts' Resentments, conflictual attitudes that are held back Web of tacit relations Dubious feelings Thriving in the fog	**Tacit and collective** Communities of practice Things are done without being explained Network of tacit understanding Collective orientation is sought Atmosphere is uncomfortable Inference and insinuation, implicit reciprocal denial Make the configuration collective Emergent attitude of knowledge sharing

Figure 4.5   *Observed behaviours*

Placebo-action (Langer, 1978; Langer et al., 1978)
Elaboration of an informal matrix of relations (Barnard, 1938; Engle, 1994)
Establishment of a new rule to clarify and control the situation
Formation of a collateral organization to confront the problem (Zand, 1981)
Introduction of an exploratory change. Trial and error (Mintzberg and Westley, 1992)
Updating, wiping the slate clean, or collective or public explanation of the situation
Implementation of new permanent or temporary organizational settings
Fine-tuning (Starbuck and Milliken, 1988b)
Mobilization of a clandestine network (Moullet, 1992)
Meta-learning, reframing, second-loop learning (Imel, 1992; Osterman, 1990; Schön, 1983)
Renewing organizational intelligence (Wilensky, 1967b) or the sociology of secrecy (Simmel, 1906)
Bounded rationality (Cyert and March, 1963; Newell and Simon, 1972)
Past successes interpreted as evidence of competence (Starbuck and Milliken, 1988b)
Rejection of a behaviour which has not proved efficient (Fritz and Marks, 1954)
Reframing all processes through revolutionary change (Mintzberg and Westley, 1992)
Socialization, contact-seeking (Nonaka and Hedlund, 1991)

Figure 4.6   *Examples of observable actions*

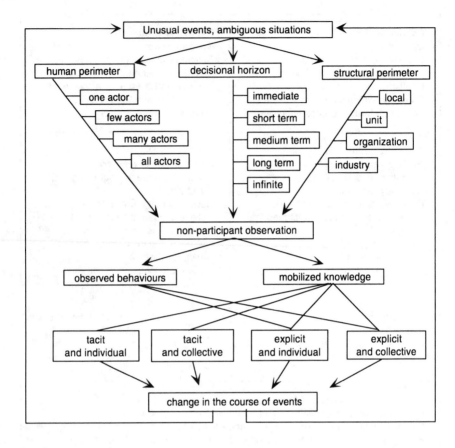

Figure 4.7   *An integrative framework of analysis*

such as the introduction of a new rule? Does it concern a more local adaptation?

We then look at the actors during the course of the action. What behaviours do they exhibit? What knowledge do they mobilize? For example, actors may turn to scientific expertise (collective and explicit knowledge) to clarify the situation; or they may do the reverse, they may prefer to mobilize their practical knowledge and tackle the problem head-on with their intuition and particular know-how (individual and tacit knowledge). What frame of mind are they in? Are they frightened by the puzzling situation that confronts them? In this case their behaviour is impulsive; the firm is marked by a collective frenzy, a heavy atmosphere in which the mounting tension is palpable, yet nobody shows express disagreement (collective and tacit behaviour). The observations have finally been grouped into an integrative interpretative diagram (Figure 4.7). This diagram allows us to describe the sequence of actions undertaken, including their respective perimeters, the behaviours

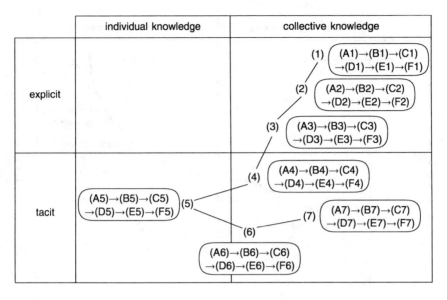

Figure 4.8 *Positioning sequences of events into the matrix*

that have been observed and the knowledge that has been mobilized. What results from the firm's actions, what is the new situation? In what way has the course of events been modified? From there we recommence the cycle of interpretation, as the Figure 4.7 demonstrates.

To establish this cycle, we proceeded to a coding of field notes, observations and archival materials. 'A code is an abbreviation or symbol applied to a segment of words – most often a sentence or paragraph of transcribed field notes – in order to *classify* the words. Codes are *categories*. They usually derive from research questions, hypotheses, key concepts, or important themes' (Miles and Huberman, 1984: 56). Each sequence comprising an event and the handling of it has been coded. How do managers react, in terms of knowledge management, to ambiguity and sudden changes in their normal environment? Why, at what moment, and according to what mechanism do they give preference to one 'knowledge base' rather than to another? Who do they telephone? What do they ask? How do they resolve embarrassing situations? It is these small observations which allow us to identify sequences in which mobilized knowledge is on the whole explicit and collective, tacit and collective or again tacit and individual. Each small sequence has been integrated into the matrix according to the knowledge that it implies the most strongly (Figure 4.8).[15]

This repeated presentation of the findings allows each of the four case studies to be read with the same coding, and comparisons to be drawn between them. Codes enable us to understand at what moment and in what conditions the 'transition' from one mode of knowledge to

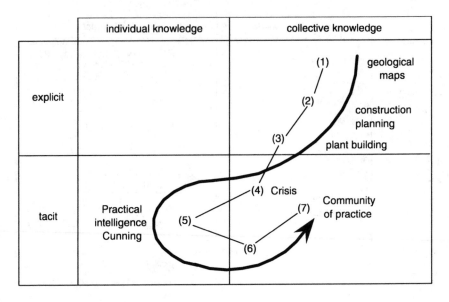

Figure 4.9   *Visualization of knowledge transformations*

another has taken place, and to connect this with behavioural and organizational components. A simplified matrix has been established for each case to enable a rapid transition reading. This matrix enables the dynamics of knowledge to be illustrated in a global movement, showing how the firm has wandered from one form of knowledge to another. A curve has been simply traced by following each sequence (numbered 1 to 7 in Figure 4.8). The result gives us an immediate visualization of the course knowledge has followed (Figure 4.9).

The cases were then compared against each other, leading to conclusions about both the observed behaviours and the particular characteristics of each organization. The analysis leads to a precise definition of the roles of the different forms of knowledge in the apprehension of ambiguous situations, and to more general conclusions about the management of organizational knowledge. The visualization method allows for a rapid comparison of each organization's management of its specific organizational knowledge (Figure 4.10).

Firms in exemplary situations

Although Eisenhardt (1989) argues that the populations of the case studies should be selected on a theoretical foundation, this method of intentional sampling is based on the selection of representative rather than exemplary cases (Lincoln and Guba, 1985). In this study cases were chosen that had encountered and recovered from uncertain situations, with the added intention of looking at cases that varied as widely as

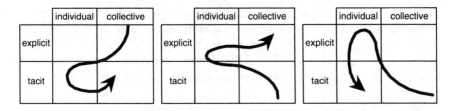

Figure 4.10   *Different patterns of knowledge transformations*

possible in their other attributes. The construction of a new theory is partly facilitated by the maximization of differences between the groups being compared, which itself increases the differences in the data obtained. The objective was to obtain the broadest dispersion possible among the studied cases, to best test the replication of results. Organizations that differed widely in size and in social conditions as well as in their goals were sought. Similarly, I avoided formulating any a priori hypotheses about them, to avoid becoming locked into any perceptual frameworks, or schemas, which could limit the breadth and suppleness of the results in the later construction of theory.

The first case is that of Qantas Airways. The idea of studying an airline came to me after reading the International Air Transport Association's (IATA) 1992 annual statement, which announced that at that time only three of the world's airlines (British Airways, Singapore Airlines and Cathay Pacific) were not showing losses. The puzzling situation was evident. Following the deregulation of the airline industry it also met the criterion of confronting a dramatic shift in the macro-environment. Qantas had experienced an abrupt change over a very short period, provoking transition and ambiguity. Having already had to cope with its recent fusion with Australian Airlines, Qantas was now facing the question of entering into an alliance with either British Airways or Singapore Airlines. From all the evidence it was an organization contending with complex tasks: the management of an airline is a classic example in literature on complexity. Qantas met all the criteria.

The second case is that of a small firm specializing in the publication of confidential newsletters. Despite its modest size, Indigo operates on five continents. It publishes newsletters touching on Africa, Asia, Europe and the US. The task is complex, as the company produces at least seven bulletins bi-monthly with a staff of only 12. It too had recently experienced a shift in the macro-environment, occasioned by the end of the Cold War, the fall of the Berlin Wall, and the collapse of the Soviet Union; which for this trade is equivalent to deregulation in the airline sector.

The Indosuez Bank equally satisfied the criteria. The bank had known strong losses in its real estate operations which had damaged its image as well as its financial returns. The financial sector itself has suffered from ambiguity, transition and puzzling situations since the 1987 crash (meeting the criterion of a shift in the macro-environment). The bank had withstood multiple internal reorganizations following the group's large financial losses, which the press had not hesitated to make public. These repeated reorganizations had made it a complex organization.

The Pechiney case is more historical, but nevertheless contemporary. The organization had been confronted with macro-economic change during the decolonization of Guinea, from 1955 to the 1970s. Once again, the situation had been unsettled, ambiguous and puzzling, as it was strongly dependent on the political instability of Guinea during this revolutionary period. Pechiney was already a firm that had mastered a complex technology.

These four organizations faced profoundly puzzling situations. The press devoted a number of articles to the difficulties Indosuez encountered when, in a deliberate attempt to learn a new trade, they recruited directors from Drexel Burnham Lambert. Pechiney's experiences in Guinea are common to many pioneering companies of international trade as they try to survive the early commercial and industrial vicissitudes of the globalization of the economy: goods are nationalized, factories requisitioned and markets diminish or escape them during the decolonization period. Indigo was a very particular case of a small firm that had to face an ambiguity intrinsic to its field, which involved selling 'positional' knowledge (knowledge sought because others do not possess it). After musing over these types of company I began to question some of them to discover whether, recently or otherwise, they had ever come up against serious difficulties with a 'dossier'. Indigo had. I now had two cases with deliberate configurations: Qantas *wanting* to deal with a perplexing environment and Indosuez *wanting* to extend its competence; as well as two cases of emergent challenges: Indigo *trying* to interpret equivocal events and Pechiney *seeking* a solution so as not to be dispossessed of its plant (Table 4.1).

The choice of multiple cases allows us to establish theoretical oppositions, to study contradictory situations in different locations. This is what Quinn and Cameron (1988) recommend when they urge the researcher to cultivate paradox rather than to avoid it. This idea of heterogeneity is also found in Astley and Van de Ven's (1983) appeal for the systematization of dialectical oppositions.

Limitations of the non-observable

Through default of inherence

Knowledge is paradoxical. The more we seek it, the more it escapes us. The more we contain it, the more it evaporates. The more we render it

Table 4.1   *The cases selected*

Company	Activity	Origin of difficulties	Environment	Situation
Indigo	Information	Incongruity of an environmental stimulus leads first to unfavourable press, then to a lawsuit	End of the Cold War The information industry	Emergent challenge
Qantas	Airline	Amalgamation of Australian Airways and Qantas entering into association with British Airways	Deregulation Only three of the world's airlines register a profit	Evident challenge
Indosuez	International finance	A newly recruited team threatens to leave	Deregulation Financial losses	Deliberate challenge
Pechiney	Aluminium production	Risk of nationalization of the plant	Decolonization (1955–62)	Emerging challenge

sophisticated, the more it simplifies itself. In short, it would be vain and illusory to claim to exhaust it: and so its study returns us to the question of our own awareness. Researchers interested in cultures know this phenomenon well, which Morin describes as knowledge's *inherence*. For the researcher comparing cultures, inherence is what is commonly called 'ethnocentrism' – the researcher's membership of a cultural reality that is ineffable, unavoidable, and present in all of their thoughts, perceptions, sentiments or attitudes. Ethnocentrism is the traditional limit of work involving comparative cultural analysis, and is of course relevant in this work too.

As Morin (1986: 205) makes clear, one must belong to a world to claim to know it, even though our capacity to distance ourselves from this world, to become both object and subject of knowledge, is equally a condition of knowledge. Despite methodological precautions, notably the care taken to effect a period of immersion within each firm before beginning the data collection, a researcher's inherence in the organizational and cultural realities of Qantas, Pechiney, Indosuez or Indigo can only ever be limited. The researcher's own tacit knowledge, their own unconscious – which is affected by their culture, their perceptual framework and their personal 'history' – permanently and continuously influences whether they perceive important stimuli, and whether these perceptions are at all distorted.

As well as the researcher's 'inherence' in a particular world, we cannot forget that the research has, in this case, been carried out in three different countries. A historian or a sociologist would certainly question the different social, cultural and historic conditions in which the four ambiguous situations have arisen. In the Indosuez case, the 'Drexelites' had come from the American culture of management, more particularly, from the New York financial culture. Similarly, the Pechiney case involved both the French post-war culture and the Guinean culture. But the very fact that identical phenomena ('floating' attention, a matrix of informal relations, clandestine management) can be observed in different cultures and places would tend to strengthen the validity of the results. It has often been stated that the management of knowledge is different in different countries. Notably, Nonaka and Hedlund (1991) have compared knowledge management in Japanese and Western organizations. As Nonaka belongs to the Japanese culture and Hedlund is Swedish, they were able to induce their conclusions from personal experience; they did not support their research with rigorous empirical evidence. It would therefore be interesting to carry out the same study in Japan to see whether their critical propositions can be corroborated on an empirical basis.

I should note that the case studies on which this study has been based were carried out exclusively within 'Western' (Anglo-Saxon and Latin) cultures, with no substantial differences being identified between them. However, I have not included cultural variables in my measurements, which very probably constitutes a limit to the inquiry.

Researchers' stormy relationships with data

The third limit of this research involves difficulties encountered during the codification of data concerning tacit attitudes (affective or non-explicit behavioural predispositions) or tacit knowledge (knowledge actors mobilize without being able to express). The lack of a research tradition, and notably the absence of methods dedicated to the study of tacit knowledge in real life situations, necessitated the establishment of a methodology (based on the works of Miles and Huberman). The codification system has been based partly on literature on tacit knowledge and unconscious processes, and partly on specific needs linked to the research questions. For example, one consequence of reading works on the role of ambiguity in politics was the consideration of the possible existence of an attitude encouraging the development of ambiguity. Apparently, ambiguity can be instrumental in politics and diplomacy as it can enable the actor to avoid taking a definite position or entirely revealing their intentions, and it can allow voters to modify their perceptions of announced measures according to their own expectations (Edelman, 1988). From this example I defined a category to identify attitudes of actors who aim to encourage a situation's ambiguous character.

Although the purpose of a review of relevant literature is to identify problems and any previously established results, it is possible that the final number of categories defined appears restrictive or reductive when compared to the 'real' range of possible behaviours or attitudes *vis-à-vis* an ambiguous situation. In total, 22 codes were defined to categorize actors' behaviours or attitudes. The assignment of behavioural data to these categories posed no serious difficulties. As the research design anticipated a study of internal documents and prolonged non-participant observation of actors before the final series of in-depth interviews was carried out, I was able to observe behaviours directly several times before assigning them to categories. But the limitations of such categorization did pose certain difficulties when it came to the codification of 'attitudinal' data.

The main difficulty involved the manifestation of 'mixed' attitudes towards ambiguous situations. In some cases actors could exhibit behaviours, emotions or positions that indicated a resentful attitude. There was no difficulty in observing the effects this bellicose attitude had on their behaviour, but no explicit conflict appeared on the organizational stage. The collectivity ignored it. The dialogue between actors was not interrupted, nor was the collectivity particularly guarded – there was no apparent avoidance of the situation, but neither did the actors particularly involve themselves with it. Such a case poses an attribution dilemma: there is at once an attitude that is collective and explicit, in the collectivity's display of nonchalance, and an attitude that is tacit and individual, in the resentment of individual actors. This paradox demonstrates the problem of the predominance of one attitude over another and, more generally relevant to all of the codings employed, the distinction between the *repeated*, the *important* and the *determinant*.

When I then came to take double, and even triple, codings, it was impossible to establish any predominance among the different attitudes noticed. This impossibility constitutes another limit. The predominance of particular behaviours or attitudes was in fact established, in relation to the frequency with which they were observed. It was reinforced by the series of interviews. However, it was not measured as it could have been had I used evaluation scales during data collection, and asked actors to clarify their attitudes and then to attribute a value to them – to attribute degrees of 'importance' to behaviours or attitudes. While this method would have been effective to a certain extent, for example to measure resentment as either a favourable or an unfavourable attitude, it would have introduced a bias in both data collection and interpretation. It could also have had an effect on these attitudes, as actors could have adopted these explanations and valuations as their own, thereby modifying their attitudes and possibly their behaviour. Yin identifies three problems of such participant observation:

First, the investigator has less ability to work as an external observer and may, at times, have to assume positions or advocacy roles contrary to the interests of good scientific practices. Second, the participant-observer is likely to follow a commonly known phenomenon and become a supporter of the group or organization being studied, if such support did not already exist.

> Third, the participant role may simply require too much attention relative to the observer role. Thus the participant observer may not have sufficient time to take notes or to raise questions about events from different perspectives, as a good observer might. (1984: 93)

Since I opted for non-participant observation so as to not to influence actors or modify their cognitive, affective and conative predispositions, rather than meddling in the evolution of the observed situation, I have taken the risk of gaining less precise determination of predominance.

As with the coding of attitudinal data, there are certain inherent limitations to the coding of 'the knowledge mobilized'. While the relationship between data and codes is fairly strong as far as explicit knowledge is concerned, obstacles do arise in the coding of tacit knowledge. For one thing, when actors invoke such knowledge they are either aware they are using knowledge but cannot explain what it is, or they are completely unaware of the entire process. In both cases, it is difficult firstly to establish the data through observation, and secondly to reinforce it through interviews or through perusal of documents. To counter this obstacle I have tried to involve actors in reflexive practice during the interviews. Nevertheless, we cannot avoid the fact that even a 'thick description' (Geertz, 1983), reinforced by many returns to the actors, cannot totally resolve the question of the robustness of the interpretation when faced with tacit phenomena.

For example, after Qantas's merger with Australian Airlines I noticed that the 'Australian Airlines people' were a mystery to the 'Qantas people'. Qantas employees regularly invented stories about their new bedfellows – some humorous, others twisting the facts or attributing whimsical characteristics to the airline and its employees:

> 'The people from Australia are going to take over our territory, we will only have landing rights at Hong Kong and Los Angeles.' (a Qantas steward)

Or, in reference to the bushman's hats worn by the Australian Airlines stewards:

> 'Those hats are stupid, they're keeping them just to be different.'

Or again, more simply:

> 'We're different from them. We don't have the same history . . .'

This last remark was particularly frequent, and always followed by a different description of the 'history' in question. Qantas's directors were aware that employees from both airlines would carry with them mythologies of this type, and tried to counter the effects of this by mixing up working teams by making successive small adjustments in both departments and divisions.

The frequency with which these small mythical tales appeared has led me to attribute this phenomenon to the temporary emergence of a 'fantastical knowledge' within the organization. Yet the body of evidence supporting this attribution consists entirely of the recurrent observation of the phenomenon *in situ*. When it comes to reinforcing the attribution through written evidence (internal documents, memos, etc.) we are confronted with an obvious fact: we are dealing with knowledge which is not 'announced' by actors; it is 'absorbed' and implicit. The strength of the relationship between data and codes here is dependent, to a great extent, on only one type of data: that harvested through non-participant observation within the organization.

The second difficulty associated with the interpretation of tacit phenomena involves the reduced possibility of having the work controlled by another researcher. While such a control is possible – and it was practised during part of the encoding – for data concerning explicit phenomena (for example actions, behaviours, explicit knowledge and re-transcribed explicit attitudes), it becomes less practicable for codings in which the major part of the attribution relies on the direct observation of phenomena. Indeed, note-taking, or re-transcription, already constitutes an explanation, or an *explicitation*, of tacit phenomena – which is by nature non-expressed and difficult to transfer. The solution to this problem would be to repeat not only the encoding but the entire investigative process – to effect a double, perhaps triple observation, by repeating both the interviews and the incursions. This brings us to an interesting conclusion about the study of unconscious processes: to ensure the validity of the research, the entire investigative process – from the gathering of the data to its analysis – should probably be carried out by a research team. As this was a difficulty which I had not suspected at the start of this study, I was not able to incorporate it into the research design.

Another consequence of a work on tacit knowledge is the difficulty of applying traditional methods of control to the codings. One of these methods, inspired by Cohen, consists of measuring the number of times in which there is agreement on a coding between different coders, and the number of times where this agreement can be attributed to chance. From this the 'sturdiness' of the coding, as a function of coding identity, can be measured and given in the form of a 'Kappa coefficient'. The Kappa coefficient is defined by the formula $K = (P_o - P_c)/(1 - P_c)$: where P_o represents the sum of the percentages of agreement obtained between coders for a given category and P_c the product of the marginal totals – those agreements that could be attributed to chance. However, in order to be able to calculate such a coefficient, data would have to be coded exclusively as one thing or another, and, as we have seen, actors can have mixed attitudes (a number of attitudes at once) or employ a number of forms of tacit knowledge (for example intuition and automatic knowledge) when faced with an ambiguous situation.

The difficulty of controlling the sturdiness of the codings by a proven and rigorous method therefore constitutes another limit to the results of this inquiry. It seems that this could have been avoided if we had been able to define exclusive categories, and important work remains to be done in this area. Also, for the utilization of a Kappa coefficient to be applicable the entire process would have to have been repeated, to enable the coders to participate independently in both data collection and analysis.

The limits of the interpretation

I have chosen to follow a method based on adduction – that is, not founded on formal logical reasoning, on formal inference, but on 'the identification of form from chaos' – and, more precisely, on the identification of repeated attitudes or behaviours. This choice is itself a source of limitation. A traditional approach to data collection would have implied what Yin calls 'maintaining a chain of evidence':

> The principle is to allow an external observer – the reader of the case study, for example – to follow the derivation of any evidence from initial research questions to ultimate case study conclusions. Moreover, this external observer should be able to trace the steps in either direction (from conclusions back to initial research questions or from questions to conclusions). (1984: 102)

Without completely abandoning this principle, I have been led to consider its limitations when it concerns the study of attitudes or knowledge involving actors' 'unconscious inferences'. A chain of evidence is entirely relevant for a study of observable facts (decisions, behaviours, actions, results of actions), but we come up against a wall when some of the phenomena are tacit; when actors cannot express the knowledge they mobilize or the attitude they develop when faced with the situation. I have therefore 'absorbed' all the stimuli that presented themselves to a dormant observation, seeking neither to establish sequences nor to assume direct relationships between the observed phenomena. The result was a large mass of data, in the form of archives, notes and interview transcripts, without any a priori allocation of links between them. This constraint has brought me to present the results in two forms:

- The first is that of a report which presents each case study in its chronological order, giving a description, based on the data collected, of the sequence of events as each situation developed and evolved.
- The second is what Yin (1984: 139) calls 'a theory-building structure', in which the analyses follow a logic that depends on the

theoretical arguments being advanced. In this second presentation of the data I have included individual sequential analyses (for case-by-case analyses), cross-case sequential analyses (for comparative case analysis), and cross-case non-sequential analyses (for the identification of which knowledge is most frequently mobilized, without considering the sequence of events).

This choice in the manner of presentation and interpretation of the data can itself be debated, and contrasted with another, more traditional, choice: the iterative presentation of evidence in what Yin calls an 'explanation-building process' (1984: 115). In this approach, rather than a re-transcription and analysis of the body of accumulated data in the development of the final qualitative analysis, evidence is introduced and analysed according to need. This manner of data presentation limits the possibility of a reading 'from conclusions back to initial research questions or from questions to conclusions' (1984: 102). The possibilities of putting forward different interpretations of inferences established from the data would then be limited as well, because of the dominance of non-participative observation in the data-collection process and the problem of non-sequential connection with the phenomena studied. For example, the reappearance of communities of practice within Qantas was simultaneous with measures taken by the organization's directors, but within the deep structure of the organization. The mobilization of these communities of practice only took place once the environmental scanning system (which had been introduced to resolve the profoundly disconcerting situation following the deregulation of the industry) had failed. Direct observation then leads us to identify phenomena – such as communities of practice – whose origin and demise are both indeterminate. In such a context it is difficult to establish iterations of evidence in relation to phenomena (and here we are once again dealing with tacit phenomena) in which the relative order of actions or attitudes taken or of other knowledge mobilized is not determined, precisely because it is indefinable.

I will now let you judge the results for yourself, as together we venture into these 'puzzled organizations' to discover how – and sometimes with what panache – they have known how to anticipate and react, to query, and to recover.

Notes

1 In the *American Journal of Sociology* in 1906, Simmel had proposed that we know more than we want to express (he was to be echoed by Détienne and Vernant in 1978), in 1966b Polanyi added that we actually know more than we *can* express.

2 In his study of informal networks within the organization, which appeared in *Social Networks*, Volume 7 (1985: 2), Barney remarked that 'it appears that the measures used to structure informal relations are chosen because they are available, rather than because they have received theoretical, that is empirical, inductive support'.

3 Montaigne, when mayor of Bordeaux, on his refusal to enter the city during the height of the plague.

4 In their 1988 paper 'Executives' perceptual filters: what they notice and how they make sense' (1988a), Starbuck and Milliken discuss how sense-making and noticing interact in the act of perception.

5 Goleman (1985: 24–5) credits Gregory Bateson with the coining of the term 'dormitive': 'He used the word to denote an obfuscation, a failure to see things as they are. "Dormitive" is derived from the Latin *dormire*, to sleep. "I stole the word from Moliére," Bateson once explained. "At the end of his *Bourgeois Gentilhomme*, there is a dog-Latin coda in which a group of medieval doctors are giving an oral quiz to a candidate for his doctoral exam. They ask him, 'Why is it, candidate, that opium puts people to sleep?' And the candidate triumphantly replies, 'because, learned doctors, it contains a dormitive principle.'"' That is to say, it puts people to sleep because it puts people to sleep.'

6 Berger and Luckmann acknowledge this in *The Social Construction of Reality* (1966).

7 Grammarians who have written on the non-expressed include McAndrews and Moscowitch (1985), Reber (1967, 1993) and Brooks (1978). On behalf of cognitive science, Helmholtz (1867) is of particular interest; this was elaborated on to a certain extent by both Gibson (1969, 1979) and Anderson (1976, 1983).

8 For instance, the works of Polanyi (1966a), of Castaneda (1968), of Greenspoon (1955) and of Reber (1993).

9 Fischhoff discusses these risks in great detail in his 1982 paper, 'For those condemned to study the past: heuristics and biases in hindsight'.

10 M. Ozouf, in an article which appeared in *Le Nouvel Observateur*, 12 February 1973 in response to René Girard's *Violence and the Sacred*.

11 This mode of functioning is also suggested by Kottkamp's (1990) notion of 'on-line' and 'off-line' – during action and about action.

12 These aspects of theory construction are raised by Weick in his 1989 paper, 'Theory construction as disciplined imagination'.

13 The internal validity of the results has in this been slightly weakened as the possibility of having several coders, in order to calculate a Kappa coefficient, loses its pertinence.

14 This distinction is discussed by, among others, Glaser and Strauss (1967) and Bowman and Kunreuther (1988).

15 As the treatment of the qualitative data involved a large amount of data and consequent processing, I have here only reproduced its outcome, that is, the matrices. Each interview and each observation gave rise to around ten pages of notes. The coding of each interview resulted in a similar-sized document.

5

Qantas, or Collective Wisdom

Plus ça change, plus c'est la même chose.

Alphonse Karr (1808–90) Les Guêpes

Qantas Airways, Sydney (1986–93)

In November 1918, only months after the conclusion of the First World War, a young fighter pilot named Reginald Lloyd announced his intention to create an airline that would fly from Australia to England, by way of the Middle East. To publicize his idea (and to illustrate his courage) Lloyd set off from Sydney in January 1919 with a convoy of motorcycles and side-cars, heading for Darwin. They were racing the postal train, and in so doing illustrating its inefficiency, and ten weeks later they reached their destination having passed through Singleton, Murrurundi, Quirindi, Moree, Charleville and Longreach. But not everyone was amused by Lloyd's stunt: 'The question of an aerial mail service is entirely unreasonable in a country like Australia,' declared Australia's then Postmaster General: 'with our population scattered over such a large territory, and given the great distances separating major postal centres, let me make this quite clear, Australia will be the last country to need such a service. This I can guarantee!' Nonetheless, many voices were to be raised against such conservatism; those of the hundreds of aviators and engineers demobilized after the First World War.

Among these veterans was one Hudson Fysh, a 24-year-old ex-lieutenant who, like Reginald Lloyd, recognized that the people of Queensland suffered from a lack of means of communication. A state four times the size of California, Queensland's broad plains and warm climate made it particularly suited for such a project, and Fysh's ideas readily gained currency. The seeds of Qantas had been sown. Not long after, the Australian government offered £10,000 to anyone who could successfully pilot an aeroplane from England to Australia in less than 30 days, and Fysh and a war colleague, pilot Paul McGinness, were attracted by the sum. McGinness had an impressive war record: at 19 he was decorated for 'outstanding bravery' at Gallipoli. He then transferred to the Australian Flying Corps in Palestine, 'where his gallantry and skill in action earned him a Distinguished Flying Cross. With seven confirmed victories, he became one of the few recognized air aces in Palestine'.[1] Fysh had served as McGinness's observer in Palestine, before gaining his pilot wings in 1919. Although the pair were finally unable to get the necessary funds together to mount such an expedition, they were taken on by the Australian federal government to supervise airfields set up in readiness for the arrival of the aeroplanes. Brothers Ross and Keith Smith, who had left England on 12 November 1919, landed in Darwin 28 days later, on 10 December 1919.

Several months later, early in 1920, grazier Fergus 'Laird' McMaster set off for a meeting of the Anti Cattle-Duffing Association – a local association formed to combat the problem of the poisoning of wells – and broke the front axle of his car in the sandy bed of Queensland's Cloncurry River. McMaster returned to a nearby post office hotel to seek help, where he met a young man about to leave on a picnic with his girlfriend. Forsaking his picnic, he immediately offered assistance and the pair struck up a friendship. While they did not speak of aeroplanes that day, the young man was Paul McGinness, and on 20 June 1920 Fysh and McGinness met with McMaster in the lounge of the Gresham Hotel in Brisbane, where they presented him with their idea of creating an airline in Western Queensland.

McMaster had fought in the war as a gunner in the Australian Imperial Forces: he remembered McGinness warmly and was enthusiastic about their proposition. He was later to write of McGinness: 'That chance accident and meeting, that true Australian help and friendship given me, perhaps was the greatest factor in the shaping of Qantas-to-be'.[2] McMaster rounded up other investors, including Templeton, a successful sheep breeder and wool dealer, and John Thompson, whose Queen Street bookshop was only a few blocks away and who immediately put up £100. Going from street to street, McMaster garnered enough funds to send both Fysh and McGinness to Sydney to buy parts for two Avro 504K biplanes, and on 19 August 1920 the Western Queensland Auto Aerial Service Limited was incorporated – a name soon to be changed to the 'Queensland And Northern Territory Aerial Service Limited'.[3] QANTAS was born.

Qantas's fledgling years, from 1920 to 1930 (when the company clocked up its first million miles), were turbulent and adventurous, and remain the pride of the airline today. The company has published a small handbook retracing in detail the meeting of the three men, their discussions, their early struggles and the opening of the first flight routes. They also sell copies of early posters dating from this period; colourful watercolours of twin-engine jets flying above the Australian continent, incarnating the epic of the company's creation. Hudson Fysh (who was to remain with Qantas until 1966) probably never imagined in

1920 that by the time the company celebrated its 70th birthday more than 40 airlines would be flying in and out of Sydney, heading for Europe, South-East Asia, the United States and hundreds of other destinations worldwide. As Australia entered the 1990s there was no longer any shortage of airlines operating in the country. The problem was rather the opposite: there were too many airlines.

In January 1993 Qantas was soon to be privatized. They had just released a public report on their efficiency, and were seriously considering relinquishing 1,835 jobs. Only the month before, British Airways had been awarded the right to buy 25 per cent of the company's stock, at $A450 million. There was a lot of discussion about the possibility of selling the remaining shares, which financial analysts had put at $A1.29 billion. The 900-page report recommended a reduction in spending of $A107 million in the following two years, with 60 per cent of the budgetary cuts to be carried out before June 1993. It suggested the number of administrative officers employed be cut by 30 per cent, and that Qantas's entire personnel could be reduced by up to 7 per cent.

Uncertainties, ambiguities and anxieties

The challenges Qantas was confronted with in the 1980s and the early 1990s were in no way unique to Australia. By 1991 the world airline industry was facing a dilemma of over-capacity, linked to an excess of supply in the face of a slow growth in demand, a situation that had locked carriers into persistent competition. Airlines were forced to refocus their activities on fundamentals – on aerial transport – and many were withdrawing from other ventures they had embarked upon, particularly from hotel management. This centring of their attention had only increased the pressure the industry had been under for at least a decade, as it grappled with an unprecedented number of difficulties, including the worldwide recession, airport congestion, a decline in aircraft resale values, alarming financial figures, weakened demand, and rapid and unexpected changes in the United States' air transport policies. Social crises arose that paralysed airports and blocked passengers, and redundancies were widespread. By 1993 the environment was shifting, uncertain and volatile. It had become polymorphic; sometimes incomprehensible, often sudden and unexpected.

Accompanying the globalization of the market was a sophistication in the itineraries of both the business and the tourism sectors, an evolution airlines had to keep up with. At the same time, neither this nor the enormous increase in aircraft capacity corresponded to an increase in the actual number of passengers flying. Companies were seeking quick returns on their investments, but the intense competition for passengers resulted in prices falling by 30 per cent in real terms over ten years, and in 1991 the industry lost $A12 billion. Many people were already predicting the self-destruction of the industry. Allan Moore,

Qantas's Strategic Planning Director, explained the conundrum he felt the industry was getting itself into: 'If the airlines keep on bending themselves to the will of the consumer, kindling price war after price war, how are we going to be able to replenish our fleets?' An increase in acquisitions and mergers was predicted, and in the industry's concentration in those sectors that had remained viable. The climate was marked by conjecture and speculation, as experts pointed their finger at the companies they felt would not survive. People in the industry began to ask: 'Are we to be bought out, or are we to be the buyers?' 'What game are we playing?' 'What are the new ground rules, and what has happened to the wisdom we once had?'

Actors were trying to make sense of a now multifaceted reality. When colleagues met they shared information, hypotheses and scenarios. The restructuring of Continental Airlines was discussed in great detail; they had declared bankruptcy, but had immediately gone back on the decision. What were they up to? Canadian Airlines announced it was ready to increase its capital, and rumours spread that they too were hiding something. The industry was beset with uncertainty, as all were plunged into an ocean of doubt without really knowing how to stay afloat. 'Canadian Airlines was going to replace their fleet to fit in with stricter world regulations,' claimed one Qantas employee. 'I can't believe it. Canadian Airlines going into Chapter Eleven' said another. Amid technical regulations, security imperatives, unforeseen alliances and reduced demand, maintaining a realistic image of the industry had become a real challenge.

Make sense, quickly!

The story I will recount here is that of a company whose leitmotiv had suddenly become 'Make sense, and quickly!' A company struggling to find a path through the dense, but changeable, fog that the airline industry had become enveloped in. To make sense of what was happening was the particular mission of Allan Moore, Qantas's Strategic Planning Director, who summarized his team's priorities as follows:

First off, we want to understand the evolution of the industry's growing globalization. Our second objective is to increase our returns so as to reduce the company's financial losses, which are at the moment of an order that prevents us even from buying a new aircraft. Our third objective is to stimulate the market. With the successive crises of the last few years [the war in Kuwait and the economic recession were particularly damaging for the industry], the market now has to be 're-stimulated', or 'rejuvenated'. And the lowering of prices has not proven to be the best method to stimulate the market. Finally, we have to supervise the development of engines, and to realize our choices of developments at the right moment. This involves keeping an eye on new technology, and adopting it when it is a source of competitive advantage.

This was not the time that such plans had been put together, but this time they had to move quickly. 1992 had been a busy year. Qantas had bought out Australian Airlines and redistributed the airline's employees under the new hierarchy. As well as coping with their new employees' identity crises Qantas's returns had been poor, and they had been obliged to have recourse to outside capital. It was a year in which the organization was forced to make a lot of important decisions under pressure, with a new decision-making structure and while disputes over role definitions continued, all of which hampered the circulation of knowledge.

The Australian situation

More than 40 regular companies operate in Australia. The business-class market totally collapsed at the end of the 1980s, an event that bore little relation to the overall tendencies of the industry. But the way in which people travelled had changed as well; increasingly, business travellers were visiting a number of cities and countries in a single trip, and Australia was generally at the end of air routes (this applied as much to Japanese business travellers as it did to European or American). The deterioration in returns was mainly affecting the smaller carriers, as larger airlines could offset any losses they made on certain routes with the yields made on more profitable ones.

In the past, Australia's sizeable domestic market has had a negative impact on Qantas's profits. By 1993, however, domestic circulation had lessened, and although most of the company's revenue came from international flights, the domestic market was now showing a profit. Qantas's yield – its per-kilometre per-seat income – was approximately 9 cents and Australian Airlines' 16 cents, figures which may seem fairly low if we compare them with those of major European airlines, which were at this time bringing in around 30 cents a kilometre; however, Australia's long distances were an important factor in their determination and must be taken into consideration. There were three major reasons for the worldwide deterioration in airlines' profits. Firstly, the cost per unit had changed dramatically. Aeroplanes had a greater capacity than ever before, and new routes were created in the hope of at least covering fixed costs. Secondly, the new 'mega-carriers' were aiming at short-term profits and a high flow of cash, with little regard for future needs – they limited investments in assets or modernization. Finally there was the economic recession, and prices became extremely elastic. Commercial traffic became another sector in decline, as firms tried to reduce their hitherto generous expense accounts. New communication technology (including computer networks and cabled conferencing) also had an impact on the slump in the business travel sector.

Disputes above the Pacific

Although Asia was already the world's most promising market for air transport, it was also a market notable for its hermetic restrictions. The earnings of national companies were carefully watched by their governments, and every airline operating in the region was heavily involved in lobbying to protect its routes. This made the opening up of new routes extremely complicated. However, Asia's global economic growth attracted a lot of carriers, and many tried to circumvent the restrictive regulations on flight routes. North-West Airlines for example had a convention with Japan to use Osaka's airport as a stopover for their flights to Australia. Japanese carriers, in cooperation with Narita Airport, then began to collect real time economic information on North-West Airlines, to protect their Tokyo–New York route. With information obtained instantaneously from the airport, the Japanese revealed that most of North-West's passengers were in fact disembarking in Tokyo. The airline had manipulated the terms of the agreement to compete on one of the most profitable routes: US–Tokyo.

North-West Airlines had launched its Sydney–Japan service more than a year earlier, in 1991, despite protests from Qantas, who had foreseen the loss of one of its most profitable routes. Since then, North-West had steadily increased its share of passengers on this route. The Australian Department of Transportation had warned North-West that it could reduce its rights to transport passengers from Sydney to Japan, claiming that North-West had broken its quota agreement. North-West declared the restriction illegal and unjustified, and replied that the issue of passenger quotas had never before been brought up – either formally nor informally. North-West also retaliated by asking the American government to restrict Qantas's non-stop flights to Los Angeles (at the time Qantas made ten such flights each week).

The threat had been conceived to attract attention to the dispute. And it worked. The debate rapidly reached governmental level. Such disputes are not infrequent in the airline industry. The capacity to handle the complex itineraries now being taken by businesspeople constituted a definite competitive advantage. Airlines quarrelled over flight routes, the length of stopovers, and maintenance facilities. The mapping of the sky became the object of negotiations and regulations, and complex agreements – but in the Asian market some carriers were more equal than others. A lot of Asian countries provided essential stopovers for both Japanese and European routes; their airlines were ideally placed to compete in both the local and the world markets, and they could prevent new actors from entering the arena. In addition, playing an important role in a number of airports and flight routes gave these companies access to a multitude of sources of information, providing a distinct competitive advantage to those companies which were not at either end of major routes. There was also a possibility for those companies situated *en route* to take advantage of the variety of paths available; making use of combined paths to compete with companies using direct flights. This is referred to as the 'Sixth Freedom Right'.

Many controversies had broken out at the end of the 1970s over this 'Sixth Freedom Right', but they had all ended the same way. Airlines could not compete against the will of consumers. The global tendency – and this was especially the case for travel in Asia – was for circuits, with stopovers in different countries. How could passengers be forbidden to use different trajectories to reach their final destination? The Sixth Freedom Right enabled certain companies to offer very competitive prices, lower even than those offered by competitors on direct routes. This paradox arises from a complex combination of high and weak returns. From a tactical viewpoint, it was in a company's interest to be able to offer different stops to satisfy the new trends. Any loss resulting from a lack of passengers on one leg of a journey is compensated by another, very profitable, leg. For example, Singapore Airlines was able to offer Sydney–Hong Kong at a very competitive price, as the Sydney–Singapore leg was predictably highly profitable; in this way they could counter Cathay Pacific's direct Sydney–Hong Kong flight. In fact there were three other indirect lines that could compete with Cathay Pacific's direct flight in the same manner. The Sixth Freedom Right also enabled passengers to bypass a direct line by making one or several stops, at a price competitive with that of the direct journey.

Being at the end of most flight paths, Australian and European carriers, however, are not able to profit from the Sixth Freedom Right. Companies like Singapore Airlines, on the other hand, can take advantage of this bill in both their Singapore–Sydney and their Singapore–Europe flights, and so compete with the Australian and European direct Sydney–London flights. Nevertheless, the European and Australian companies did lobby their own governments to protect the market from new competitors, making authorizations and rights more difficult to obtain.

Companies like Singapore Airlines, Cathay Pacific and Thaï International were then very well placed to compete with European companies. The result of this was that now one could fly from Europe to either Singapore or Sydney for approximately the same price, even though the distance from Europe to Singapore was much shorter. There were two principal strategic implications of this:

- as the Europe–Singapore route was shorter, returns on it were proportionally higher;
- as the route was then more profitable, Singapore Airlines generated a cash-flow that allowed it to be competitive on other South-East Asian routes.

Following the same strategy, the fusion of two companies could have lasting consequences on their long-haul flight strategies. For example, once British Airways controlled 25 per cent of Qantas, Air New Zealand, of whom Qantas already owned some 19 per cent, would be faced with two options. It could either join with British Airways and Qantas, and perhaps disappear, or enter into a partnership with Ansett and its network of smaller airlines. Ansett Airlines was at the time looking for new partners on the Australia–Great Britain route, to replace Qantas, which had merged with its rival on the domestic market, Australian Airlines.

An increasingly unpredictable and complex environment

The multiplication of such alliances did nothing to improve the clarity of the environment. 'We have to change the company's mind-set,' stressed Jennifer Le Gassick, who was responsible for new project development. 'We have questioned a lot of people working in the company, and they don't see the logic behind the organization's methods and strategies any more. The major part of the evaluation of any new idea is made within financial criteria. We need to make our involvement more transparent. We would like to develop our training and educational programmes, so that people can become more involved with the company.' But the task was not easy. The competition's globalization, accompanied by a complexity of flight paths, had led to an increasingly unpredictable environment. All Nippon Airways (ANA) and Japan Air Lines (JAL), for example, were two companies with offices in the same street in Tokyo. The companies had been competitors for a long time and had developed in parallel. During those years they had developed tacit knowledge of each other's intentions – a capacity for anticipation. The companies had become mutually predictable. But in 1992, ANA were rudely surprised. They had never suspected that JAL had encountered the severe financial losses that they now realized had been the case. This realization shattered the 'cognitive community' that these companies had shared for more than 20 years. The element of surprise rendered the two carriers unpredictable to each other. 'That is why we have to change our mind-set,' continued Le Gassick. 'The circulation of knowledge is too bureaucratic, too anchored in tradition. There is the "old boys" network of pilots and operations managers, but they are completely undisciplined. They talk a lot amongst themselves and they know a lot about what goes on, not only in this company, but also in other companies, but this is nowhere near enough any more.'

The growing number of alliances in routes, in Frequent Flyer pro-grammes, in catering and even in crew-sharing also complicated com-panies' perceptions, and rendered the environment still less predictable. These changes concerned the majority of airlines. In 1992, the most profitable routes were transatlantic: Japan–United States, Australia–Japan, Australia–Hong Kong and Australia–South Africa. Operating jointly with other companies could here be a means of procuring a competitive advantage. JAL initiated partnerships with Alitalia, Swissair and Iberia, going so far as to make use of their aircraft. As British Airways and Qantas were in the process of merging they were sure to come to an agreement on European routes. All of this was very complex for airline personnel, and especially for those who had been with a company for some time, those who had passed the major part of their career before the deregulation of the sector. Things had been clear then. One nation had one airline, or perhaps two or three sharing the work, and a yoke of governmental rules protecting the lot of them. 'People applied one simple rule to their work: "You do things right, and I'll do things right",' explained Le Gassick. 'They only knew about that which was related to the accomplishment of their own tasks, and as complex as these were, they were their own tasks. There was a culture that protected each member's individual knowledge. After the merger with Australian they have to share their knowledge, they have to develop the transverse knowledge which we need today, which we haven't needed in the past.' But new personnel-sharing agreements were disturbing. 'We are losing a bit of our soul,' one of Qantas's stewards confided to me. 'Japanese passengers don't really appreciate having Spanish or Italian crews, and I don't know how we will react ourselves if we have to fly on a Japanese plane one day.' In less than five years from the beginning of deregulation the very outlines of the organization had become blurred and ambiguous. 'Not only do we have to deal with internal rifts, with differences between groups within the company – flight staff, marketing and finance – but we have to develop in an environment that is not our own, and to act as though it were,' added the steward. With the tendency towards sharing catering and crews, and even sharing aeroplanes, the majority of the actors complained about an industry they found bewildering.

'She'll be right, mate'

'Knowledge is very compartmentalized,' explained Derek Sharp, the new Property Planning and Development Manager. Sharp is one of the 'old boys' of the Australian airline industry. He knows everybody, even though he came to Qantas from Australian Airlines. 'My job is to determine what Qantas needs and where it needs it. I look after airport accommodation for our teams, so I buy, modify and sell property, and I try to convince the owners of the airports to build as well.' Sharp was able to respond to Le Gassick's attacks. Le Gassick was well respected in the organization; she was directly responsible for the installation of Qantas's Executive Information System, and Sharp had a terminal on his desk, but admitted he used it very rarely. 'But she did a great job. Look at it. It has a tactile screen and you can select menus.' He recognized that many things had changed, yet insisted: 'I still work with the same people I knew in the past in other departments. The same

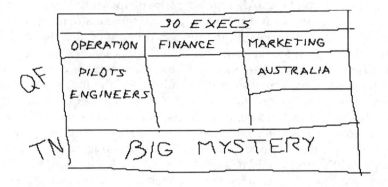

Figure 5.1 *Derek Sharp's drawing*

personal networks. Yes, it's true I have fewer and fewer contacts within the expatriate networks. Most of my personal contacts there have disappeared. And since the reorganization and the mixing-up of Australian Airlines and Qantas personnel, there are a lot of people even on this floor who I don't know. Except within a ten metre radius, of course.' He then took a piece of paper and sketched a simple diagram (Figure 5.1).

'TN stands for Australian Airlines and QF for Qantas,' he explained. 'And the small square marked "Australia" refers to the guys from domestic marketing. They describe what they do in mysterious terms. I don't really follow how they describe themselves.' Sharp then explained the 'thick walls' dividing those who worked in operations, finance and marketing, and the 'great mystery' that the Australian Airlines people were for many at Qantas. 'Perhaps we should distribute more historical information on Qantas. We could set up a database that the public could access by modem. Happily, we do have the Company Directory, which includes 9,000 people from Australian Airlines and 17,000 from Qantas, that itself wasn't easy to achieve. But this thing here really has been done well. You can access anyone's details by name, by function or by department, and they might be anywhere in the whole world.

'It is difficult to know what is going on now,' he comments. 'Ah, yes, I forgot, there is the Yellow Peril,' he continues with an ironic smile, picking up a sheet of yellow paper. 'This is a dispatch Public Affairs circulates every two or three days.' He then points at the wastepaper basket filled with yellow paper.[4] 'In fact, I learn a lot more about what is happening in the company by reading the press service's news clippings.' Nonetheless, Sharp is not unduly anxious. There is a popular Australian expression that sums up fairly well the attitude the 'old boys' had towards the great upheaval the company was going through: 'She'll be right, mate.'

Where is the wisdom we have lost in knowledge?

Even so, Sharp did find the recent changes somewhat disturbing. 'Aviation's history is a history of a pioneer spirit, and this doesn't seem to be understood any more. We used to call our planes "vessels", like in the navy. We didn't take holidays, we were "on leave". Our whole jargon was borrowed. And what we all had in common was that we had successfully lifted these planes off the ground,' he remembered with emotion. 'Today, it's only the guys in operations who remember a bit of this. They're the ones who keep our traditions alive. If truth be told, around here we often refer to the guys from finance as "bean-counters". I suppose we see them as being second-class citizens. We call the people in marketing "hired commercial representatives" – they're smooth talkers. Today, everything is expressed in figures, it's all a question of finance,' he goes on. 'Then you look at Australian Airlines, they've preserved their spirit from the start. It's a bit of an old man's club, with grey cardigans and so on, but the atmosphere is relaxed, you're called by your first name, and nobody is preoccupied with the kind of divisions you find here. Taking a domestic flight is like taking a bus, or catching a train. No doubt that's why Australian is different. They're a lot less bureaucratic. When something needs to be done, it's done, without making a fuss over it. The widely held vision is that Qantas functions on two principles: that of nepotism, between friends and relations, and that of patronage.' He then explained how the rationalizing of activities had led to the loss of the spirit employees had previously brought to their jobs. Employees were feeling frustrated, and new recruits were being taken from technical colleges rather than the large universities.

Sharp had the impression that the coordination of activities had become a lot more formal and complicated. (Other personnel also shared this opinion, as one of them had already confided to me: 'William Dix, our boss, is an avowed interventionist, and he's very strict about financial costs. He is very attentive to details. He always wants to prove that the numbers are right, to the point that people spend weeks doing calculations to present to him.') After a short moment of silence, Derek Sharp stood up and led me to the door of his office: 'We have lost a lot of wisdom,' he concluded.

Where is the knowledge we have lost in information?

It was in a context that was not yet uncertain and puzzling that, in 1988, Qantas's management expressed the need for a system to analyse their environment and their competition. This was not though a propitious time for the creation of expensive new departments. The idea was to set up a computerized news-clipping service, within an executive infor-mation system. Allan Moore recalled the reasoning behind the project: 'We were tapping a huge amount of data, but were still starved of information. We wanted management to mark the difference between data and information.' Bob Cain (he later left the company to join a consultancy firm) and Jenny Le Gassick (who by 1993 was responsible for new project development) were put in charge of the project. 'We had to install the executive information system (EIS) for managers who hadn't been part of the computer revolution,' recalls Le Gassick. 'We decided to have touch-sensitive screens to avoid having to use a keyboard.' Their idea was to construct competitive profiles on 18 airlines, profiles that would evolve with time. Data was collected and then classified by theme: positioning, investment, resources, strategy and so on. Senior management could consult the information very rapidly on their screen, and at their own leisure.

The EIS turned out to be quite different from original expectations. The person in charge of the project was buffered by four others who selected articles from the press, typed synopses of them, and then entered them into the system. The system involved personal computers with tactile screens on which there were six large squares carrying titles like 'Financial Results' and 'Routes and Traffic'. The sixth title was 'Competitive Analysis'. Simple pressure on the screen would give one access to different menus containing the latest information available on Qantas's major competitors. The design of the system and the software had been realized by the company's engineers, who were very proud of their work, and had put special effort into the system's ergonomics. There had never before been anything as easy to use in the company.

The system was, however, very costly to operate. So costly that Qantas could only equip the first 20 levels of their hierarchy with terminals – and it was rumoured that the selection was made by the company director, or someone close to him. It became a mark of pride within the company to be the favoured possessor of one of the little blue screens, which were carefully placed in full view on executives' desks. The real tool of their job, the classic PC with no tactile screen, was generally pushed to the far side of the desk. 'That was quite characteristic at first,' recalls John Gilchrist, who directed the operation. The utilization rate declined fairly rapidly. The team was reduced. Soon there was left only the person in charge of the project, who had to find all the news items alone and enter them into the system. Six months later both the service and the project were abandoned. 'The only result was we realized that if something is given to a particular person to take care of people have a tendency to think that it is no longer their responsibility,' commented Roger Robertson, Qantas's Strategic Planning Manager. 'Appoint someone, put a system in place, and people will pass blame on to that person or that system.'

According to Fiona Balfour, Qantas's Chief Information Officer, in 1993 there were still blue screens on some desks. 'And people do use them, but you rarely see a manager lingering around them.' At British Airways they had recently found a double-page review, with hand-drawn graphics, tracing the company's comparative analyses of different airlines' performances. 'It's ugly, but very interesting,' commented Allan Moore, with an ironic smile.

An ambiguous situation

'The circulation of knowledge is not a problem that is very well understood by organizations; no more by ours than by any other,' notes Allan Moore. 'There is a lack of acceptance of its importance. Of course, we understand it exists, we see it happening around us and we even create it, but this doesn't necessarily imply that we always respond to it consistently. Most of the time, we change our interpretations the moment we make them, depending on our degree of confusion, or the extent of the confusion we may find ourselves working in.' Allan Moore had been in the company for a long time, he knew the way it worked, its cliques, its language and its ceremonies. 'Nobody lives in isolation,' he continued. 'Of course, there are different internal cliques, and of course that can appear a bit chaotic from the outside, and sometimes a bit rigid, but knowledge gets around. We don't always know how, but we end up knowing more than we thought we did.' Each month, Allan Moore and his team would prepare a special report for the company's president and its management. In it they presented, in a precise fashion, recent contributions to the knowledge the company had about its environment. Although relations were sometimes strained between Bill Dix and his executive director, John Ward, the information flow was maintained within Qantas's management: 'John Ward develops the plans and the general approaches . . . and Bill Dix confirms he is an interventionist director. But you can see that in our business plan, in our role definition,' concludes Moore. 'Luckily this is only a surface phenomenon.'

'Yes, we have been through ambiguous situations, and had to make some difficult choices,' recalls Robertson. 'How did we deal with them? The most recent case is without doubt the choice between merging with Singapore Airlines or British Airways.' Robertson, as the company's Strategic Planning Manager, was part of the small team who, together with Qantas's president, were charged with evaluating their options. 'The first question we asked ourselves was, of course, what their strategies were. British Airways' plans were clear: globalization as fast as possible. There were strong signs of an impending agreement with US Air, which would complete their global dimension. On the Singapore Airlines side, we recognized the web of connections they had from their alliances with Swissair and Delta Airlines, but as to whether they had any great plans for the future, that was another story. There were four or five of us evaluating the different options. The big question was what the loser would decide to do. What options could they take? Our deliberations were directed by the Chief Executive, and we were helped by two people external to our group, both of whom were retired: an

Figure 5.2   *Roger Robertson's sketch*

ex-employee of Qantas, and another man who had a lot of connections in this industry. There was a lot of controversy, and nobody knew the answers. We seemed to have a lot of minor information, which we tried to put in the right places. We all made a lot of presumptions, and believe me, these were rarely the same. We tried to simulate what was going to happen, according to different hypotheses, using tables that we didn't throw away. We decided, I can't remember exactly when, to adopt the technique of decision trees. We were finally convinced that this was the direction to take.' Robertson explained the process with gestures and a small sketch (Figure 5.2).

As our discussions progressed, we would repeatedly go back over different hypotheses, that is to say, we would climb up and re-descend the branches of our decision trees. In fact, we also went back and forth continually between the decision-making table and studies we were all carrying out individually. The two external advisers gave their hypotheses, and we discussed these in turn. This is the "close-off" technique. You tell yourself 'This is where we are,' and a month later you end up with a single final report that can be presented to the board. There were a lot of telephone conversations, because after that everybody had to look over something that could have an impact on their activities. They thought we should go back over one part of our estimations, and so we did.' The decision was finally taken in favour of British Airways. 'It is not easy to think strategically at difficult moments,' concludes Robertson. 'Something occurs in the environment, and one has a tendency to use it as an excuse.'

Epilogue

'One always remember difficult situations by faces and voices. It's curious, isn't it?' confides one of the longest-serving employees. 'When you don't know where you're going any more, you want to hear someone's voice, you don't want to read about it. And when nothing is going right, you want to be face to face, not looking at a screen. The difference between us and machines is that we sometimes discover things that we didn't know we knew, and we say to ourselves, "Yep, I knew that." Machines only know what we already know. Hey, that's why we put it in the machine, isn't it?'

A practice-embodied knowledge

The Quantas case shows us an organization facing an evident challenge. Rather than emerging as events unfold, here an existent ambiguity has served as a motive for the installation of a knowledge management system. This ambiguity was not a result of the equivocal nature of separate incidents, but of the abundance of unfamiliar incidents – events which were all explicit, yet their interpretation remained complex and puzzling.

Refutation of the redundancy principle

This observation contradicts the hypothesis advanced by Nonaka, who contends that:

> Redundancy . . . the conscious overlapping of company information, business activities, and management responsibilities . . . plays a key role, especially in the process of knowledge creation at the level of the organization. Redundant information can be instrumental in speeding up concept creation. (1994: 28)

According to Nonaka, redundant information, or 'the existence of information above the specific information required by each individual' – *the multiplication of information* – entails sharing extra information among individuals, and 'promotes the sharing of individual tacit knowledge'. Yet we can see that the airline industry had a great amount of very detailed information at their disposal, that they all had access to this information, and that the organization itself (Qantas) inundated its managers with this information. On the other hand, we see that the arrival of a system that enabled this information to be explicitly distributed within the organization, that encouraged the sharing of information, (1) was not the success one might have expected it to be, and (2) did not modify in any way the tacit knowledge held by individuals, nor the ways in which this tacit knowledge was shared. Moreover, it was precisely because there was an overabundance of information that the situation was puzzling, and that the company decided to take organizational measures. Allan Moore, Qantas's Strategic Planning Director, put it this way: 'We're overrun with information, but we're dying for lack of knowledge.'

Nonaka has said that 'When members share overlapping information, they can sense what others are trying to articulate. . . . In this situation, individuals can enter each other's area of operation and can provide advice. . . . In short, redundancy of information brings about "learning by intrusion" into an individual's sphere of perception' (1994: 28). Yet Nonaka's analysis lacks empirical support, and rests on two misinterpretations:

- A surprising confusion between information and knowledge. Information is within the domain of the communicable (as one divides it, transports it, stocks it), whereas learning, as Polanyi and Dewey especially have shown, lies in the sharing of experience, that is to say, the sharing of knowledge that itself is tacit.
- An implicitly erroneous definition of perception. The field of individual perception cannot be reduced to the exchange of information. As we saw in Chapter 3, perception is a complex phenomenon, of which the visible part is deceptive. A large part of any exchange of knowledge is unconscious.

On top of this, redundancy of information does not necessarily imply that this information will be shared. Qantas devoted a part of its resources to writing an informative newsletter which it distributed to every member of the organization. But the newsletter was nicknamed 'The Yellow Peril' by personnel (because it was printed on yellow paper, and because it was unwelcome), many of whom would throw it straight into the wastepaper basket.

Tacit repertories of knowledge circulation

From this case study we can observe that knowledge is exchanged according to 'tacit repertories of circulation'. These tacit repertories stem from 'communities of practice' (Lave and Wenger, 1991) which have formed over the course of the organization's history. The first repertory identified is that of the pilots and their 'retinue' – those who manage the company's operations. They form the pioneer body of the company; in their vision, they are the airline itself. This group's leitmotiv is: 'An airline is nothing but a company that picks people up at point A and takes them to point B.' Knowledge circulates then in the framework of 'cognitive territories', whose existence I touched on in Chapter 1. Qantas's second tacit repertory of knowledge circulation is that of its financial community, and we observe the same automatic circulation of knowledge among its members. The third tacit repertory of knowledge circulation involves Qantas's marketing sector.

Each of these communities brings to bear a particular mythology upon the others. They each have their own language – confirming the existence of multiple constructed realities within the organization – and they each exhibit institutionalization, distinct symbolic universes, and idiosyncratic language.[5] From a desire to increase the information available to each organizational member there developed, in response, a strengthening of these existing communities of practice.

Individuals within an organization have, of course, their own preferences – concerning both who they transmit their knowledge to, and how they transmit it. The dynamics of organizational knowledge creation is equally subjected to these preferences: personal preferences as to the composition of teams, preferences in their interactions, or in the adoption of one way of doing things rather than another. These preferences may be conscious or unconscious. Conscious preferences can form in opposition to new organizational measures imposed from above; as the flight steward put it: 'Not only do we have to deal with internal rifts, with differences between groups within the company – flight staff, marketing, and finance – but we have to develop in an environment that is not our own, and to act as though it were.' This is where we find the collision of the tacit and the explicit. This model of management, which operates from the top down, is explicit; it allocates resources according to hierarchical repertories, it produces manuals, it places the accent on the processing of information, and it amasses knowledge in computerized documents. But communities of practice, conjectural knowledge and repertories of thought inscribed in practice are all tacit.

A transition from the explicit collective to the tacit collective

As we have observed, individuals express a preference for a less constrained and less explicit circulation of knowledge, and this is what they bring into play. In our matrix, which is reproduced here (Figure 5.3), the organization moves from the upper right-hand square to the lower right-hand square: from the explicit collective to the tacit collective. It is clear, however, that 'human behaviour may, in any individual case, be a symptom of ignorance, obtuseness or deviousness. But the fact is that such patterns of behaviour are fairly common among individuals and institutions' and this suggests that they might be sensible under some general kinds of conditions – that 'global ambiguity, like limited rationality, is not necessarily a fault in human choice to be corrected but often a form of intelligence to be refined by the technology of choice rather than ignored by it' (March, 1978: 45).

This is exactly what we witness at Qantas. The refusal on the part of the personnel to make use of the knowledge management system could be qualified as 'obtuseness' or 'deviousness'. But, as March makes clear, behind this apparent obtuseness (the personnel simply returned to the repertories of knowledge circulation they had always used) lies a form of intelligence. Going even further, March maintains that individuals 'know that, no matter how much they may be pressured both by their own prejudices for integration and by the demands of others, they will be left with contradictory and intermittent desires partially ordered but imperfectly reconciled' (1978: 45).

Our investigation of Qantas has distanced us even further from the dichotomies proposed by Nonaka between organizations that do not authorize chaos (and instead strive for a rigid management of their knowledge) and those that do authorize chaos, and from this successfully engender creativity and the mobilization of an 'organizational spiral of knowledge creation'.

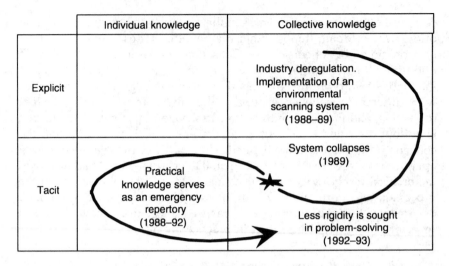

	Individual knowledge	Collective knowledge
Explicit		Industry deregulation. Implementation of an environmental scanning system (1988–89)
Tacit	Practical knowledge serves as an emergency repertory (1988–92)	System collapses (1989) Less rigidity is sought in problem-solving (1992–93)

Figure 5.3   *An inertia of tacit processes (Qantas)*

Conversely, we have moved closer to Hedberg, Nystrom and Starbuck's (1976) principle of 'antithetical processes guaranteeing organizational wisdom'. We have seen that individuals reactivate personal networks, in fact counterbalancing expected outcomes of events so as to obtain a harmonization of the sharing of their knowledge. Being unable, in a strongly hierarchical organization, to explicitly counterbalance imposed measures with their own measures, they instead employ *registers of actions and of tacit knowledge*.

Inherence and inertia of organizational knowledge

We can complete this first analysis, declined in terms of conscious preferences, with an analysis in terms of *inertia* in the realm of the unconscious. Two types of tacit knowledge can be distinguished from our study of Qantas: *present* tacit knowledge and *reminiscent* tacit knowledge. The present tacit dimension is that of the community of practice: the tacit knowledge which is developed in learning through practice. The reminiscent tacit dimension is that of organizational culture: that which is registered in organizational memory and 're-emerges' when someone tries to introduce a change in the organization. It is a body of knowledge which we remember unconsciously, but which we cannot express. When Qantas merged with Australian Airlines care was taken to mix up workgroups, but when we look at the circulation of knowledge within the new organization we find that it adopts a course reminiscent of the original two organizations.

This observation accords with Morin's analyses of knowledge's inherence. Knowledge develops within a knowable world, defining its possibilities: 'Knowledge of physical things presupposes membership of the physical world . . . knowledge of cultural phenomena presupposes membership of a culture' (Morin, 1986: 205). Which translates in simple terms as: 'Knowledge of Australian Airlines presupposes membership of the world of Australian Airlines.' Thus, there is no single generic body of organizational knowledge, but a number of different bodies of knowledge within the organization. When two bodies of organizational knowledge mix, they do not automatically hybridize. Accompanying the phenomenon of inherence is a phenomenon of inertia.

What do we learn from this case?

The ambiguity that Qantas saw as a challenge came from a lack of hybridization between organizational elements belonging to distinct knowledge modes: to current communities of practice (operations, finances and marketing) on the one hand, and stemming from the reminiscences of organizational communities on the other. Because the new explicit dimension offered to the collectivity appeared foreign to it, the collectivity took refuge in the only reality that appeared familiar – that which lived on tacitly below the surface of the organization (Moullet, 1992). In this way diverse forms of management emerged behind the façades that people displayed to each other, together with repertories of knowledge circulation that were almost invisible to the company's higher management.

Organizations often overlook behavourial inertia, as such cases as the *Challenger* disaster (Starbuck and Milliken, 1988b), or the Three Mile Island catastrophe (Perrow, 1984) may suggest. Qantas, however, is paying careful attention to its organizational behaviour by implementing processes which put together managers from different origins in joint socialization processes. Hence, even when behavourial inertia is attended, knowledge inertia can remain, and may continue to prevent socialization processes from consolidating. As ambiguities develop, upper management multiply codification experiments and large-scale and unilateral decision-making. Five major characteristics of the management of puzzling situations that can be deduced from this case are:

1   Redundancies of information, and overlapping organizational processes, do not foster better socialization, as the consolidation of socialization processes relies on tacit grounds which escape codification.
2   Tacit repertories of knowledge are much more resistant to change than behaviours, attitudes and codified knowledge. The more collective these repertoires, the stronger the resistance to their modification.
3   Collective tacit knowledge may embody most self-designing processes in organizations. Behaviours might not be consistent

with expectations of a self-designing organization, yet behind the façades and below the organizational surface the tacit organization is self-designing its adjustments.

4   Reorientation plans might have to take collective tacit knowledge into account, and prepare to separate implementation programmes for the explicit and the tacit processes of intended change.

5   Finally, this case also suggests that organizations tend to ignore, or to take for granted, their communities of practice, while these communities preserve and improve critical knowledge for their survival.

Notes

1 *Beyond the Dawn: A Brief History of Qantas Airways*, Qantas publication, 1995, p. 4.

2 Ibid.

3 McMaster went on to become the first chairman of the company. He led the campaign to secure government airmail contracts, and with the exception of three drought years (1923–26) remained chairman until his retirement in 1947. He was knighted in 1941 for his contribution to Australian aviation, and died in 1950.

4 'The Yellow Peril' is a term that gained currency in Australia in the 1950s and early 1960s in reference to a then-current conservative fear of Asian immigration. The term has since then slipped into vernacular to refer to anything unwanted and yellow, often in ignorance of its racially offensive origins.

5 Berger and Luckmann discuss these definitive elements of social groups in *The Social Construction of Reality* (1966).

6

Indigo, or Navigating in the Tacit

To reach the point that you know not,
You must take the path that you know not.

Saint John of the Cross

All truth is a lie.

Pablo Picasso

Indigo, Washington and Paris (1984–94)

Situated in Paris's Sentier quarter, incongruously both a centre for international press and finance operations (including the Paris Stock Exchange) and one of Paris's seamier inner districts, Indigo Publications is a remarkable little company. With an annual revenue of 12 million francs ($US2 million) and a team of only 14, Indigo manages to surprise those who are surprised by nothing, to inform the most well-informed, and to interest the most blasé. Founded in June 1981 with a capital of 10,000 francs by a fervent devotee of investigative journalism, Indigo specializes in the production of confidential newsletters. It publishes the *Indian Ocean Newsletter, La Lettre du Continent, Maghreb Confidential, Africa Energy and Mining, Africa Confidential, East Asian Affairs,* and the *Intelligence Newsletter.*

Indigo's world is a world of intrigue: of doubt, mystery, secrets, confidences, ambiguities and systematic questioning. It furnishes its readers with difficult-to-obtain insights, casts an unexpected light on events, and lifts the curtain on a reality that had hitherto been concealed, misunderstood or secret. I interviewed a number of its readers to find out what it was that made this tiny company and its young founders unique – and they too were baffled at Indigo's success: 'I have no idea how they manage to produce all that,' admitted one devoted reader, a French company director. Others wondered as well. Many professionals in the intelligence community are assiduous readers of the *Intelligence Newsletter,* and the rumours came thick and fast. 'Who is really behind it?' 'How can a small team like that have access to all this knowledge?' 'There has to be some foreign intelligence service behind it all,' suggested one suspicious intelligence professional. 'They know a thing or two, they get around, they've got connections,' commented another.

A heavy, stifled atmosphere reigned at the Washington Omni Sheraton on 3 November 1993. Numerous small meetings were being held in the hotel's lobby and on the sunlit steps of its southern entrance. Visiting cards were exchanged, many of which carried only a name, a postbox address, and the name of a division of the 'DOD' – the United States Department of Defense. Nine hundred professionals from the areas of diplomacy and intelligence (including information brokers and hackers) had settled in for the Second Symposium on Open Source Solutions: the central theme for the day was the defence of national competitiveness through the privatization of intelligence capabilities. Two members of the Indigo team, Maurice Botbol and Olivier Schmidt, had come along to this conference that united their readers and their sources of information with stories unfolding in real time. For me this was a unique opportunity to directly observe Indigo at work.

The discussions turned on the possible declassification of government documents, which would make them available to private companies. The hotel was buzzing with questions. To what extent can a government involve itself in the defence of private interests? When can one evoke the national interest? How can the motivations behind declassification be monitored? What about the risk of collusion between individuals working in governments and those in large national companies?

Botbol and Schmidt listened intently to all the expert presentations, although they took few notes. Hoping to attract subscriptions, Maurice Botbol had set up a little stack of copies of the *Intelligence Newsletter* in the hotel's ample foyer, and between presentations he and Schmidt would approach participants, soberly greeting the many they already knew. Over the three days of the conference they would create new contacts and strengthen existing ones: 'We try to maintain a constant flux between a rational, exhaustive and complete approach to events and a more intuitive approach,' explained Botbol. 'The ideal would be to employ both approaches at once. We try to avoid the trap of spending more time on the exhaustive than on the intuitive,' he continued. 'Even though the intuitive approach demands more effort and imagination, it often pays off more as well.' Indigo does not have a lot of resources – it is a small organization, of small means – but to publish as it does one newsletter every two weeks it must constantly produce new material: 'We read what others publish so as to know what is publicly known; we use it indirectly to seek information that is not published – in order to devote as little time as possible to what is formally known, so that we can then spend more time on the informal dimension.'

Later that evening Botbol, Schmidt and myself joined a group dining at a nearby restaurant. We were shown to a round table in an alcove to the rear of the main dining room. The atmosphere was friendly, and the meal began without any sensitive issues being broached, creating a climate of confidence. There was soon some light discussion of the progress of the conference and of the more interesting, or controversial, of the day's contributions. We were all digging around, looking for common ground. Yet at the same time they were clearly testing each other, trying to uncover motivations, the true intent behind this informal dinner. Each one hoped to learn something that evening – which was of course why they had come along: they wanted to add to the knowledge they had or to find out something completely new, something they had never suspected before this meal, and this was to be done by putting the pieces of the jigsaw together, those they already had and those others could give them. If no knowledge had been created among them that evening nothing would have been lost. They would have passed a few agreeable hours together, and acquired impressions, intuition. They would at least have been able to judge whether they were on the right track or had taken a false turn. 'Why do people give us what we're looking for?' Botbol replies to my question after the meal. 'Because they are sure of it. If they had any doubts, the whole thing would be off the record. They all know that if they don't want to be implicated they only have to tell us. They often have something they want to say, to express their disagreement over something perhaps, but if they feel this would go against the interests of their countries they want to do it without being openly associated with their comments. For a normal journalist it is more incisive to be able to say: 'Minister X told me that . . .', but we function differently.'

As the meal went on, the atmosphere became more relaxed. Whenever Botbol engaged in conversation, Schmidt would sit back quietly. He seemed to take in everything that went on, not only what was said, but how it was said: he watched people's body language, looked for signs of embarrassment or pride, and saw when subjects were avoided. When anyone became too ill at ease Schmidt would deftly shift them on to another topic. Then Schmidt would step in, and it would be Botbol's turn to listen attentively. There was never a lull in the conversation, in fact there was a certain dynamics to it all. The evening was lively; it felt like a group of old friends out for the night and we would not have stood out in the crowded restaurant – we were no more and no less rowdy than other tables, and no more and no less serious. From time to time there were even bursts of laughter, that mixed in with the general clamour. 'Trust is very important,' Botbol explained later; 'it's established on the basis of several things. The usual way to gain anyone's confidence is of course never to betray them. We respect confidentiality, the "off-the-record", no matter what. We are more interested in the relationships we develop. What we really want is to gain long-term confidence, even though that itself can be fairly dangerous if this confidence becomes complicity, or collusion. We're interested in piecing together history, in tying up loose ends. This will always involve both aspects – it has to.'

During the meal, Botbol and Schmidt did discover unsuspected relationships between the elements of the puzzle they were here to solve. There was no real intention of discovering them, but they came out in the course of the discussion. One of the people at the table mentioned a then current dossier and spoke of those involved in it, referring to them by their first names. Little by little the nature of the relationship that linked them became more explicit: what had led them to work together, how they had met, how their relationship had progressed. There was nothing really secret in this, nothing sensational, but this tiny piece of the puzzle of how people were connected could uncover a hidden reality: 'People are blocked by their own position. They never have complete knowledge. They cannot come into contact with the other camp. Our range of vision is much wider than theirs. When you have this type of attitude, and you have to be very clear on the fact that you are not a "friend" of everyone involved, the circulation of knowledge is easier,' explained Botbol.

Navigating the press

Back in Paris things ran somewhat differently. At the Indigo office people were busy archiving, classifying and preserving knowledge. The archives were all grouped in one room, carefully guarded and protected. Each day would begin with the traditional perusal of the press: 'The way we run through the press is complicated, but informal. We know how to read newspapers: such-and-such a publication has such-and-such a tendency, is under such-and-such an editorial constraint.' Of course, none of this was written knowledge. There were no memos saying: 'When reading *Le Monde*, think of its publisher's commitments, of its journalists' connections with personalities X and Y, of its editorial line that includes A, B, C and D.' No, these are things you learn but they're difficult to put down on paper. Firstly, all of this is constantly changing, it's uncertain and the field is vast. Journalists leave and others arrive. A newspaper is a complex thing, full of contradictions, internal oppositions and cliques. Botbol gave an example of this: 'In Kenya for a while it was taboo to directly name any particular ethnic group, even though the ideology was all too obviously entirely ethnic-based. Instead of saying that someone was from this or that ethnic group, they would say they were from this village. You would then have to decode the information. We had to read the press knowing how to link the villages with the different groups. Everything was implied, not stated outright, and the heart of the problem was never revealed for what it really was.' Acquired experience of what is not said allows one to follow what is meant.

African newspapers too are social constructions, neither more nor less than *Le Monde*, the *Guardian* or the *Washington Post*. Journalists express themselves in language that is understood in a given social construct, a construct they share with their editors and their readers. 'In the Ivory Coast and Senegal, all audiences with the chief of state are public. Nobody ever repeats what is said at these audiences, but everyone knows what they talk about.' This is not a paradox, pointed out one of Indigo's editors: 'There are some countries where the symbolic has as much value as the knowledge associated with it. If we read in a newspaper that the President of a particular African country has received a French delegate, we try to build up a scenario, we use our imagination. What background knowledge do we have? If we also know that the delegate in question has some connection with a company that operates in the country, even if the delegate is neither formally nor explicitly part of this company, we try to understand the nature of the non-formalized relationship between the delegate and the company,' says Botbol. 'In short, we try to group together the non-formalized knowledge that we are sure of and that which we are still guessing at. We gather information, we read a lot, and we try to make connections. If the daughter of the minister is a shareholder in the company, or if she is on its board, the minister's foreign visit might have a different meaning. You often need quite a complex body of knowledge to determine the real meaning of things.'

Accustoming oneself to ambiguity

All of this is routine for Indigo: navigating ordinary ambiguity to unearth an extraordinary meaning. Indigo's environment is of course far more uncertain and puzzling than what one would call 'routine' in another organization, but even so, the perception they have of it is that of a routine. It seems that there is a phenomenon of becoming accustomed to a degree of ambiguity that others would find incomprehensible. In other words, what is ambiguous to us is perhaps not at all ambiguous for them. We look at the same reality, or probably the same reality, but we don't read the same thing into it. But does Indigo seek Reality with a capital R? No, theirs is no quest for absolute truth. Between the deceptiveness of their evidence and the complex reality of the events they are concerned with, a reality which is probably not completely understood even by its protagonists, there exists a spectrum of increasingly 'true' versions of reality. To move along this spectrum is definitely an important element of Indigo's motivation, but is it possible to reach the end, if there really is an end? Is it desirable? Is there any sense in it?

There are, no doubt, many ways to answer these questions. But Indigo is not in the philosophy business. It is answerable to the weaknesses of its resources and the imperative of selling its newsletters. This does not necessarily imply compromise, in fact it all falls into place quite naturally – in the dynamics of exigency, in its well-thought-out approach to a dossier, in apportioning time and in the level of pertinence aimed for – before it can answer the single most important question 'Can we write it?'

For Indigo's editors – paradoxical as it may seem – actually write very little. 'Although we are journalists, we're quite unlike others. Most of them have to publish a lot of material just to survive. Often they stick to a single source, which is a risky thing to do,' explained one Indigo editor. 'The other pattern you find is the journalist-counsellor. "What do you think I should do?" the politicians ask them. Here, we refuse to get involved in that kind of thing. Our problem is making them accept that even though we may have a relationship of confidence with them, this won't prevent us from saying things that may not always please them.' If the situations they get involved in are ambiguous and puzzling, the relationships through which they attempt to clarify them are entirely explicit and direct. 'It's a bit like what we're taught at journalism school, but here, I don't know, it's different. We apply the same rules, but without excess formalization, and we're very pragmatic, we don't lose touch. We try to have a deep understanding of the person, and of the relationship that is in the process of being established.' Indigo's founder is more precise: 'The newsletters that I have created are based on the idea of a press that works differently while still being viable. That is, a press that is economically profitable but not biased, without being totally at odds with the system. In other words, to understand while staying behind the fence, without being completely cut off from the other side.'

Although Indigo accustoms itself fairly easily to an ambiguity that is customary for it, the same cannot be said for those in its environment. It seems some find it very ambiguous that Indigo does not feel the ambiguity they feel! As there is no 'natural' explanation for their success, mythologies circulate. The Indigo team is young – the oldest was not yet 40 when interviews were conducted in 1994 – something that upset the rationality of expertise, of the accepted wisdom of 'sly old foxes with connections in the political and industrial arenas'. They publish eight different newsletters with a staff of only 14, and with only two directors – Maurice Botbol and Olivier Schmidt. Botbol and Schmidt have been through it all, including conjecture on the derivations of their names, invoking mysterious Middle Eastern or German origins, and stories about their supposedly secret pasts. Even when everyone knew perfectly well which journalism school Maurice Botbol had attended, for example, a minor break in his studies always attracted comments: 'But what was he doing then?' I posed two simple questions to people in the industry: 'Do you know who Botbol and Schmidt are? What did they do before Indigo?' Some told me they had both changed their names, that they were not really 'Botbol' and 'Schmidt'. Everyone I spoke to was suspicious of Indigo's success. 'There's something fishy about it, that's for sure,' said one, unwilling to say any more.

'At the beginning, I tried to explain things,' says Maurice Botbol; 'but, firstly, people usually wouldn't believe me; and secondly, if they did believe me it would frighten them. If readers see grand conspiracies behind it all, secret services pulling the strings, clandestine alliances, they equally see it – because their belief in the explanation that they have invented is so strong – as an unequivocally reliable source.' In other words, the Indigo myth is indissociable from its credibility. 'These days I just tell people "You're free to believe what you want, but subscribe",' he adds, with a smile. 'Once they become subscribers they change their opinion of us. Once they've taken the time to recognize our abilities.'

Non-partisan observers

'There is one important thing you should understand about us,' stressed Botbol. 'Our whole approach can be summarized by the idea that we are "inside" without being "insiders". When we go to see people, or when we write, we don't do it from a plane that you would call exclusively "rational". We are not culturally partisan, either towards France's interests, nor those of the third world. Our neutrality tends to be complete. The *Intelligence Newsletter* is an exact translation of the *Monde du Renseignement*, to the word, to the comma. We are very careful not to have any "national" positioning, not in the sense that we want to please everybody, but because we don't want to join any one camp, we don't want to lose ourselves.'

What was at the beginning intentional – wanting to keep their distance – had become an automatic reflex, part of their mind-sets. 'A lot of journalists in Paris treat Africa from a particularly French point of view – they take the French side. I don't believe they're even aware they do it. We try to distance ourselves from our origins as much as possible. The fact that we write in two languages helps us to do this.'

To reach the point that you know not . . .

'Our work involves navigating backwards and forwards through knowledge, we have to read between the lines, to read what is implied or latent as if it were an open book, and to prepare the field so that we can uncover what hasn't been said,' Maurice Botbol explained. 'We manoeuvre through muddy waters, and when we get hold of something we don't let go, we cling on until we can make some sense of it.' Botbol recalled what he referred to as 'The Seychelles Affair'. His company had been very young then. He was really the only member of the organization: 'At that time I was learning the ropes. I'm still learning, but ten years ago I had no idea how much I had to learn. Today, though, I have a vague idea.'

There was one habit he took up very early: that of not writing too much, so as not to 'stifle' anything: 'When you write, your attention focuses on what you've written, and you tend to push anything else to one side. The synopsis you've put to paper becomes the "truth" and the rest, well you risk forgetting it. It doesn't bother me to keep everything in my memory. I accumulate whatever I can, I chew it over, I let it develop, until I see it's all coming together.' Botbol remembered the day he had seen a photograph of the President of the Seychelles in a local newspaper that he subscribed to. He noticed in the background the figure of the Seychelles Foreign Minister, and next to him 'the Seychelles Ambassador for the Order of Malta': 'I looked at it for a minute, then I cut it out,' he remembered; 'and I found it strange.' It was the incongruity of an ambassador from the Order of Malta being in the Seychelles which struck him. But why? He was by no means an expert on the Order of Malta, but the situation caught his eye all the same: 'From time to time I put questions to those who might know something. How is it that there is an Order of Malta in the Seychelles?' He decided against publishing anything as, after all, there was not much to say. Why not? Why shouldn't there be an Order of Malta in the Seychelles? 'I then learnt that the ambassador in question was one of the most powerful businessmen in the Seychelles (he was involved in tea factories, hotels, and granite mining and export projects). I found out that he also guaranteed the President's personal security and provided him with an armoured vehicle, and that he arranged phone-taps on opponents of the regime.' The more information he obtained, the more the situation seemed ambiguous. The more his knowledge increased, the less he understood. He was faced with a sum of facts which went beyond his comprehension. He was looking for something, but he did not know what.

. . . You must take the path that you know not

His search for meaning followed a number of random paths. It seemed he knew more than he could say, but how much more? He had a few ideas for scenarios, but it all seemed either impossible or ludicrous. The incongruity that had attracted his attention only led to further incongruities. One day he discovered another track 'in the small opposition newspapers they have in the Seychelles, that gave fairly precise information about this man, including publishing photocopies of documents', which led him to Italy, where the businessman, the ambassador of the Order of Malta, seemed to have had a past. At this time Botbol was waiting for the answers to some questions he had sent to Malta 'about the representation of the Order in Africa, and the verification of the nature of the Seychelles Order of Malta's "incorporation" which, quite bizarrely, had taken place in New York'.

'For the moment, I still didn't publish anything. I had accumulated a lot of things and I just sat back and took it all in.' A few months passed, and Botbol had met with a lot of people, absorbed a lot of stories, and been confronted with a lot of different attitudes. At one point the opposition to the Seychelles government, based in London, 'began a very precise campaign against the same businessman'. The pieces of the puzzle were falling into place, but he still could not really make satisfactory sense of it all. And then the leader of the opposition was assassinated.

At that point he decided to publish what he knew: 'This was partly because it had suddenly become news, and partly because a series of things had fallen into place in my mind. For some time I had been interested in something less exploitable, of no apparent profitability, but then it revealed itself as being important.' Botbol describes himself in this period as being a 'floating eye' – not necessarily attached to the pursuit of anything precise, but navigating left and right, collecting elements of sense; always uncertain, unstable, even disordered: 'At the start there is always an intuition'; what keeps it going is the non-communicable, the transient. The ambiguity is not fundamentally resolved, but he touches on something new: by creative induction, by adduction from a few of the small and unusual elements he collects. 'I think you have to have the intelligence to take an interest in a certain number of things that are not interesting at first glance, but that will one day become so,' he explained. 'Well before the first paper, before the discovery of the false Order of Malta – even before the assassination – I had met with some Seychelles ministers, and I asked them what they knew about the Order of Malta.' Indigo typically dives headlong into the sea of doubt; to taste the flavour of it, to measure its temperature and its consistency: '95 per cent of the time what we do is quite simple, but you have to be able to say to yourself, "Hey, look at that, that's an interesting thread to pick up on."'

The paper was finally published. 'We had a web of presumptions which all tallied up.' There was the bugging of the political opposition. The links were often weak, but they were there. 'We could have left it at that,' Botbol recollected, 'but there was a court case, and everything seemed to shift. It took on a new amplitude. There was a second, then a third court case. We were destabilized.'

Collision of the tacit and the explicit worlds

With the affair brought to the courts, Indigo was forced to defend publication of the article. They had to go back over everything, to unravel one by one each step of the course they had followed: 'We had to do it all again, but it was different. This time we were looking for proof. It was less oblique, more direct. We couldn't accept approxima-tions, we had to keep focusing on the idea of proof.' The defamation trial turned the pyramid upside down. Everything that had previously been tacit had to be made explicit, tangible, black and white. There were now no rules of discretion about their sources. 'We discovered a thoroughly crazy world. How were we to explain it? At the start, our attorney really took us for complete fools.' Indigo lost the case on a very minor point, and had to pay a token penalty, 'as we had at least proven that there were some troubling elements. We could demonstrate the truth of the connections we had made, but we couldn't prove what Scotland Yard itself had been unable to prove. But the trial had some repercussions. Articles appeared in the *Independent* and the *Sunday Times*. The ambassador of "the Order of Malta" had closed up; he'd left the Seychelles and gone to South Africa.' They later discovered his key role in managing the Seychelles as a fiscal paradise, incorporated in Zurich. The reality of Indigo's discoveries was finally disclosed, although the case had already been firmly closed by the judges.

Epilogue

'All the stories we do, we work alone – we have to, there aren't enough of us to do otherwise. Each publication has its own editor-in-chief. The Seychelles case, which all happened around 1985, was one of the first newsletters we published, and I was the only one who worked on it. We are in a system where the personality of each player is very important. It is not only intuition; the "intelligent" part of it, in the sense of comprehension, is the ability to have an inkling of what's going on, of when something is happening, and to be aware that we are always at the threshold of something else. We're really a cottage industry – we have very limited means and we work on an individual scale – but we achieve a lot, and often a lot more than better-organized structures do.'

An exemplary 'management' of knowledge

The Indigo case reveals an aware and exploratory mode of approaching ambiguity. Aware, Maurice Botbol refuses to write, 'because later on, you retain only what is on paper, you lose the global impression, you become falsely guided by details that have been accentuated by being put to paper'. Exploratory, Botbol's approach eschews pre-emptory hypotheses or closed scenarios – he avoids anything that could stifle exploration. When he finally decides to publish a story, the decision is based on a 'consonant web of knowledge', of which the concordances are often intangible. His approach is 'adductive'. He puts a certain trust in the workings of chance; by not developing any specific quest, yet including – 'in the background', he notes – a preoccupation with a subject. We notice also that through legal pressure (the court case) Indigo was compelled to resort to explicit knowledge. The situation was then apprehended collectively, and all of the organization's efforts went into unravelling a predominantly tacit mode of operation to respond to the demands of the accusations directed at them. In this, there was no

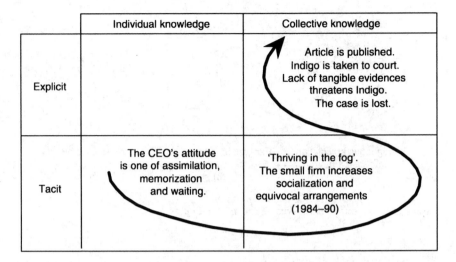

	Individual knowledge	Collective knowledge
Explicit		Article is published. Indigo is taken to court. Lack of tangible evidences threatens Indigo. The case is lost.
Tacit	The CEO's attitude is one of assimilation, memorization and waiting.	'Thriving in the fog'. The small firm increases socialization and equivocal arrangements (1984–90)

Figure 6.1   *Navigation within tacit knowledge*

phase in which ambiguity gradually lifted; the situation's resolution was brutal, it was knocked on the head by the judge's gavel. This allows us to characterize Indigo's mode of apprehending ambiguous situations. We can say that the organization, being small and flexible, 'navigates within tacit knowledge' (see Figure 6.1).

A mutable and blurred management of knowledge

Once he recognized the incongruity of the Order of Malta's having an ambassador in the Seychelles, Maurice Botbol became alert to the situation's wider environment. We note that he began with a 'determined repertory': he did not want to write; he refused any rigid positions; he maintained a sort of 'imprecision' in his approach. This is this same repertory that is developed in a process of socialization. Each meeting, each element obtained during contact with others, unconsciously enters into this 'fuzzy' knowledge base. The conscious motivation behind this effort is not to lose information. Maurice Botbol could instead have applied an exhaustive approach: a systematic and detailed treatment of each clue, one by one – but he refused to do this. He did take clippings and photographs from the press, which he put aside as 'archival', but these were not part of any formal analytical process. His approach was one of trial and error, he felt his way along without there being any point where he could clearly say how far he had gone, or how far he had to go. From the beginning to the end of this intangible quest it was impossible to identify any 'steps', until the final moment when the discovery was made explicit. The quest was constructed and inscribed in practice.

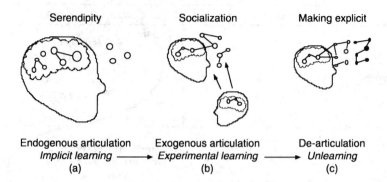

Figure 6.2 *Several forms of knowledge articulation*

Articulation of tacit knowledge

We can distinguish three phases in Maurice Botbol's articulation of his tacit knowledge. The first phase began at the moment when he 'knew more than he could express'. His initial approach to the situation was intuitive; he was able to imagine an eventual coherence and convergence of elements on their own terms. This articulation is *endogenous* – we can say it is a 'closed circuit' (Figure 6.2a). The articulation feeds on impressions and intuition – on a *phantasmagoric* knowledge – and there is no search for any supplementary stimuli.

During this first articulation, knowledge is represented in an abstract manner:

> Abstract codes contain very little, if any, information pertaining to the specific stimulus features from which they were derived; the emphasis is on structural relationships among stimuli. . . . Exactly how the various components of this kind of representation are coded with respect to each other is still an open question. (Reber, 1993: 121)

My interviews with Maurice Botbol confirmed this. If there is a process of knowledge classification involved – which he does not reject a priori – Botbol says he is unaware of it, and that he is not 'unduly preoccupied' with it, his objective being 'to accumulate impressions'. The learning that occurs in this first phase is implicit.

In the second phase, Botbol deliberately confronts his 'impressions' – still not clearly defined, still uncertain and unstable – with what he refers to as 'the dossier's temperature'. He enters a phase of deliberate learning, still conserving a tacit mode of knowledge apprehension. In this he employs socialization, which corroborates the work of Nonaka (1991b) – although there does seem to be some confusion in Nonaka's conceptualization: it is the people who socialize, not the knowledge.

Socialization is a means of galvanizing the transformation of knowledge, but it is not the transformation itself. This is why I prefer to speak of the *articulation* of tacit knowledge, as the term applies just as well to endogenous methods (imagination, induction, mental elaboration) as it does to exogenous methods (socialization, non-formalized interaction, observation, sensation). It is therefore in the course of diverse socialization that the subject (Botbol) will effect an 'exogenous articulation' of his tacit knowledge (see Figure 6.2b).

In a third phase, the articulation that has stabilized into 'a complex web of convergences' gives rise to explicitation: it is put into explicit terms. In the Seychelles case this explicitation was contradicted by a third party, and proceedings were instituted against the company. Maurice Botbol was then constrained to dearticulate – or unravel – what had become a stable body of tacit knowledge. The trial was difficult: Botbol remembers his attorney's reaction when he presented the case to him: he was incredulous. The attorney found the story completely implausible. For one thing, the connections that had been made between apparently isolated events seemed extraordinary, and on top of this was the story's stunningly perfect correspondence with reality. However, to translate the product of multiple articulations assimilated from tacit knowledge into combinations of explicit facts is an arduous task. Botbol had to backtrack, to 'unlearn', to be able to make his knowledge explicit (see Figure 6.2c).

A fluid memory

As we have been able to observe, Maurice Botbol refused to 'fossilize' his knowledge. The entire process of articulation was carried out in his memory, in an abstract and dynamic fashion (elements that could flesh out the elaboration, whether creatively constructed or more or less unconsciously perceived, being articulated as they appeared). This memory is fluid. It stores articulations that remain open and 'fuzzy', and is under continual revision – it continually substitutes or appends other articulations, themselves of a fluid nature.

Such a memory is organized in terms of perceptual frameworks: of scenes (Mandler and Parker, 1976), of ideas about self (Markus, 1977), about events associated with an actor's goals (Lichtenstein and Brewer, 1980), or about other people. The first 'scene' memorized was that which was suggested by the photograph 'of an ambassador of the Order of Malta being in the Seychelles, standing with the country's leader'. The scene was memorized and served as reference for the inductive elaboration of various articulations. These articulations were in response to the incongruity of the apparent situation. Botbol also adopted a tacit approach to the situation with regard to his framework of 'ideas about himself'. He frequently returns to his conception of how he does his work, of how he developed his approach, of what makes him different from other journalists. This framework is also a basis for his articulations. The desire not to 'fossilize' or 'stifle' things is central to it, and repeatedly directs his analyses of the situation.

Finally, he has a perceptual framework about 'businessmen'. It is clear that the incongruity he sensed was a result of the image he had of the archetypal 'businessman': 'He cannot be an ambassador from a humanitarian organization and have such industrial and financial connections.'

A psychological principle of economy

What is it that directs the processes of reconciliation, association or contradiction between these different frameworks? The first thing we notice is that all of these frameworks are open: the original perception of the scene (which started the process off) will be modified according to different impressions (tacit knowledge that he cannot express) of other events that may contradict or confirm it. The three frameworks concerning the scene, the people and their purposes are going to be fleshed out by Botbol's socializations.

But the Seychelles affair is not the small organization's only dossier. Indigo publishes seven bi-monthly confidential newsletters, involving dozens of similar dossiers each month. For each one, Indigo's approach is identical. The same script (Schank and Abelson, 1975) is applied to all ambiguous situations. A script is a body of mental representations organized in sequences, concerning the achievement of a task (in the fashion of a cinematographer's script). Memory, in its organization, includes frameworks and scripts. Repeated episodes form scripts, and learning these scripts, brings us closer to procedural knowledge (Polanyi, 1966a). Direct observation shows that these scripts are submitted to what Freud (1960/1905) called a 'psychological principle of economy'; the economy comes from the avoidance of psychological expense in apprehending a phenomenon. In fact: 'there is an important class of physical principles involving economy, such as that of least time, which Fermat expressed as "Nature always acts by the shortest course"' (Jones, 1975: 10). Knowledge is equally submitted to a principle of economy: in its harnessing (by a selective perception), in its creation (by organizing it in the form of messages: Dretske, 1981), in the way we store it and call it up (by abbreviating it to ideas of 'goodness' or 'truth': Berry, 1983).

It appears that there is also a principle of economy underlying Maurice Botbol's concern not to 'freeze' his knowledge. Once knowledge is 'frozen', it takes on the status of a 'truth'. But this abbreviation then becomes inconsistent with other tacit knowledge acquired after it, and forces this new knowledge to become frozen as well (to become explicit), so that it can 'fit in with' the knowledge already frozen and abbreviated to 'truth'. In a context of sense attribution, the effort of combination is more costly than the effort of articulation. Knowledge which has not been 'frozen' (tacit knowledge) permits a greater malleability *vis-à-vis* a fluctuating reality. 'The articulation of tacit perspectives' is, as Nonaka (1994) says, 'a mobilization process', and 'a key factor in the creation of organizational knowledge'.

Maurice Botbol does not want to write things down because he does not want to stop the process of the mobilization of his knowledge. But on top of this, this mobilization is realized by economizing on appeals to thought-processes, as we saw in the example, in Chapter 2, of human behaviour during a tornado ('you don't see, you know'). Botbol himself speaks of 'letting what is going to happen, happen', and in this his attitude could be described as *laissez-faire* – he follows a 'wait-and-see' policy. We can speak here of an organic configuration of knowledge, perhaps of an auto-configuration (to the extent that numerous articulations are being unconsciously elaborated).

What do we learn from this case?

Why and how was ambiguity tolerated throughout this process? The ambiguity of the situation was due to the impossibility (for Maurice Botbol) of attributing a likely interpretation to events of which he was the observer – an incapacity to render events explicit, to come up with an intelligible explanation. The events were equivocal. Furthermore, we see that the ambiguity was at its peak when the two dimensions, tacit and explicit, 'collided'. Because there was a legal imperative (the trial) to make knowledge explicit (to 'fossilize' it), the ambiguity – *the disparity between possible interpretations* – increased. Once the possibilities were checked – once an interpretation was 'frozen' – the ambiguity subsided.

Nevertheless, before the trial episode the ambiguity seemed to be perfectly tolerated by Botbol and Schmidt. In their socialization, for example during the meal in Washington, not only do they tolerate but they generate ambiguity. Their behaviour is equivocal. Although, in a reflective manner, they say they must 'keep the boundaries clear; we're not "pals" with everybody we're involved with', direct observation reveals behaviour that is less cut and dried. For one thing, they do not announce this principle. They do not say to their interlocutors 'We're not pals.' They do, however, reassure them of their respect for the confidentiality of any information they provide them with: their respect for the 'off-the-record'. There is a desire 'to make them feel they can trust us', but observation shows that it is precisely their friendly attitude, the emulation of a psychological proximity with the interlocutor, that enables them to obtain the knowledge they seek. One can therefore speak of behavioural ambiguity. Their attitude reveals a 'mutable management of the mutable' (Détienne and Vernant, 1978).

Finally, five major characteristics of the management of ambiguity can be gleaned from this case study:

1 repudiation of acclimatization (whereas the determinant role of acclimatization in the *Challenger* space shuttle catastrophe was demonstrated in Chapter 2);
2 the refusal to 'fossilize' or 'stifle' knowledge, a refusal to establish 'abbreviated truths' too rapidly;
3 thorough reflexive practice on Botbol's own knowledge preservation and development;
4 an 'organic' configuration of knowledge;
5 and Maurice Botbol's role as 'articulator'.

7

Indosuez, or Elusive Know-how

Information blockages are a lot more serious than blockages
of machines or utensils.
Indigestion of signs, more serious than food-poisoning.

R. Ruyer

Bank Indosuez, New York (1986–94)

The reasons behind the relatively puzzled atmosphere that reigned in the New York offices of Bank Indosuez at the end of 1986 were twofold. It was partly exogenous, linked to the deregulation of financial markets, to the globalization of economies, and to the economic recession; and partly endogenous, linked to a growth strategy which the bank entered into at the end of the 1980s, and which did not give the results they had expected. 'We have taken the necessary steps to adapt to the changes that have occurred in our industry,' wrote Sir Antoine Jeancourt-Galignani in the traditional Chairman's Message. 'An institution like ours, concentrated but of an international stature, cannot allow itself to underestimate the extent of the transformations that are necessary to adapt to these changes.' At Indosuez, 1987 was to be marked by contrasting events. The bank's privatization was marred by the turbulence of the October crash. Following exhaustive preparations, the privatization was a technical success. But their success was uneven, notably on the large financial markets where 'the path will be incontestably more difficult, where we do not always have the same roots', explained Antoine Jeancourt-Galignani. 'But we believe that in these large markets partnerships with businesses or teams with a similar profile and similar ambitions to ours could be an attractive solution.' The vocabulary, the wording of these annual reports, give the impression that the bank is trying to reassure itself as much as its partners of its *raison d'être*: 'Our vocation is very much that of a French and international investment bank, endowed with a coherent and clear strategy of development at the international scale' (Annual Report, 1989: 7). Could the 'very much' in the middle of this affirmation suggest that there may be some doubt about this? Could the 'coherent and clear' imply that the clearness and the coherence of their strategy could also be the object of doubt? On the next page of the same report we read: 'this is our strategy – we will not move from it . . . this satisfaction on our part in the mobilization of our Group on a coherent and clear strategy of development, at a worldwide scale, of our eight areas of interest should nevertheless not mask the existence of certain nuances met with in reality,' we read a few lines further on. Could this 'reality' be something different from 'things are fine'?

'So, a year of intense effort, but also of deep concern and disappointment, draws to a close for Banque Indosuez,' the Chairman's Message in the 1990 annual report opens. The anxiety stemmed from the invasion of Kuwait; this shook the bank which has operated on the shores of the Arab-Persian Gulf for nearly half a century. 'Despite the anguish and innumerable problems caused by the war, we did not want to destroy, by withdrawing, the network of friendship and mutual confidence established in that region,' explained Antoine Jeancourt-Galignani (page 5).

'Our disappointment stems from the results of the Bank in 1990. Last year we celebrated breaking the billion franc barrier in the net results recorded by our shareholder Compagnie de Suez, and the market crash on 19 October made it a disappointing and frustrating process for our many shareholders and supporters around the world,' commented Antoine Jeancourt-Galignani in the Chairman's Message that year; 'Nonetheless, privatization has opened up many exciting future opportunities, by providing Banque Indosuez and its sister companies within the Suez Group with renewed access to the enormous resources of the capital markets and by strengthening our ties with French and international partners of the highest quality. Through new cooperative ventures and synergies in France and abroad, Banque Indosuez and its partners can work together to develop our respective activities to mutual benefit.'

In 1988 Indosuez undertook an intensive strategic study, outlining an ambitious project in its '1988–1992 Business Plan'. The bank wanted to achieve a level of excellence in three financial sectors: international banking, capital market activities, and financial engineering. These activities were to be conducted 'in France and abroad, particularly in the US, the rest of Europe and the Far East, regions where the bank is traditionally strong.' In the 1988 Annual Report we can also read: 'Our new activities might well prove more volatile than what we have been accustomed to in the past. However, the decreasing contribution of traditional intermediation activities should enable us to overcome inertia in parts of our organization, where the routine nature of certain types of conventional lending has dulled the entrepreneurial spirit.'

By the end of 1989 the mood at the bank was one of satisfaction, which was reflected in the tone of the Chairman's Message of that year: 'Banque Indosuez growth has benefited its parent, Compagnie

Financière de Suez, and all its shareholders; our valued associates at all levels can justly be proud of Banque Indosuez's financial performance,' wrote Jeancourt-Galignani. Nineteen eighty-nine also marked the launching of the bank's Development Charter – and the first results seemed encouraging. The bank seemed to be able to accomplish anything: 'Bank Indosuez demonstrated its power in all of its chosen fields: it took a new leadership in project management, aircraft and ship financing, as well as in securities brokerage. Yet this year we are recording a 10 per cent drop in these results. . . . Numerous factors have led to this decline: a weakening of the quality of our loans portfolios in the United States, in Great Britain, and in Germany; various falls in currency values, especially in Tokyo where W.I. Carr had invested heavily; and the difficulties in the Middle East,' commented Antoine Jeancourt-Galignani (1990, page 5).

In 1991, the tone became a little more embarrassed: 'The results of 1991 as they are presented in this report must be examined with caution,' we are warned in the first line of the Chairman's Message (page 7). After numerous details of new successes in Asia, Latin America and Great Britain, there is a very sobering line: 'However, the deterioration of the Parisian real estate market has led us to fix an exceptional reserve of 650 million French francs on a single building in that city.' The bank recorded a further drop of 13 per cent in its net shareholder results.

A series of disturbing events

In the Indosuez case we witness a disconcerting situation where there is no question of the 'isolation' of the disturbing factor: it centred on the integration of a team of financial experts from the Drexel-Lambert company. Indosuez's aim was to bring knowledge to the organization, which drove the bank to privilege integration rather than exception. Starting from an analysis of this initial situation, I will explore the role played by this 'oblique' knowledge in the bank's everyday activities, and look for the lessons drawn by its management from what I will call the 'Drexel-Lambert' affair.

Towards the end of the 1980s the Compagnie de Suez was engaged in a policy of intensive acquisitions which almost tripled its size. In 1988 Suez acquired the Société Générale de Belgique, and in 1989 the Groupe Victoire, for 27 billion francs – the largest external takeover in France's history. The acquisitions created a vast group acting in real estate, insurance, banking and international finance; but it showed a loss of 1.87 billion francs in 1992. At the heart of the group, the Bank Indosuez itself experienced difficulties when, in 1989, it attempted to take over the British commercial bank Morgan Grenfell. The many ups and downs which the group experienced finally brought about a restructuring of its organization.

Restructuring: how knowledge was managed at Indosuez

When I questioned Jean-Claude Gruffat about the restructuring and what it meant for the bank's original strategy, he replied: 'the difficulties that we experienced confirmed the accuracy of our strategy. They were consistent with what we had perceived and undertaken to deal with.' The reorganization of the bank had begun in 1986, and the results were summarized in the bank's Development Charter, some aspects of which are included in directive 88/06 of 29 November 1988. This was followed by readjustments described in directives 90/01 of 27 December 1990, 91/04 of 7 October 1992 and 92/06 of 31 December 1992.

In 1992 the second five-year charter was instituted within the bank, with the support of the Boston Consulting Group. The charter emphasizes products. The reorganization enumerates the product lines as follows:

- trading in debt and exchange instruments;
- corporate finance (share issues, mergers and acquisitions);
- brokerage (quotations);
- financial management (private banking);
- financing assets.

Questioned on the reorganization, managers saw it as 'putting down on paper the tasks that the bank was already carrying out before the reorganization, but without knowing it.' The bank had previously been organized on the basis of responsibility to its customers, and 'had done everything the client asked'. Before 1987, the quality of the relationships between customer and financial consultant was the seat of the bank's 'strategic orientation'. Those at the frontier of the company's development, those who might be called the 'boundary spanners' (Daft and Weick, 1984) in the profit centres, were readily recognizable – credit managers and customer relation officers – as were those in the cost centres – the technical committees. Organization according to product lines imposed management by profit centres (products), the cost centres being situated, however, in the sale costs of the products. In the 1980s the historic dimension was predominant: bank executives were proud of the bank's long history, and as the bank moved from being a customer bank to being a trading bank many of the people I questioned had the feeling that 'the bank had changed its perception of itself'. For some, Indosuez had to 'find a new identity in a world where previously well-established situations are disappearing'. In deregulating credit, the 1980 banking reform was one of the first signs of this profound change in the macro-environment: deregulation was synonymous with the end of statutory recognition.

The banks were no longer subject to a classification that defined their area of competencies, but each competence they did have had to be proved against that of rivals in a market context. Such competencies are established either by specialization according to clientele, or by specialization according to products, and the dilemma that confronted banks is summarized well by the philosopher Clement Rosset in *Reality and its Double* (1985): if all roads lead to Rome, then no road has any meaning. If all banks offer universality in services, then no bank has any real identity as against another. (Banks like Citibank, Credit Lyonnais or Deutchebank have all followed the path of universality, with its associated ups and downs.)

The second profound change in the macro-environment was undoubtedly the weaker value of acquired inertias. In a regulated environment, statutory advantages allow for easy deployment. For example, Credit Agricole, benefiting by the opening of local branches in a regulated environment, created for itself an image of proximity which had a strong intrinsic value as long as the environment remained regulated. This value is relative today, and will certainly be so in the future. Bank Indosuez had, during the 1950s, obtained the licence to print French francs in several countries, which conferred on it a privilege of presence analogous to that which Credit Agricole had at the domestic level. Unilateral deregulation of the environment not only jeopardizes advantages currently being acquired, but also abruptly dislodges acquired inertia. It affects not only market logic, but also identity.

The reorganization of Indosuez into a trading bank raises several questions about the management of knowledge. Its clientele remained the same, even if their financial needs became many-sided, as a result of far-reaching changes in the macro-environment. A scanning of product literature risks reducing one's perception of the strategies of customers to their product strategies – that is, it gives a partial and fragmented perception of the customers' real intentions. In an organization founded on the client–consultant relationship, a thorough knowledge of the client is to be achieved only through a higher level of intimacy between the client and their consultant. The problem that remains to be resolved is the macro-environmental perception of product evolution – a problem to which Indosuez seems to have responded by a reorganization of its activities according to its products. Numerous managers who were interviewed felt that 'this vision centred on products ought to have been moderated – it can lead to an impoverishment of the relationship we have with the client'. Such a focus on products is based on concepts of proximity of access to services, and on product standardization, whereas a focus on services is based on the quality of the relationships between clients and their consultants.

Another concern that arose from this compartmentalized system was the existence of transverse offers, which involved the combination of several products – like credit financing which required the management of the supplementary debt. A third concern arose from the veracity of the macro-economic changes that justified the reorganization. The globalization was not unilateral, and was sometimes even embryonic in certain areas of the bank's activities. For example, the American market was a very 'domestic' market. In this case, the size effect (as a major domestic player) is essential in the United States, and the network effect (taking up exterior resource opportunities) very relative. Within the industry, the conviction was that the network effect would, in the long term, constitute a decisive comparative advantage, a hypothesis that is difficult to confirm today. A corollary concern relates to the coordination costs of managing such networks. If such a network is to survive it must generate profits across the board. At Indosuez in 1983 everyone carried out their own activity in their particular country, and so each county's particularities were incorporated into the bank's activities. But becoming a world player does not wipe away local realities, nor does it efface their singularity. A trading bank is by nature an opportunist bank. When attention is directed to the transaction (the product), competitive advantage is reduced to its explicit expression (the product), whereas a customer relationship always involves multiple dimensions, tacit and explicit.

If we return to the example of the financing of assets, we find that these are physically very localized. Even if Total invests in the United States (a transnational activity), the reality of the investment will be domestic and will risk being strongly contingent on the domestic market. The network effect loses its value. The bank tried to counteract these obstacles by holding repeated internal meetings, to enable them to extract a 'customer' vision from several 'product' visions. When questioned about this practice, managers saw it, in the words of Pierre Bouniol-Laffont, Manager of Asset Finance, as 'a useful aid to the representation of the environment' which allowed them to 'see what was going on in the outside world' and 'gave meaning to our professional life'.

Direct observation and in-depth interviews within Indosuez's back office provide us with a supplementary view of the functioning of the bank. The back office monitors market risks. It is, in theory, centred in Paris, but the New York back office acts as intermediary. A database called 'Global' was developed in New York, then set up in all branches. It enabled all of the bank's products to be followed, and it responded to the growing need for sophisticated analysis. The relationship with Paris was often maintained over the telephone 'because we needed to pass on qualitative information on the risks', explained Jean Luc Eymery. The back office's activities relied on a thorough familiarity with what was happening within the bank in terms of flux, of the books, and even of what went on in the trading room (from which it was separated by a glass wall). It also had to evaluate each trader's fundamental strategy, not in human terms, but simply to understand why they were in a customer section which generated a certain profitability. 'Our work is basically rationalization,' explained Eymery, 'but generally after the fact.' The back office would assess the fiscal risks; it would quantify the market risks while it qualified the compensation. The information handled by the back office was then coded, articulated in report form, and entered into the system; 'but relationships with employees couldn't be too formal. We were often confronted with people who thought that we worked only with hard facts. It was actually a question of scale. The management wanted information that had already been digested, already made intelligible. What we did too was to transform hard information into soft information for management,' explained Eymery. The people I interviewed saw their organization therefore as a very organized institution, but one which tried to promote creativity.

A deliberate learning

The bank entered the American market for the first time, not in New York, but in Chicago, with the purpose of acquiring expertise in futures trading. In the 1980s it was engaged in business loans, a segment it moved out of in 1988. Leibowitz (1993: 20) wrote: 'when I arrived in the United States, I realized that our trading operations were not really profitable, that our loan activities were going nowhere, and that we had no significant relational corporate network'. In March 1990, the Indosuez Bank bought out a team of talented professionals in structured finance (SF) from Drexel Burnham Lambert, which was experiencing serious financial difficulties. The operation of structured finance can be summarized as an operation of 'de-packaging' and 're-packaging' of financial instruments, according to the financial needs of the clientele, and the acquisition of this team was followed by the inauguration of ICM (International Capital Markets), a branch of Indosuez specializing in structured finance. It is here that our story begins. On one side we have a bank wanting to develop its expertise in a developing sector, in which expert knowledge is in the hands of a limited number of people. On the other, a group of young competitive experts, wanting to continue doing what they do best and to profit from it.

The complexities of 'structured finance'

Knowledge of derivatives, which are the instruments of 'structured finance', is 'positional knowledge' – which is to say that it is knowledge whose value lies in the relatively superior position which it confers on its possessor. The limits of positional knowledge are also very well summarized by Hirsch: 'If everyone stands on tiptoes, no one will see any better' (1977: 5). 'Positional' does not mean 'rare' in absolute terms, but rare relative to the availability of the information in a given environment. For example, knowledge of the basic principles of accounting is not strongly positional in the United States, where accounting methods are taught in all universities. It becomes positional knowledge, for example, in the industrial sectors in Czechoslovakia that have operated for several decades under Soviet systems of management. Whilst this example concerns an explicit positional knowledge (accounting methods), other forms of positional knowledge do exist. For example, the experience of an industry – of its rituals, its rules, of the in-depth knowledge its members have of it, of the game rules between these members – is tacit positional knowledge.

'Our job is to offer to our customers structured financial products which are not available on the open financial markets,' explained Ravi Trehan, formerly of Drexel-Lambert and now director of Indosuez's department of structured finance. This is an activity that demands creativity and innovation. Whereas on the traditional bonds and equities markets the price and the quality of the relationship with the client essentially dominated the transaction, in structured finance it is the creativity and the appropriateness of the specialist's ideas which will ultimately convince the client. 'It is a dynamic activity. We have a good idea one day, the next day the competition does,' confessed Trehan. The business is highly sporadic. There can be two or three months of mediocre activity, then suddenly it can all start off at once. The channels of information are very informal. Decisions rely on an intangible knowledge of the environment: 'This activity requires a different attitude towards management. Monthly performance statements have no meaning, and nor do budget-planning processes,' commented one executive.

The team occupied two offices at Indosuez's US headquarters in New York's Rockefeller Center. One of the two offices was completely empty. The team worked in the other room, in a tumult that contrasted starkly with the relative order of the bank's other offices. 'The most important thing is to have access to a good informal network within the industry. Every bit of information matters, even an apparently insig-nificant comment made by one of our clients,' explains Trehan. The techniques for 'feeling the market' are informal, and managers cross-check by assigning particular executives to each operation 'to preserve the focus'. As this activity really only began in 1983, there is little 'history' involved: there is no real history of the development of the product, which would not really have much significance until at least ten years had passed; notwithstanding, there was a desire not to 'reinvent the wheel', and to try as much as possible to link up the creative process with past experience. However, the products were complex and very much relative to the situation and the specific needs of clients. The emergence of derivatives activities related to a deeper trend in the banking occupation. In the past, the dominant concept had been that of the 'universal bank' and its traditional banking services. These derivatives activities corresponded to the creation of 'boutiques' to cater to the complex and shifting needs of customers, often on a transnational basis.

They concentrated a large amount of knowledge in the minds of experts who devised the products according to the needs of their clientele. The experts compared their job to that of a brain surgeon: 'The clients are not concerned about what goes on behind the curtain. Working in bonds for example is transparent, but for our part we are not worried about transparency,' confided one executive. We can distinguish here two key elements of this role: positional knowledge, and creation in the course of action – or 'action generated' creation (Starbuck, 1983). A third aspect is the necessity to 'be continually on the lookout', to continually observe the client and the market. The job requires a global vision: 'according to a configuration of events in one place in the world, we re-package the proposal for another part of the world. We creatively re-articulate the product. It is a completely different configuration of priorities,' explains Ravi Trehan.

The integration of structured finance (SF) activities into the bank was in itself a challenge, in a profession which is not subject to dramatic changes, and therefore is hardly receptive to these changes. SF activities 'could serve to identify business opportunities for the bank's management, but its integration into the fabric of the bank's activities remains incomplete to this day,' continued Trehan. The main fear of experts in SF was that the operation might become 'institutionalized', that the department would shift its direction and follow the aims of the other bank departments: 'The landscape is always changing for SF, whereas the landscape is always the same in the other banking activities,' concluded Trehan.

The genesis of an ambiguous situation

In the growth strategy that Indosuez adopted, the *modus operandi* was that of acquiring knowledge from outside by buying out institutions (purchasing parts of Morgan Grenfell in 1989, and joining into an alliance with Blackstone in 1990, for example) or by luring away executives who possessed positional knowledge in other institutions (Pierre Daviron, acquisition expert from Morgan Grenfell in March 1990, six experts in debt trading from Citicorp in March 1991, and Richard Sandor, from Drexel-Lambert in March 1990).

The acquisitions, or attempts at acquisitions, were sometimes very aggressive, and experienced mixed success. The attempted acquisition of Morgan Grenfell in 1989 failed. But it is Indosuez's appropriation of experts from Drexel-Lambert, negotiated in the space of one weekend in March 1990, which is of particular interest to us. To fully understand the course of events we also need to understand the culture of Indosuez. Indosuez owes much of its strength to its history, beginning as the Banque d'Indochine et de Suez, and to the links which it has kept with the Middle East since its historic involvement in the construction of the Suez Canal in the 1860s. The bank's prospectus features a photograph of a colonial house on all main pages: the 'seat' of the Banque d'Indochine in Saigon in 1875. This attachment to its history is not unrelated to the bank's determination not to 'be an insignificant player'. 'The challenge is not only in New York. What we want to become in New York is what we want to become in the major financial places, including France. If we were not participants who are successful in commercial banking and trading in our basic market we would be taken over by someone else, or we would become a minor player' (Jean-Claude Gruffat, interviewed by Leibowitz, 1993: 21). The contradiction lies perhaps in Jean-Claude Gruffat's conclusion during the same interview: 'We just want to be another Wall Street organization.'

But the 'rules of the game' in Wall Street are very special. Salaries are very high and the mood is particularly entrepreneurial and competitive: very different from the French banking culture and its more conservative management style. When Drexel-Lambert had financial difficulties in February 1990, the opportunity was seized immediately and Richard Sandor's team of specialists in 'swaps' and SF were 'bought' by Indosuez. The terms of the transaction promised autonomy, high incomes and privileged access to Jean-François Lepetit and the bank's two presidents in Paris. From this point Indosuez could become a textbook case for understanding the difficulties of 'cross-cultural management', but we will turn our attention rather to the resolution of ambiguity and the role that 'oblique processes' played in this.

In the institutional culture of a French bank, the 'Drexelites', as I will call them, stood out from the crowd. At the start, Indosuez was surprised by the 'on the spot' decisions of the Drexelite team, as the bank was used to 'an exchange of memos between Paris and New York' before making any important moves. This is not only because of a difference in culture. As we have seen above, the operation of SF and of derivatives is one that is erratic, rapid, creative: carried out 'in the fire of action', was Ravi Trehan's expression. Undoubtedly, Indosuez's second error concerns the feasibility of such a raw transfer of knowledge.

Knowledge of derivatives is flexible, tacit, held by experts – as opposed to 'hard information' which could be the subject of an operational manual or a theoretical course. 'They thought we possessed this "black box", and that they could learn and acquire certain technology. But we were not interested. They had the wrong idea,' recalls a former Drexelite (interviewed by Leibowitz, 1993: 22). For Gruffat, the rationale behind the acquisition of the Drexelites was the bank's commitment to globalization.

Despite an underlying ambiguity and the obvious fact that the 'Drexelites' knowledge was thoroughly idiosyncratic (which was apparently not consistent with Indosuez's desire to acquire external knowledge), the operations of Indosuez Capital Markets (ICM), the Drexelites' independent branch within Indosuez, showed a good performance without problems in its first year. Wendy de Monchaux directed derivative trading, Ravi Trehan directed SF, Bob Shingleton was in charge of settlements, and Sandor was responsible for the ICM group, in the role of President and Chief Executive. External analyses however reported that ICM was not as aggressive as might have been expected, even though its charges were more or less consistent with standards in the brokers' market. Other analyses (Standard & Poor's) attributed a grade AA to the bank at this period – which helped it to access certain transactions that had been more difficult to obtain since it had been recategorized at grade A following the real estate losses of its parental branch. Trehan led a team of 12 people, and senior management were satisfied with their results. But the underlying ambiguity which I have mentioned, as to the idiosyncratic and positional nature of the Drexelites' knowledge, was not slow in producing its effects. One could certainly debate the decisions to create ICM, to give autonomy and the presidency to Sandor, and to emphasize the singularity of the Drexelites within the group. The decision to create an autonomous structure undoubtedly emphasized the isolation caused by the rarity and specialized nature of the knowledge possessed by the Drexelites, who barely interacted with the rest of the bank: 'Indosuez wanted us to become part of the bank, and to take part in management conferences. We were sort of independent Americans, and at the end of the day I don't think the French were really happy with that. We felt we had a protected status because we were making money. The profits we were making were not important, though, as the average employee of the bank was not benefiting from it' (ex-Drexelite, interviewed by Leibowitz, 1993: 23).

The underlying ambiguity was transformed into a disconcerting situation when the group recruited Marc Schmitt, a veteran of 18 years at the Dresden Bank, to run the Paris international funds operations – with a direct link to Jean François Lepetit and Alain de Korsak. Schmitt's position gave him control of Sandor in ICM, and de Monchaux in derivative trading. Jean-Claude Gruffat outlined the reasoning behind Schmitt's appointment in the following way: 'The President did not want to be on call at all times to approve new clients or products or to settle New York's problems' (Leibowitz, 1993: 24). But the idea of having their operations controlled by Paris had no real meaning, particularly for the Drexelites, since the bulk of the operations took place in the United States. The situation had reached an impasse, to use Détienne and Vernant's term. Schmitt had his own ideas on the organization of the business of derivatives, and conflicts with de Monchaux became frequent. The situation became so uncomfortable that the outcome was unpredictable, and could well have resulted in the dissolution of the organization dealing with swaps – the Drexelites.

The emergence and collapse of tacit and conjectural knowledge

The swaps group – the Drexelites – maintained an 'informal matrix' of communication with Jean-Claude Gruffat, who could approve increases in credit lines although he was not responsible for the operation as a whole; this responsibility remained centred in Paris. The Drexelites still feared being absorbed by the Parisian bureaucracy, and communication between these two parts of the organization was limited by a mutual avoidance of spelling things out: each feared that a too direct or too piercing statement might jeopardize the fragile equilibrium that was reached from time to time.

The whole organization was aware of the problem, and while some thought the bank was making too much of the Drexelites, others thought (privately) that the young Drexelites were asking too much as well. But New York swaps constituted by far the most profitable segment of the bank's derivative activities, and this was entirely the work of these same Drexelites (Leibowitz, 1993: 24); in 1992, the small team produced nearly $US60 million in profit solely from derivative operations. The Drexelite group had become accustomed to special treatment, including not having to deal with the bank's hierarchical structure and being able to meet directly with Jean-Claude Gruffat whenever they felt it was necessary – which is undoubtedly what enabled them to continue their cooperation with Gruffat below the organizational surface. According to some, they had a sort of automatic understanding, even though relations between them had at times been strained.

When Sandor left the bank things seemed to return to normal, much to everyone's surprise – and this is a little the impression one has today on meeting the ex-Drexelites still with Indosuez. Indosuez's manage-ment became even more distant towards disagreement. Schmitt con-centrated on the swaps group, and other New York managers simply avoided having too much to do with him, although this was never made too explicit. All the same a kind of tacit fabric remained – a trace of what had happened, but only detectable by those who had lived through the events – a tacit fabric which was more painful for de Monchaux than for others. Above all since after Scott's arrival she had been asked – explicitly this time – to pay more attention to Hong Kong's position, and to absorb the costs of widening swaps operations in the rest of South-East Asia (Leibowitz, 1993: 25). For a group like de Monchaux's, which based its profitability on flexible short-term movements, this was at the very least irritating.

Relations between Schmitt and de Monchaux deteriorated rapidly, culminating, in June 1992, in a 'closed door' meeting between the two in New York. Insiders later described this meeting to Leibowitz as 'a turbulent exchange'. Schmitt being above de Monchaux in the bank's hierarchy, it was decided that de Monchaux would leave the bank: but no detailed explanation was given for this decision when it was presented at a meeting held soon after. This meeting brought together actors who had until then exchanged only indirect communications and more or less tacit definitions of their respective positions. According to various sources, several traders threatened to leave the bank, but Schmitt stayed firm. After de Monchaux's departure, Richard Stein temporarily took charge of swaps until, in October 1992, Indosuez recruited Philippe Gautier from Banque Nationale de Paris, where he had been responsible for swaps and capital markets: a recruitment which Leibowitz argued was an unambiguous message that swaps were to be controlled by Paris (1993: 26).

In three moves, Indosuez had shifted from a kind of ambiguous tacit flexibility to an explicit uncompromising rigidity; they had jostled about between two worlds, to end up in that of the collectively accepted explicit. Following Gautier's appointment Stein, Leon Bemell (the bank's best swaps trader), arbitrage specialist Bob Shingleton, and marketing expert Andrew Langerman all took a week's leave to reflect upon their respective options.

Re-emergence of the tacit dimension

Indosuez was in the following situation. They had navigated ambiguity for some time and established a matrix of informal relationships, below the organizational surface, which allowed them to deal with this ambiguity. Then a meeting crystallized what had been changeable and fluid, while actually preserving a certain 'status quo', in a confrontation over rules (hierarchy and strategy) and the territory of the explicit (definition of roles and division of responsibilities). The explicit domain being always more confining than its tacit equivalent, the game shifted to become 'black and white, win or lose, in or out', as one of the people I interviewed put it. The ex-Drexelites were thrown into an ambiguity that was obstructive because it had been exposed – the cards were on the table. They could no longer control the situation by allowing it to remain fluid, so they took a week's leave; they withdrew from a reality which had become too explicit. Their isolation was a question of survival.

At that point, Jean-Claude Gruffat, who I should point out had already taken the initiative of following an 'informal matrix', tried to negotiate the return (or to avoid the departure) of these key actors, the Drexelites, who were from beyond the organizational terrain and who had kept their distance and made their own choices. Speaking to Leibowitz (1993: 25), Gruffat commented that his primary goal was to convince the Drexelites to continue working within Indosuez. Gruffat recognized the problem posed by Indosuez's hierarchical structure, and decided that the solution was to 'find a way to keep them on board with a different environment'. But the environment which the Drexelites had been privileged to work in had already been very different from the general Indosuez environment, as they had been offered autonomy and responsibility at the outset. A hierarchy directed from Paris had then been thrust upon them. What could be done? Was there a third way around this situation, an 'oblique' way?

Apart from Langman, who rejoined de Monchaux at Bear, Sterns & Co., every other Drexelite agreed to stay on board on the condition that they report to Norbert Graetz, who was in charge of Indosuez Funds in New York, and who was in turn to report to Gruffat at the Paris office. Although this combination of explicit circuits did not exactly replicate the articulation of what had been tacit (and seemed to work), these new official channels did closely resemble the tacit articulation and the first informal matrix which Ravi Trehan and his group had developed with Jean-Claude Gruffat, and which bypassed Schmitt. Although it was never made explicit, this new articulation of their knowledge reinforced the fabric that had formed tacitly when the ambiguity was at its peak. Gruffat had saved the day. The ex-Drexelite traders ended up working on the same projects they had been involved in when the ambiguous situation and the ensuing crisis first arose, even if the formal and explicit definition of their field of activity had changed in the organizational diagram.

Epilogue

It seems that some learning was involved in the delicate task of assembling this expertise. In March 1993, Indosuez again recruited a team of six people who specialized in derivatives, but this time from BNP Capital Markets. This time, led by Carolyn Jackson, who rejoined her old boss Philippe Gautier, everything went smoothly. Of course, many of the same characteristic reactions arose; some people saw it as an easy way out for management to bring in external teams to resolve internal problems. But this time, events unfolded in a different and more innocuous way.

When the bank's officials looked back at what had happened, and tried to make sense of the events, they certainly did invent problems in order to justify solutions. In trying to explain the reasons for the considerable ambiguity and the crisis which followed it, Schmitt comes to mind, and one former executive comments: 'He tried to take over all operations as far as he was able to. He tried to control swaps and he failed.' But a close study of the unfolding of events does not support such a reductionist explanation. Schmitt's comment on the subject is perhaps closer to the truth, though very simple: 'There was no right answer to the problem.'

And in fact, it seems that the problem did not lie where it seemed to: rather it lay behind the management styles, behind the culture, hidden in the depths of the organization, in behaviours, in different attitudes towards knowledge. Schmitt was later to say: 'I was not brought up in the Drexel style. My way of looking at things is to go from point A to point B with the minimum cost. Sometimes you have to give a little to get more, and this is indeed the problem of global organizations. You have different cultures around the world, and there is an art to making people work together' (Leibowitz, 1993: 27). But it is not at all certain that differences of national culture really played the role that Schmitt attributes to them. New York's Indosuez office is a subsidiary where only English is spoken. American and European managers coexist there, and direct observation does not pick up any significant differences in their attitudes or in the exchange of knowledge. As for the difference in culture between Paris and New York, we should note that Jean-Claude Gruffat travelled enormously: he could quite readily have been perceived as a Parisian element in New York, and as a New York element in Paris. And yet he was neither of these, although he played a decisive role in the flexible coordination, beneath the organizational surface, which saved the situation.

One of the most interesting phenomena is undoubtedly Jean-Claude Gruffat's public comment on the whole affair. He admits that he had a share of the responsibility, and that he should have recognized the problem earlier on and 'been more assertive at the time' (Leibowitz, 1993: 26). Two problems can be identified in this statement. On the one hand, there is the question of recognition. The problem was not identified at first, we can say that it was not recognized, in the sense that one recognizes a person from a distance in the street without distinguishing their face, through their posture and a general impression of their gait. The process of recognition is instantaneous. Within it we cannot identify phases, a sequential search or a bounded rationality. It is a crystallization. The second aspect raised is that of a lack of assertiveness: Gruffat feels he should have been 'more assertive'. This refers to two things: to both his intervention and to the form of this intervention. The choice of the word 'assertive' suggests a mode of intervention which is both direct and informal. It is also noteworthy that those who were the key elements in Jean-Claude Gruffat's informal matrix expressed the most contentment in relation to their actual situation within Indosuez in New York. Interviewed by Leibowitz, Ravi Trehan declared that Indosuez provided the environment they needed in order to continue to carry out SF in an 'entrepreneurial spirit', and this is confirmed by my direct observation of the conditions in which Trehan and his small team work today – harmoniously chaotic, with the empty room next door, and clashing markedly with the rest of the floor, yet all the same without appearing to be isolated. There are no walls on this wing of the floor, only a 1.5 metre divider which separates the small team from the back office a few metres away. As for Liebermann, he is perfectly content with the absence of a weighty hierarchy.

Incompatible knowledge?

Through the 'Drexel-Lambert affair' Indosuez 'learnt to unlearn' (Hedberg, 1981), and traces of this learning could be found throughout the organization once the ambiguous situation had been resolved. The shifts and crises of ambiguity followed one after another, but Indosuez had been confronted with other ambiguous situations over its history – such as the Suez Canal affair in 1956, when the Suez Company lost ownership of the canal, which was taken back from it by President Nasser of Egypt. And traces still remain. Understanding spreads in an organization like a drop of oil. One learns by what one sees, sometimes as much as by what one does. The learning process is simply different. It circulates in a narrative tradition, in collective beliefs, in a community of practice.

In October that year, the franc was attacked on all sides. Indosuez's treasury in Paris established permanent contact with the small group in New York, including Gruffat, employing all of their telephones, beepers and portable phones, and this contact was maintained until the situation of flux and ambiguity was resolved. Leslie Harrison explained how this worked: 'The aim is for management to understand thoroughly what is actually going on. We discuss our interpretations together. No one sits working alone in his corner. A continually changing flow of information is maintained with Jean-Claude Gruffat so that he can intervene and react in the decision-making process.' This approach to knowledge permeated all levels of the company.

The trading room manager was based in a glass office, which allowed him to watch what was happening and to respond to calls for assistance. The 'top traders' would be near the entrance of this office so as to always be at hand when necessary. Rumours were tracked back to their source, and then the question would be asked: 'How many times has this person been right and how many times have they been wrong?'

This assessment is really based on a tacit knowledge of the trader, drawn from the manager's experience; as manager Carolyn Jackson put it, she saw her role as 'sparing others from errors, on the basis of my 15 years of experience'. As earnings for those working in the market room are indexed on the profit they realize for the bank, they are very sensitive to errors. Jackson describes her role as one of continual monitoring, based on practical experience of the financial scene: 'I know what price we should get.' Asked about the process which guides her in filtering environmental stimuli, she says: 'Never listen to the opinion of others.' The traders learn by doing.

The training period for these traders lasts for five years, during which they develop their judgement with small transactions. The value of these transactions increases progressively according to the performance of the trader. Asked about the selection of traders at the outset, Leslie Harrison declares: 'I only engage people I know, referred by people I respect.' The 'education' of the young traders begins with instruction in banking operations, through which they learn the necessary book-keeping skills. 'We try to give them a sound knowledge of the mechanisms of information transfer within the bank, so that they understand the overall environment they are in. They have to learn to carry out several tasks at the same time if they are to attain good results in their trading.'

Two essential factors can be identified in this training: a mastery of mechanisms, and the development of judgement. 'But to understand the thinking, you have to feel the pain,' adds Harrison. When asked about the role of increasing the funds at stake, she corrects me by arguing that the size of the funds involved does not play a determining part: 'The pain is the same, because it occurs at different stages in the trader's development. Whereas ten million dollars can be a big stake for a young trader, it is not so much for an experienced trader, although 100 million dollars is.' Learning through mistakes is very important: '90 per cent of our activity is in problem-solving,' she adds, 'and the number of variables involved in this problem-solving are always greater than they seem on first impression.' The explicit instruments of risk evaluation – such as Cook's ratio – evaluate only 'black and white' knowledge: the wealth of the required knowledge is much greater than its explicit expression.

Distinguishing the routine from the unusual is a difficult thing to achieve. It is clear that here the education of perception is developed through routine and is inscribed in practice. When I introduced the question of a disagreement between the principal trading areas of the bank (London, Paris, New York) on what strategy to follow the responses from my interviewees were immediate and universal: emergency procedure consists of calling a meeting to ensure a thorough sharing of information. Maintaining informal collaborative relationships with a few people in Paris and London allowed them to broaden their field of understanding.

In the preceding cases, we have seen that tacit and conjectural knowledge is deployed through collateral processes, even when there are fundamental differences between the collateral organizations. I have noted that the term 'clandestine management' could suggest a value judgement regarding its collateral processes, attributing to them a secret, extraordinary, immoral nature which would be misleading. The tacit circulation of knowledge, and its use as basic support for decision-making and the resolution of ambiguous situations, are quite common and normal within organizations. There is no question of immorality in this form of information management; on the contrary, it proves to be an extraordinary resource for the organization. Whereas we were examining individual skill in managing and dealing with the tacit and oblique dimensions of knowledge within Indigo Publications, with the Indosuez case we will explore collective skill, or more precisely, the role of oblique processes in comprehending disconcerting situations involving several people.

This case enables us to shed light on the functioning of collateral processes – 'parallel with, not instead of' the organization's formal and explicit processes (Zand, 1981: 58). We will focus here on identifying when and why these processes are deployed. In the Indigo case, the 'oblique' process was adopted as a result of a breakdown in the normal processes used by the organization. The process adopted responded to a logic of isolation.

Following a rather long period of incubation and maturation of the ambiguous situation, the deployment of the process finally amounted to a personal decision. This was followed by a series of manoeuvres involving only one 'metistic' individual, and the situation that confronted him. The organization as such was absent from the process, perhaps voluntarily placed on the sidelines. This does not imply the creation of a new reality for the company; more the isolation of a 'disturbing reality' within a well confined area.

A significant reorganization

The bank had to face up to the volatile nature of the Drexelites' results alongside the fixed level of its general costs. This was a structural problem tied to the nature of its activities and the structure of its revenue. There was also some uncertainty as to the guarantee of the bank's continual presence in the sectors in which it was dealing, and a perennial problem regarding the existing staff on one hand, and the staff required for the longer term on the other hand. Confronting an uncertain situation, Indosuez's management multiplied its instructions regarding the distribution of roles and the definition of tasks. Employees followed a set of explicit rules, which were reinforced through regular meetings. The bank moved from a system that was compartmentalized according to services, to a system that was compartmentalized according to products. The predominant mode of managing knowledge was explicit and collective. A set of formal rituals and of rules made interpersonal relationships hierarchical, and imposed both measurement systems and a language.

The confrontation of the two modes of understanding

When the Drexelites arrived, they did not expect to attend meetings. They did not see any use in them. They rarely looked to the collective rules as guides to behaviour. Their method of acquiring knowledge was tacit, their articulation of it personal and difficult to transfer to others. Their dominant mode of knowledge management was tacit and individual.

In a knowledge mode that is principally explicit, knowledge is modified by its combination (Nonaka, 1991a). Indosuez proposed a new 'knowledge combination' when it initiated its reorganization. Adjustments to these combinations took place at internal meetings. In a knowledge mode that is principally tacit, knowledge is circulated through socialization. The Drexelites' group was important within Indosuez because their knowledge was difficult to divide. From direct observation we discover that the Drexelites' work space was not compartmentalized, it gave an impression of chaos. The single office (leaving the second office that had been allocated to them empty) served to isolate them and concentrate their activities. Their tacit individual knowledge organized itself within their own space of socialization.

The bank tried to support them by giving them statutory and decisional autonomy. It reinforced their 'closed' form of socialization. The transfer of knowledge to the rest of the bank never took place, but the team did achieve striking results. The Drexelites' tacit knowledge did not articulate itself so as to integrate with Indosuez's explicit knowledge mode. Vice versa, Indosuez's explicit knowledge mode was never interiorized by the Drexelites. A cohabitation of these two modes of knowledge circulation was produced: socialization within the small group of the Drexelites, and combination within Indosuez as a whole. When the bank initially engaged the Drexelites it thought that their knowledge would be transferable to the organization, because Indosuez's explicit and collective mode of managing its knowledge led it to see the Drexelites' knowledge as a transferable object – a perception that the Drexelites found startling. The situation lasted for one year, until a new derivatives director was named in Paris, at which time the pressure on the Drexelites' mode of knowledge circulation became stronger. They were asked to articulate their knowledge within the knowledge of the group as a whole; a demand that led to the crisis.

The articulation of the Drexelites' knowledge within Indosuez was completely infeasible, as it would necessitate an extension of their socialization from a closed unit to much broader socialization, which could only have been realized in New York. The situation became unpredictable and ambiguous. Jean Claude Gruffat then took the initiative of instigating a 'matrix of informal relations' below the organizational surface. In this crisis Gruffat realized the articulation that was necessary.

The situation of the Drexelites within Indosuez cannot be described using Zand's term 'collateral organization' – as this defines a parallel organization, which coexists with the organization, and which a manager can use to supplant the existing formal organization. Oblique processes do not 'supplant' the organization, they complete it, perhaps even shift it somewhat, but they leave the functioning of the organization, its identity and its structures, intact. They proceed furtively perhaps within the organization, but do not substitute for existing processes. In the Indosuez case, the motivation behind the recruitment of experts from Drexel-Lambert was a transfer of knowledge. This expertise was perceived by Indosuez as an explicit expertise (in Polanyi's 1966b categorization, 'communicable'). An unpredictable and ambiguous situation emerged from:

• a crucial difference between the modes of knowledge management employed by the Drexelites and by Indosuez. While Indosuez saw

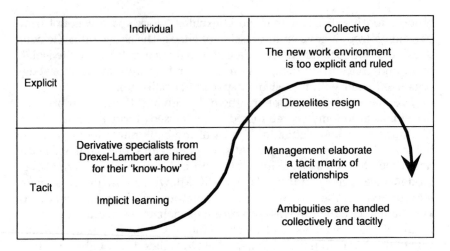

Figure 7.1   *Shifting knowledge modes at Indosuez*

knowledge circulation as explicit and collective (strict rules, bureaucratization, hierarchy), the Drexelites valued tacit and individual
knowledge (self-worth, the singularity of knowledge);
- the Drexelites' know-how was finally not communicable. They
  found that it involved individual and tacit knowledge. The passage
  of the individual-tacit to the explicit-shared is difficult, and a crisis
  arose (Figure 7.1).

The organization successfully extricated itself from the ambiguous
situation by finding a tacit and communal way of managing the situation
(an 'informal matrix of relations' between Gruffat and the Drexelites).
Without the intervention of Gruffat, the situation would almost certainly
have worsened, according to those involved.

What do we learn from this case?

Any entry into a new field requires a 'thick understanding' of the way
in which knowledge is generated in it. In the case of Indosuez, the
evaluation of the feasibility of transferring the required knowledge was
made under the conviction that this type of knowledge (structured
finance) would be transferable to the organization.

When two dominant modes of knowledge management are in
opposition, an effort should be made to find the connections between
them. In the Indosuez case, the Drexelites had been isolated from the
organization (they had autonomy, Indosuez Capital Markets had been
created for them, and they had a different way of calculating their
remuneration). Such isolation is not favourable to the creation of
connections between the two knowledge modes. There is no doubt that

this isolation was one of the sources of the crisis that ensued. In a financial world in which rare and positional knowledge are the keys that determine the success of the bank, the integration of such knowledge should include a precise characterization of its nature. Finally, there are five major characteristics of the management of ambiguity that can be learnt from this case:

1 Tacit knowledge can constitute an obstacle as far as a transfer of knowledge is concerned. Here, the Drexelites' knowledge was difficult to imitate, or to articulate with a body of explicit transferable knowledge. It was 'organic', and supported an organizational dynamic which was itself organic (that of ICP).

2 Indosuez's management, faced with tacit knowledge that was difficult to grasp, took measures to 'thaw out' the organizational environment which received this knowledge.

3 Individuals with different cognitive styles have very different tolerances towards ambiguity.

4 In absorbing the tacit repertories of those about him, Gruffat imposed himself as an articulator of tacit knowledge, and alleviated the ambiguity.

5 Antithetical processes developed in the tacit dimension to counterbalance the rigid processes adopted in the explicit dimension.

8

Pechiney, in a Too Explicit World

It is so! Century of speed! So they say. Where is this?
Great changes! So they speak of. How is that?
In truth, nothing is changed.

Céline
Voyage to the End of Night (1932)

Africa was for us a challenge, a blank page.
How were we to approach her. . .
As ethnologists? As anxious technicians?

Jacques Bocquentin,
Cahiers d'Histoire de l'Aluminium, Winter 1995

Pechiney, Guinea (1950–70)

The three preceding case studies – Indigo, Qantas and Indosuez – were direct observations of companies facing ambiguity. Indigo's active interpretation of an uncertain and mutable environment resisted ambiguity – in an environment that resisted investigation. Qantas was entangled in the demands of a rapidly changing environment; simultaneously coping with the deregulation of the airline industry, with a difficult merger with Australian Airlines, and with the intricacies of choosing a partner for its privatization. Indosuez attempted to move into unknown territory; it tried to acquire new knowledge – new know-how – and new competencies but failed to resolve internal disputes and personal conflicts, and could not effect the necessary articulations of its knowledge.

This fourth, and final, case study was chosen to provide a longer-term perspective on organizational ambiguity. Doubly disconcerted by its displacement into a lesser-known environment – by Guinea itself – followed by the country's decolonization (which commenced in 1958), Pechiney's experiences enable us to understand the profound modifications that such ambiguity can provoke over the course of 20 years in those who work for the company, and in the evolution of the

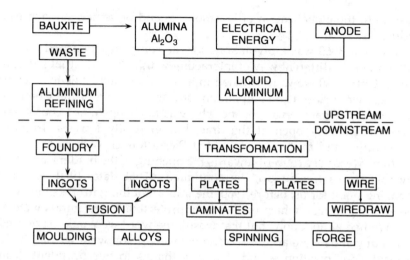

Figure 8.1 *Bauxite's route to aluminium*

organization's structures and strategies. Pechiney is today the world's second-largest aluminium producer, with an intensive focus on transformation (e.g. acquisition of American Can). Because of the historical nature of these events, the research method adopted was noticeably different. Closer to the historical method, it consisted of comparing witnesses' accounts with other written records: as well as interviewing those few actors still available, recourse was necessarily made to the company's archives, to contemporary newspaper articles, and to previous accounts of the events concerned. Immersion of the organizational milieu was very important. The following account represents one year of interviewing, of comparative reading of archives, of looking for clues and cross-checking.

The quest for water and bauxite

The production of aluminium necessitates two unavoidable ingredients: bauxite and electrical energy. It is here that we find the industry's upstream (Figure 8.1), and here that our story begins . . .

Pechiney's history can be broadly divided into four phases, corresponding to four major movements – four changes in its environment. From its beginnings and its first plants in the French Pyrenees and Alps, Pechiney began to extend further into France when it descended from the mountains into the valleys seeking hydraulic energy. From this essentially 'mountainous' period Pechiney would conserve a certain pioneer spirit until the end of the 1950s. This pioneer spirit accompanied it into its next phase, its first international developments in North America, Africa and Greece. But by the end of the 1950s Pechiney had to face up to the globalization of its resources and of its new downstream industries.

The year 1960 was a pivotal one for the company. It opened on to a different era, a different way of interacting within the industrial environment: 'Until 1960 we were closeted in a very protectionist State. . . . Our channels were closed to competition, and the creation of the Common Market was felt as – even for me who was fairly open, or I considered myself reasonably open at the time, but in reality I was a frightful conservative and protectionist,' added Pierre Jouven with a smile; 'my reactions were very reticent towards the opening of the borders, and also towards prices freeing up,' he continued. 'That date, 1960, was the changing point for us: before 1960, the important thing for Pechiney was the internal market, which was entirely protected, so our minds were at rest. We had a monopoly, but that wasn't the word we would have used then, our minds were at rest because we were doing what we had to do to justify our position – and that was thanks to our president, Jean Matter. We've always sought technical progress. To be number one on the technical side of things, that was President Matter's ambition, which allowed us to keep our costs down. You see, we could always defend ourselves on the economic plan. But we were still apprehensive because we knew we were small fish on the international market. So we had a tendency to be a bit over-cautious. Within three or four years of 1960 we found ourselves confronted with competition for what was really the first time.'

Pioneer knowledge

How can we define this 'pioneer knowledge' which forged part of the group's philosophy from the post-war period through to 1960? The two important markets at the time – for Pechiney, a French company – were those of France and the US. The rest of the world was by contrast a hunting ground for bauxite and electrical energy, perhaps to be partially transformed on site to produce semi-finished products. Pioneer knowledge is assembled from the notes and verbal accounts of travellers and explorers, in which they explain what they have seen, who they have met. They were small teams of two or three men who explored foreign lands: geologists and engineers. Some of their assignments would take a number of years, and the company would often have several geological projects under way at one time. These men would set up the initial camps, draw up maps by hand, take photographs. Theirs was a narrative, rudimentary knowledge. They would also try to keep track of the activities of their rivals, as evidenced by this British Aluminium Company report, acquired by Pechiney in 1951:

Over a number of years we realized more and more the necessity of prospecting to discover new and abundant sources of raw aluminium [bauxite].

Because of the great amount of cheap electrical energy needed for the process, it became apparent that the sources for the metal had to be found in under-developed regions. Exploration was then carried out in a number of points around the world. The missions would comprise ten members, of which five were from the British Aluminium Company, and five were from Aluminium Limited. After preliminary discussions in London, visits of around one month in each case were made to North Borneo and the African Gold Coast. On the field, a mission would splinter into technical teams, each team studying that part of the project that most directly concerned it. Potential sites for power stations, dams, factories, roads, railway lines and ports were all inspected.

Everything had to be done from scratch – pioneer knowledge develops on unexplored and virgin land. 'Questions of available labour, and of productivity and price, were discussed with government representa-tives as well as with private companies and people working in the industry. Diverse public works companies were consulted to secure information needed to prepare estimates on the construction costs for each site. . . . Studies of meteorological and hydrological data were carried out to determine the amount of hydraulic energy available in each colony, and flights were made over the prospective sites of reservoirs and transport routes.' In this great hunt for natural resources solutions were invented as problems arose. Such knowledge is fluid, rapid, even euphoric. Specific information was not sought, as the field was open and full of possibilities, of projects that had to be managed as they emerged: 'You have to recognize that at that epoch information was not seen in itself as being essential,' recalls Pierre Jouven: 'It went without saying, we were accumulating information without recognizing it. Each one of us had a particular role which involved collecting certain information, but that was just part of the normal role of a group of people working together and pursuing the same objectives, everybody had a duty not to let anything slip past them. As far as transmitting information that could have been useful for others, well there is a difference between not letting something slip past and actively seeking it – between doing something systematically and doing it "naturally".'

With the encouragement of Jean Matter the company organized productivity missions. There was so much to learn, so much to do, so much to build that everybody was busy discovering and creating new knowledge. It was a race forwards, with seemingly no limit to the resources waiting to be tapped. There were capricious rivers asking only to be mastered. Ore was waiting to be taken by whoever arrived first, and again, sense was made of events as they unfolded. Pechiney's early 'scouts' were two men named Sabot and Lévian, sent to Africa by the company in 1942. Sabot landed in Africa on the same day as the military landing of Alger, and was to remain cut off from France for two years, working only during the dry seasons and disappearing some 500 kilometres into the bush each time. To succeed meant to be open to the environment, to have a 'floating eye', and the major discoveries were made through chance meetings and the luck of the explorer.

The creation of pioneer knowledge is an activity that is directly productive of wealth. The link is immediate. Each discovery gives rise to a new local economy, establishing the foundations from which a new community develops. Such pioneer industry follows a logic based on the division of responsibilities, on what Oury (1983) termed an 'economy of vigilance'. Oury explained that, because railway lines, dams, factories and smelters develop simultaneously with knowledge in this pioneer environment, so various people involved in the project 'concentrated their attention on supplies or markets, others on the proper use of their machine, still others on the functioning of the services of which they are in charge.'

It was the United States in fact that had offered Pechiney the opportunity to develop its first large-scale application of this 'economy of vigilance'. From just before the Second World War, and continuing after its conclusion (following productivity missions in the US) Pechiney structured its knowledge in response to the urgent imperatives of the unique market the US represented for the aluminium industry. Pechiney, at that time known as la Compagnie de Produits Chimiques et Électro-métallurgiques Alais, Froges et Camargue, was already a veteran of pioneer expeditions, and of the quest for new knowledge. In a memo dated November 1946, the number of visits Pechiney had made to the US was communicated to Vitry, Matter, Jouven, Serruys and Loeffel. This included Rube's visit from 27 August to 26 September that year, and Serre and Pyzler's visit in October. On 30 May 1946, Perieres submitted his report on wages and standards of living in the US.[1] Once again we find that form of knowledge we can call narrative, resembling a collation of travel diaries; in this case records made by the engineers and scientists who shared in the discovery of new technical frontiers.

A technical culture spearheaded by Jean Matter

Pechiney's technical culture focuses on ore, energy and manufacturing processes: on mastering technical systems of combining natural elements. From 1947, Pechiney tried to formalize the creation of knowledge within the company. In view of the number of memos issued dealing with the creation, modification and frequent restructuring of Pechiney's documentation service, it is easy to guess that the ideal service foreseen in 1947 could not function to perfection at that time. But structures other than those dependent on the General Secretariat assumed similar functions, such as the management committee created in 1948 which defined its principal goal as 'to provide useful advice and to coordinate the company's multiple activities'. The committee's founding statement also remonstrated that: 'until now no session of the Committee has been devoted to estimates or predictions. . . . Several committee sessions should be devoted to forecasts of the future. In the same vein, it would be useful to add to the agenda a twice-yearly (in principle December and July) statement on the evolution of organizational questions.'[2] We can appreciate the difficulty of obtaining from a population of engineers information of a nature quite unlike technical data. But we should also note Pechiney's preoccupation, from the postwar period, with the need for immediately accessible information.

There is of course a great difference between data stored in a documentation service and the knowledge to be gleaned from engineers' travel notes. The information that the company amassed in Paris was comprised of figures, data, quantities, descriptions of chemical processes, and technical designs. In their initial statement in 1948, Pechiney's management committee showed their recognition of the difference between this data and the knowledge produced by the productivity missions, and their concern about this discrepancy: 'Information to be given to the committee should not in principle be presented in figures, it should be comprised of precise and faithful accounts of salient facts and urgent intelligence.'

The Guinean experience

Pechiney's Guinean experience was above all that of a handful of men battling an unsettled and disconcerting terrain. The key men involved were Pechiney's President, René Piaton; its Vice-President, Raoul de Vitry; Jean Matter, who was at that time Assistant General Manager; Jean Chantreuil, responsible for African Affairs; Pierre Jouven, who headed the Aluminium Division; Jacques Marchandise, representing France's territorial bank; the Governor of Guinea, M. Parisot; and M. Ribadeau-Dumas, Director of the African Society for Aluminium Research and Study (la Société Africaine de Recherche et d'Étude Pour l'Aluminium). (See Figure 8.2.)

The Aluminium Division, directed by Pierre Jouven, remained Pechiney's largest and most important, and this chart should be read as René Piaton would have read it: 'Our strong points as far as foreign competition is concerned are, concerning aluminium, the coexistence within a relatively confined perimeter of bauxite deposits, alumina extraction plants and smelters – and a definite advance on the technical side of things, as demonstrated by the sale of our reduction cell patents to American producers' (Piaton, 1955). Aluminium was at the centre of the organization's activities, and Pechiney's technological achievements in connection with its production contributed to reinforcing this centrality.

Pechiney's presence in Guinea was originally a result of the discovery of large bauxite deposits at Kindia and Dobola (400 kilometres from Konakry). As the first deposits found were judged to be 'fairly mediocre' in quality, it was decided that the mining of it would only be economically viable if the ore was milled and processed on site; which

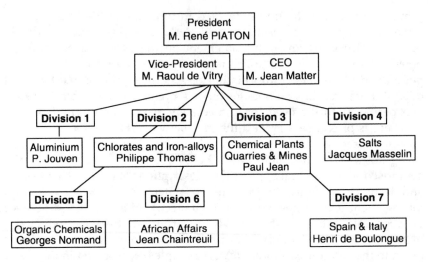

Figure 8.2 *Pechiney's organizational chart in January 1956*

was conceivable given the proximity of the Konkouré river, a putative producer of energy.[3] This initial constraint posed by the ore's quality was later to prove to have important consequences for the company. When the situation becomes 'unsettled, ambiguous and disconcerting', one should keep in mind that the ore was not exploitable in the 'healthy' economic conditions outside of Guinea.

Pechiney was therefore brought to conceive the establishment of an aluminium smelter deep in the Guinean bush, with production running to 100,000 tonnes. Relations between Guinea and France were stable during this period; it was the natural environment which posed the difficulties. The flow of the Konkouré river is extremely variable: 'it can reach 1000 cubic metres in the wet season and diminish to ten cubic metres in the dry season. It was therefore necessary, in order to normalize the flow, to build a very large dam – and the scope of this project demanded serious study from all sides' (Gignoux, 1955: 227). No maps existed of the region, and geological research was carried out in Guinea from 1942 to 1945 both to discover bauxite and to draw up such maps. Studies of the most suitable way to extract the alumina were also undertaken, with good results being obtained very quickly. It remained to determine, with precision, whether the 'Konkouré kilowatt-hour' would be of a sufficient order to enable aluminium to be produced at a competitive price.

Through miners' eyes

France and Guinea share a long history. In March 1931, after eight years of geological study, a mining engineer wrote in his report: 'We believe that when the commercial and industrial crisis that rages currently in the world has provoked a normal resumption of international trade, and we have returned to sensible pre-war economic ideas, the iron and bauxite mines of Guinea will assure the colony of splendid revenues, by bringing to these regions the amelioration of living conditions and the happy procession of works and charitable realizations that have always been the flag of the mining industry, always enamoured of justice and social progress towards its workers.' His analysis was based on the activities of Alcan, Pechiney's Canadian competitor.

Upon his return to France, Segaud, who was in charge of one the first assignments for Pechiney's African Affairs department, was to write in his report:

> If I have correctly understood what has been said to me, the goal of the mission, at least on the mining and geological side of things, was to carry out an intensive study of all of French Guinea's bauxite deposits, excepting only certain areas inaccessible to mining and some others that have been reserved for State bodies. . . . I write this on 31 August 1943, and what have we achieved to date? We must acknowledge that our results have had a destructive nature, and have left none of our initial data unscathed. The lode discovered in the Moyenne-Fatale is of an inconsequential size, interesting only for scientific hypothesis.[4]

Hence, in 1951 the first conclusions of a study undertaken in conjunction with the French national electricity company (EDF) seemed favourable and Jouven, visiting Fria, was 'seduced by the bauxite deposits' (Marchandise, 1990–91: 84). The same year saw the creation of SAREPA (Société Africaine de Recherche et d'Étude Pour l'Aluminium), directed by Matter and Ribadeau-Dumas. In 1955 the AFRAL company was created to examine the possibilities of developing aluminium smelters in Guinea. In 1956 too, the Société de Fria was created, although it was not fully incorporated until the following year. These first ten years were dominated by a technical agenda: the search for sources of hydraulic energy and bauxite. But one can well ask why this technical evaluation continued, given that in October 1958 Guinea declared its independence.

The imperative to resolve local decisions should not be looked upon as being entirely the wrong one, but rather due to a lack of knowledge. The escalation of Pechiney's financial commitment had reached a point where 'to continue or not to continue' had become the question. This involved an 'economy of vigilance', focused on the finalization and implementation of production projects already well under way. The question we must ask is whether the changes in the Guinean political environment were taken into account within the circumscribed parameters of Pechiney's industrial project in Guinea. The mode of knowing that was employed from 1951 to 1958 was technical. Certain facts are very significant: 'The English asked if we knew anything about changes in salaries since independence. Our response? "We have no information on that subject; it does not seem that any changes are to be made"' (Marchandise, 1990–91: 85). In the period that we have called Pechiney's 'mining' period, the parameters evoked for the resolution of projects (involving prospecting for bauxite and locating sources of energy) did not appear to be threatened, as Jacques Marchandise's note about salaries testifies.

Emergence of a disconcerting and ambiguous situation

It is in this context of the superposition of two agendas that the first signs of disagreement between Pechiney and the colonial government in Guinea appeared:

> At the technical level it is already well known that the lateritic grounds are exploitable under good conditions. . . . At the political level the agitation that resulted from the explosive situation in Kouilou, where the plant had been launched clumsily and without adequate preparation, has been brought up at a recent session of the Territorial Assembly, with decidedly political intentions. It does not seem to me that there is any cause to take this question seriously. The studies should be continued in a calm, composed atmosphere, without any preconceived notions. . . . Everything taken into consideration, there is no evidence to suggest that those who support the construction of the plant on the Kouilou river will finally win out over those who argue for Konkouré. (Guinet, report dated April 1955)

Until 1955 the reports from Pechiney's Guinean operations focused on technical matters – departing only from this agenda to catalogue the potential social and economic benefits of their activities. The appearance of reports showing any real interest in the local population was coincidental with the 1957 appointment of Jacques Bocquentin as director of the plant under construction. At the same time a difference of attitudes was emerging among Europeans in the colonies, between 'conformists' who tried to avoid the political situation by focusing on technical agendas, and 'optimists' who truly believed in change: 'The conformists, represented above all by middle managers and people involved in trade, estimated that the difficulties were of such a scale that it would be useless to try to resolve them, that it would be better to accommodate them – although fearing that they would lose their prerogatives' (Bocquentin, 1994–95: 79). As for the optimists: 'they considered that they had come to Africa to serve the people and the colony'. In this double transition (of attitudes and of knowledge) the first key date was perhaps 23 February 1955. On this day the president of the Permanent Committee for the Territorial Assembly of French Guinea, Framoi Bérété, wrote to Colonel Antoine, president of the Administrative Council of Electrical Energy in Guinea (who lived in Paris):

I know that you are favourable towards the execution of the works on the Konkouré river. This is why I have called upon parliamentarians to intervene in the financial and governmental communities in France, and on territorial councillors to intervene with the local population in Guinea to calm the populace and to create a climate of confidence, that is indispensable for the investment of capital.[5]

The double articulation – of technical and social ambiguity – became then not only explicit (and therefore not to be mentioned implicitly in reports) but indissociable. Social preoccupation was perceived as a factor constraining other factors on which the industrial project was constructed – as the expression 'to calm the populace and to create a climate of confidence' demonstrates – as social agitation would constitute an obligation to modify the parameters of the industrial agenda.

Belonging to a group of moderates, M. Bangoura Karim wrote to the Minister of Overseas France on 14 March 1955: 'From information we have gathered, the persistency of which is itself proof of its accuracy, it seems that the English have commenced construction of a dam on the Gold Coast, and the Belgians another in the Belgian Congo. In allowing ourselves to be overtaken by either of these nations, we would unwittingly contribute to the reduction of our chances on the world aluminium market, those who employ this material being very limited in number.'[6] Karim's letter illustrates the superimposition in the 1950s of the two economies of vigilance (local: the agenda of industrial decisions; global: the globalization of the markets). We can see a marked change in this period in the contents of correspondence between Pechiney and its expatriates, and between the French government and both the Territorial Assembly and the Electrical Energy Company of Guinea: the miner's eye gives way, bit by bit, to the eye of the economist, concerned about the local industrial environment and mobilized by aggressive English and Belgian competition. These were perhaps the first signs of the ascendancy of a new economy based on global knowledge, on the internationalization of markets. As Jacques Marchandise emphasizes, 'it became apparent that, as time passed, the debates became less and less technical, and more and more financial. The time had arrived when future production costs moved into the foreground of Pechiney's preoccupations' (Marchandise, 1990–91: 86). The Electrical Energy Company of Guinea (EEG) had a not insignificant role in this evolution. Whereas it is possible to limit geological and mining work to technical studies of the physical environment within a very limited perimeter, the arrival of electricity necessitates a broader perimeter of activity – the conception and implementation of a truly spatial economy concerned with towns and cities, and with transportation channels for the electricity: with the infrastructure and the future of the community as a whole. It demands a broadening of perspectives.

In introducing the electrical infrastructure in its understanding of events in Guinea, Pechiney was gradually brought to embrace the full

Guinean reality: the company's investment in the country had taken on a new aspect, and a psychological barrier had been crossed. Colonel Antoine, president of the EEG, wrote on 3 March 1955: 'It is obviously of vital interest to the Electrical Energy Company of Guinea that such a decision [the construction of the dam] is taken at the opportune moment, as it would entail the considerable development of general activity in the Territory.'[7]

But just as everything seemed to favour the acceleration of Guinea's industrialization, Pechiney hesitated between two sites for its dam, which entailed studies and delays. In his report of his trip to Guinea in March 1955, Pierre Jouven wrote:

> I would like to recall briefly a certain number of reflections we made on 24 March . . . I was amazed that a group like Pechiney was relying for its choice of electrical equipment on the randomness of discovery: Konkouré, Edéa, Kouilou – perhaps the Congo tomorrow? I regret the lack of taste for risk-taking among French industrials. I estimate that the realization of the studies into the Kouilou river will demand a tremendous amount of time, and it seems that if we were to wait until the completion of this study to make a decision it would be in order to allow procrastination, or for other unconfessed reasons. . . . While the political situation is calming down in the wake of stringent measures, the Governor appears to be disgusted with the incertitude of administrative directives. . . . We have been reproached in some quarters for coming here only to make money. Any financial aid from France would for them only represent a reimbursement of that which has been taken from them by the FAO and other commercial groups of this genre who have been exploiting the country for almost 50 years now, and who are continuing their exploitation with no change in their basic conceptions.[8]

In another report from this period, in April 1955, Guinet comments:

> M. Bangoura Karim indicates that the politicians are determined not to allow anything to hinder the Territory from achieving that which they consider to be a right, namely the equipment of the Konkouré and the production of aluminium in Guinea. He has accepted the notion of a relay system until the installation of a 45,000-tonne capacity dam in the Camaroon is completed. His confidence has however, been shaken by learning recently what has been going on behind the scenes, notably with the Kouilou question, from which he has the feeling that Guinea is being duped. . . . But it is impossible, in the current circumstances to say whether it would be preferable to manufacture the aluminium in Guinea or elsewhere. This is a problem that involves several parameters. It is a task that necessarily takes time. Guinea's hopes depend upon the quality of these studies.

It was, then, well into spring 1955 before the weaknesses of an understanding of the situation based purely on a technical agenda became apparent.

Disconcerting situations and the multiplication of problems

Two deposits were finally identified, one in Sangarédi, in the Boké region, the other in Kimbo, 147 kilometres from Konakry: 'The French auxiliary of Alcan (Aluminium Limited of Canada), Les Bauxites du Midi – which is at present mining the almost exhausted lode on the island of Kassa – envisages the production of 1,500,000 tonnes of bauxite per year at Sangarédi' (Camara, 1976: 136). The Kimbo deposit led to Pechiney's alumina plant project at Fria.[9]

The decision to construct a factory in Fria dated in fact from the end of 1956, 'and this even before the signing of the establishment convention, in February 1958, decided on the conditions of the project – conditions that had to include, as well as the alumina project itself, the construction of a hydroelectric dam on the Konkouré river' (Larrue, 1990–91: 37). The project was on a grand scale: 'It included stipulations that agricultural production was to be entirely rethought, that new roads were to be built rapidly, and that the inflation generated by the influx of investment would be regulated' (Larrue, 1990–91: 40). All of these aspirations lacked realism. People working on the field had a very divided attitude towards the entire project, some being critical of such grandiloquent plans. But Pechiney's engineers were men of action, and construction of the plant was completed in a little less than three years, between 1957 and 1960.

By 1957 a technical agenda had been fixed and the local industrial logic set in motion, and the ambiguity that surrounded the choice of the Konkouré or the Kouilou river seemed to have been resolved. Yet tensions with the Guinean workforce were frequent. There was talk of imminent revolution. But by sticking as close as possible to the local agenda of the construction of the plant, Pechiney's employees did everything they could to maintain a relaxed atmosphere. Jacques Bocquentin played a decisive role in this: 'By analysing the different attitudes of the Europeans and the Africans, it seemed to me that we had to definitively avoid a conformist attitude, because the Fria project would lead to such upheaval that the traditional attitudes of the colonial period would be swept away' (Bocquentin, 1994–95: 81). But on 28 September 1958 Guinea, under the leadership of trade union leader Sekou Touré, was the only West African colony to reject continued association with France in General de Gaulle's referendum on full independence or membership of the French Community.[10] The vote for independence was 1,130,292 – to 56,959 against. To the complexity of their technical agenda, and the increasing complexity of their tasks, was added a new agenda that none could avoid. The result was brutal.[11] A new, unpredictable, dimension had crossed swords with the engineers' predictive skills, as Jacques Bocquentin who had been given the responsibility of overseeing the construction of the plant, recalls: 'At every step we had to look in new places for our solutions. From

September 1958 Guinea's independence surged over the construction site, driving any problems into a new political context. I do not believe that anyone who did not live through this experience on a day-to-day basis could really grasp the full sense of it; because at every turn people mattered far more than ideas. Legal concepts, logical reasoning, acquired habits or customary reflexes mean nothing when you are confronted with an angry throng who want to force a decision. The solidarity between men from the same country, the power of the collective sentiment in Africa, the fanaticism of crowds politicized by charismatic chiefs, and the bewilderment of men with little formal education in the face of the complete upheaval that industrialization brought, all contributed to smashing the established frameworks of their existence' (Bocquentin, 1994–95: 79).

The technical-economic understanding that Pechiney had of Guinea was no longer applicable: 'After the independence of Guinea in October 1958, several events led to such questioning within the company as could never have been estimated initially. It seemed as if the operation itself was slipping from the control of its initiators, and that it was being left to the men "in the field" to reconcile the urgent aspect of the project with the new, and entirely unanticipated, imperatives of the Guinean administration and a civil society in a state of permanent revolution' (Larrue, 1990–91: 37). The element that had not been anticipated was the irreversible and unilateral change of the Guinean environment. Nothing could be planned any more, no roads or expansions, without the misgiving that acceptance by local authorities could not be guaranteed. Technical reality was reduced to a fabric of endeavours torn by the complex jumble of ramifications of the local political situation – of this chaotic revolutionary environment marked by local power struggles and the euphoria of independence. This was also the year of the first tensions between a Guinean administration imbued with its new-found power and the local representatives of an industrial group confronted with the magnification of uncertainty. New technical assistants arriving from Soviet bloc nations to 'support' the young revolutionary government only added to the complexity and ambiguity of the situation. 'While the October 1959 expulsion of Jacques Bocquentin, the first manager of the plant, could not be formally attributed to these Eastern European experts, there were indications that the argument he had had with the Governor which had led to his expulsion had been purposefully provoked' (Larrue, 1990–91: 45).

Circulating knowledge of a new nature

Yet in one way the situation was not entirely new to the company. The crisis that had crystallized around the Konkouré–Kouilou question had already provoked a change in their approach to the situation. The geological and technical reports of the period 1942–55 had been super-seded by visits and numerous organized meetings with people outside the organization. When Pierre Jouven first met with Governor Parisot on 25 March 1955, he was warned that he would come across 'many people who have negative intentions', who believed that heavy industry in Guinea was fraudulent – that it 'drained the country of its wealth and left only a minimal profit for the local population' – and that Guinea was in need of industries employing a large workforce.[12] Parisot explained that some people were 'embittered' by the delay in com-pleting the works on the Konkouré dam, which they had been assured would progress rapidly. Pechiney had surely learnt something from this experience, even if this learning was not explicit: and nor was it made explicit through the institution of permanent rules. Behaviours had evolved. There had been a fear that Pechiney would fall behind if it did not actively push ahead with its research into the site for its plant, a fear Guinet had expressed in his report. When in 1956 they decided to begin construction it was on the tacit understanding that a convention would later be signed, an event that did not take place until February 1958: they had learnt to accept an agenda that was not based on an exhaustive explicit knowledge of the situation. This represented a complete depart-ure from their earlier, prudent, agendas – in which each evolution had been meticulously supported by geologists' reports, contracts, conven-tions and figures. They were well aware that they were taking a risk, but built their new reality on trust.

It was not only the nature but equally the form of their knowledge which had been modified, and this surely helped them through the intensely disconcerting and ambiguous situations to come. There was a decisive change in the style and content of memos and reports, which was also reflected in the letters exchanged between personnel in Guinea and Pechiney's management in Paris. But the reports written by Pierre Jouven stood apart from those of his colleagues.

Whereas his colleagues limited their reports to the technical and economic analyses carried out by the company since the first geological missions, Jouven always found room in his for anecdotes and complementary information. His style was fairly informal and he was not attracted by rigidly thematic forms. His reports were written more in the style of a travel log; they were vividly chronological and always described the relationships and connections of the people he met, often quoting them or writing that he had 'had a long chat with them on a plane'. He would describe their attitudes: 'worried', 'enthusiastic', 'relaxed', 'friendly reception but seemed a bit finicky, a bit nervous', and would add details about the atmosphere of his meetings: 'It was the two parliamentarians who spoke most. They were grateful for the explanations we gave them of our project and our propositions. I thanked M. Delage heartily.' With Jouven's reports the geological documents of 1942 to 1955 were replaced by documents that were almost ethnological. The knowledge he circulated was noticeably denser and richer than that circulated by his colleagues and forebears.

The Guinean outcome

'Of all the grand industrial projects, only the Fria project in Kimbo (that of Pechiney) was to be realized' (Camara, 1976: 139). All of the others failed. The Les Bauxites du Midi company (a subsidiary of Alcan), suspended its works at Boké late in 1961 – they were nationalized on 6 November 1961. Pechiney's success, which at the start could be attributed to a handful of men (such as Guinet, Bocquentin, Jouven or Ribadeau-Dumas), spread progressively throughout the organization: people learnt to manage disconcerting situations – they 'unlearned' the need to plan every last detail and to authorize every step, and they put themselves in contact with a reality hidden by such measurement. A flexible management had gradually settled in. Delicate situations were handled by exchanging memos containing richly developed information. People moved past an understanding that was purely technical, to embrace reality as a whole. 'Our approach had become more subtle,' remembers Jacques Larrue. Finally, Raoul de Vitry, Pechiney's general manager after the Second World War, and president of the Fria Company until 1968 – the last year of its activity – 'obtained from the Guineans both an agreement on the company's capitalist industrial activities, which were to continue through all the jolts and starts of the revolution and, from this, their respect for the promise they had made in 1958' (Larrue, 1990–91: 39).

As Pierre Jouven explained: 'There was some uneasiness in the company about these African affairs. They had been entrusted to a man whose dedication had no limits, who had always done his job without trying to promote any personal interests. . . . We created an African organization for him, it was the company's idea, but what did it really mean? What were we doing in Africa? When a precise activity presented itself – and this was very early on, about 1942 – M. de Vitry sent company representatives to Africa to look into the possible development of the aluminium industry there, that is, to look for bauxite and sources of hydroelectric energy. Two men set off, a miner – M. Sabot – looking for the bauxite, and an engineer – M. Lévian – looking for electricity. M. Lévian was a man who was extremely open to the world about him; he had a brilliant career and did not stay with the company for long, but even so he made his mark and made quite a few important discoveries, and drew attention to some important things. Sabot began his explorations in Senegal, where he didn't find bauxite, only alumina phosphate. He then moved further south, along the east coast, and on to Guinea. We knew that the Canadians had already claimed some sizeable bauxite deposits there, so Sabot looked in other parts of the country – bauxite is everywhere in Guinea. But the Canadians had been mining since 1920, and they had already claimed the best sites' (interview with Pierre Jouven, 16 May 1991).

Pierre Jouven continued: 'Pechiney's African Affairs division was neglected a little, to the profit of the people in France. . . . You have to realize that in 1957 our role in Africa was not entirely clear, it was disputed – between the guys who worked in smelting, the electrometallurgy department, and the guys working with alumina, which I was one of.' What was the precise role of this division of African Affairs, of which the directive announcing its creation specified its importance as a source of information? 'But what is written in these papers does not always correspond to reality, and I think they were trying to bolster up the African division by exaggerating its general responsibilities and activities, by which I mean information and public relations, instead of just sticking to the concrete issue, the installation of operations. In Africa it was difficult to work in tandem, you needed to have someone taking a central role. The department responsible for Africa and Information on Africa was very quickly pushed aside in favour of the aluminium department.'

Despite very strong inertia, knowledge structured itself progressively. As a key player in its Guinean operations, Pierre Jouven had learnt the important role that a richer, better circulated, knowledge can bring to the company. During his interview, he clarified this: 'the defining characteristic of the company I joined in 1943 was the existence of what you could call very "personalized" departments – but this word is probably a bit excessive – let's just say that there were a certain number of very strong personalities who had their own departments, their own territories, and who carried out their business independently of each other, and they all had their own knowledge that was internal to each department – I'm certain about this, because I suffered as a result of it – at the limit of what was acceptable, and everything was kept secret.'

A knowledge lost in its explicitation

Two readings were initially brought to bear on Guinea. The first was that of the mining engineers in charge of the geological assignments: the technician's eye. The second was one of profitability, of financial planning and the course of commodities markets: the economist's eye. This first technical-economic phase was in keeping with the problems posed by the isolated locations of the two lodes discovered, together with the need to develop hydroelectric energy for Guinea's needs and possibly to power an aluminium smelter. When they were presented with two choices for the site of the dam, the decision dragged out and disputes emerged. Local groups sent letters of complaint to Pechiney's Paris offices. Did the restructuring of the company in 1956, and again in

1958, preoccupy its Parisian office and force its managers to deal with internal questions ahead of more distant issues? Interviews seem to invalidate this hypothesis. 'The reform of 1958 was simply a response to the transformations France was going through at that time. The French market was moving into an internationalized system, and by 1964 it was confident it could defend itself worldwide. By 1964 our installations in Greece were already under way, they were the first plants we had set up outside of France and its territories,' explained Pierre Jouven. 'Until 1958, that is to say, until the Guinean affair, the market for us had been France and the Empire. It was Sékou Touré who disencumbered us of this error. We went through a hard time, but it completely changed our point of view. From 1958 we said to ourselves, if we want to grow, the only way we can do it is outside French borders' (interview, 3 February 1995).

As we have seen, Pechiney's managers in Guinea were aware of Alcan's strong presence in the country. They realized that they were posing questions that the Canadians had already posed, and that ambitious projects were already planned on the Gold Coast by these same Canadians. At this time, Pechiney was still in its pioneer phase – as it sought to establish new plants – but this was reaching its end. Pechiney realized that the best bauxite deposits had been claimed by the Canadians in 1920.[13] The company did not differ in any respect from the other aluminium companies; as the nationalization of Kaiser's construction in Ghana demonstrated, the industry itself in Africa had, by the 1960s, been forced into a new management of their economy of vigilance. The international pressure on the industry to direct their efforts of vigilance and their decision economics towards globalization is illustrated by the example of Pierre Jouven. Attention was given to the industry itself, and the channels of information flowed naturally towards the electrometallurgy and the alumina departments. The quest for efficiency by settling decisions at the local level entails a regulation of knowledge that can only be established within the limited local agenda of industrial decisions. This increasing rationalization of the effort of vigilance leads however, as we have seen, to a 'territorialization' of the activity of knowing. We are here in the domain of the combination/compartmentalization of knowledge: division of tasks, division of knowledge (see Figure 8.3).

What do we learn from this case?

Whereas all of Pechiney's efforts were directed towards the acquisition of a scientific knowledge of Guinea (maps, plans, reports), reality was progressively 'hidden by its measures'. A less tangible, more unsettled and changing part of the situation escaped the engineers' attention. The question is not only to distinguish 'true' from 'false' (Ekman, 1985,

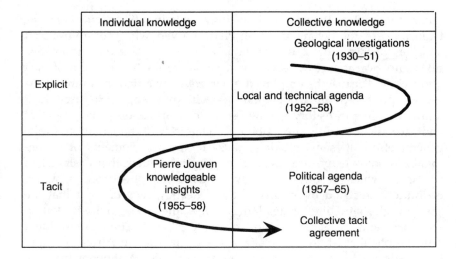

	Individual knowledge	Collective knowledge
Explicit		Geological investigations (1930–51) Local and technical agenda (1952–58)
Tacit	Pierre Jouven knowledgeable insights (1955–58)	Political agenda (1957–65) Collective tacit agreement

Figure 8.3 *Towards a tacit and collective agreement*

underlined the fragility of these two concepts), but to identify the role of the tacit and of the explicit. An excess of explicitation, within a rigid framework, can curb the fluidity of socialization, which is how tacit knowledge circulates.

Critical knowledge thus remains in the domain of the unspoken, and is not 'digested' in the form of agendas or programmes of action. This result is corroborated by analysis of the group's archives: the tacit dimension of knowledge escapes the formal organizational memory. The organizational memory will retain an entirely different story: one of successive combinations of explicit knowledge, concealing the dynamics of such knowledge. That is how it articulates itself tacitly with other knowledge which itself is intangible. To borrow an expression from Riveline (1986), all that is remembered is 'the body of knowledge that a Cartesian approach supports: objective and methodically inventoried facts, natural laws, language, rational approaches – in brief, everything that is long-term and is not based on the subjectivity of the people involved,' in other words, 'hard knowledge'. If, on the other hand, we consider 'soft' knowledge as 'that which cannot be understood by a Cartesian approach, because there is no indisputable truth in the areas it concerns' (Riveline, 1986), then we can say that tacit knowledge in the context of the organization belongs to this domain of 'soft knowledge', which generally escapes collective memorization. Consequently there is a gap between the institutionalized history, and events and behaviours that really happened.

If the firm does not retain in its memory the tacit passages in the evolution of its knowledge, this is simply because it does not pay attention to them when they happen, or because it tends to deliberately ignore them when it comes to retracing events in official reports. In the Guinean case, the behaviour of M. Pierre Jouven, who tried to transmit a richer, denser font of information rather than something more distilled and overly sorted, served as a palliative for this evasion of tacit knowledge. Because he employed a narrative style rich in commentary, Jouven provoked an articulation of tacit knowledge. He used tacit knowledge in a transitory manner, so as to re-articulate knowledge that had been dislocated by the ambiguous character of the situation. In the general effort of 'sense-making', these temporary elements of a non-fossilized knowledge are 'islands of respite', rather than 'islands of certainty' which would not justly describe the phenomenon, as no certitude is reached by means of these fleeting rays of light that are shed on the situation. Instead they allow the decision to be left in abeyance, and the situation not to be 'fossilized'. These intermittent articulations that M. Jouven realizes during his trips to Africa, and that he broadcasts to the organization in an oral presentation of his new understanding, become part of the organization's 'live memory', its 'RAM' – to use computer terminology. As a computer can be productively employed without having a precise knowledge of its internal construction, so can the organization be operated without a clear understanding of its knowledge structure. This structure is not visible to us, however we know that it receives the knowledge we create. To use another metaphor, borrowed this time from mountaineering, these are the 'handholds' on which we know we cannot put all our weight (as they are not strong enough) but which we can use to reach the next hold. These transitory tacit articulations fulfil an analogous function in the domain of the intangible. They allow other articulations. They answer to a logic of mutation. To again borrow Maurice Botbol's vocabulary, they are 'impressions', 'feelings', they form a 'web of presumptions'.

Finally, we can retain four major characteristics of the management of knowledge in ambiguous settings from the Pechiney case:

1   A principle of inherence of knowledge to different agendas: on one hand, to an international agenda (that of the movement for self-determination in France's territories in the 1950s); and on the other, to a local agenda (that of technological combination and the progression of the plant's construction). This inherence to agendas hampers the management of ambiguity.

2   A reality 'hidden by its measures' – or in other words, a 'crushing', or 'stubbing out', of the tacit dimension by the explicit dimension – which fossilizes knowledge. This is a matter of the domination of 'hard' knowledge over 'soft' knowledge. Such 'crushing' hampers the management of ambiguity.

3   Pierre Jouven's role as transitory articulator in the resolution of the ambiguous situation.

4   The importance of a 'thick understanding' of events. This understanding is reached by means of a penetration of conjectural and
tacit knowledge.

Notes

1 R. Perieres, *Rapport sur les salaires et le standard de vie aux États-Unis*, 30 May
1946, Pechiney's archives, Historic Collection.

2 Memo, 'Rôle et fonchonnement du Comité de Gestion', 20 December 1948,
Pechiney's archives, Historic Collection.

3 This first assessment was later to be proven inaccurate. Before the
employment of helicopters, teams of geologists and miners progressed into the
bush at a rate of 100 kilometres per year. The helicopter played a decisive role in
enabling the rapid development of a more 'tabular' knowledge. Source:
interview with Pierre Jouven, 13 January 1995.

4 M. Segaud, 'Mission en Guinée', report of 8 November 1943, Direction of
African Affairs, Historic Archives, Pechiney.

5 Framoi Bérété, president of the Permanent Committee of the Territorial
Assembly of French Guinea. Letter to M. le Colonel Antoine, president of the
Administrative Council of l'Énergie Électrique Guinée (EEG), 23 February 1955,
Pechiney's archives, Historic Collection.

6 K. Bangoura, Territorial Assembly of French Guinea, Letter to the Minister
for Overseas France, 14 March 1955, Pechiney's archives, Historic Collection.

7 A. Antoine, president of EEG, Letter to Framoi Bérété, president of the
Territorial Assembly of French Guinea, 3 March 1955, Pechiney's archives,
Historic Collection.

8 Pierre Jouven, 'Voyage en Guinée du 22 au 28 Mars 1955 de Pierre Jouven
et Ribadeau-Dumas', Pechiney's archives, Historic Collection.

9 Four financial partners were associated with the project, under Pechiney's
direction: the American company, Olin Mathieson; the British company, British
Aluminium; the Swiss company, Aluminium Industry; and the German
company, Allemande Werke AG.

10 In Brazzaville on 24 August 1958, General de Gaulle proposed to the
African Territories that they replace the French Union with a new association
under the impending Fifth French Republic. De Gaulle encouraged people to
vote for this by promising internal autonomy, the creation of a large political
institution, and the prospect of further negotiation of the possibility of
independence. Guinea was the only territory to vote against this.

11 Lacouture, in *Cinq hommes et la France* (1961: 349) tells how General de
Gaulle, as soon as he was seated in Mr Mauberna's office, asked him point-
blank: 'Well then, *Monsieur le gouveneur*, what do you think about this
referendum? It will go whatever way Sékou Touré decides, won't it. But I don't
think we could say yet what this will be. I don't think the decision will be taken;
and the speech we are going to hear today will not enlighten us.' Mr Mauberna
passed him the printed text of Touré's announcement, on which he had
underlined in red the most significant passages. De Gaulle rolled the paper up
without glancing at it and, holding it aloft as if it were a marshal's baton, asked
for Mr Sékou Touré to enter'.

12 Pierre Jouven, 'Voyage en Guinée du 22 au 28 Mars 1955 de Pierre Jouven et Ribadeau-Dumas', Pechiney's archives, Historic Collection.

13 Reinforcing this technical preoccupation, evaluations made at that time were forecasting that the bauxite to be found in France would run out in 20 or 30 years. This added to the interest in Guinean bauxite. As Guinean bauxite was based on trihydrates, unlike French bauxite which is based on monohydrates, it can be treated at 130°C instead of 200°C. This encouraged aluminium producers to treat it at the site, and convinced Pechiney to construct a smelter in Guinea. Source: interview with Pierre Jouven, 13 January 1995.

9

The Tacit Foundations of Organizations

'The question is,' said Alice,
'whether you can make words mean different things.'
'The question is,' said Humpty Dumpty,
'which is to be master − that's all'

Lewis Carroll
Alice Through the Looking-Glass

Executives and tacit knowledge

The first thing that strikes us when we compare the four cases is the difference between Indigo and the other organizations. In their approaches to disconcerting events, Pechiney, Indosuez and Qantas did not have spontaneous recourse to tacit knowledge. Their first reaction to a disconcerting situation was to try to make it clearer, to rationalize it, to 'put what we are sure of down on paper'. In these organizations, and particularly in the two larger ones (Pechiney and Qantas), managers often tended to neglect conjectural and local knowledge when trying to escape ambiguity − the managers I observed tended instead to uselessly multiply measures and procedures. In the Indigo case, on the other hand, the tacit register served to support its approach to the disconcerting situation. On the matrices we can clearly see the dynamics of Indigo's knowledge departing from the tacit dimension to surface in the explicit, whereas the other organizations take an opposite path (Figure 9.1).

We notice that the two largest organizations, Pechiney and Qantas, follow a similar path on the matrix. These two organizations also present similar organizational characteristics: they are strongly hierarchic, even 'mechanistic'. Decisions come from the top (as in the introduction of a management information system at Qantas, and the decisions about Guinea which were made by Pechiney's Paris-based upper management). In these two organizations, the ambiguity came from the gap between the explicit framework adopted (or which management wanted to see adopted) and the tacit reality of the organization: which I will call

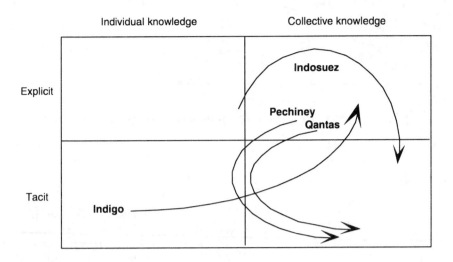

Figure 9.1   *Four knowledge trajectories*

a collision of the tacit and the explicit. They both attempted to introduce procedures, and failed (the maintenance of agendas for Pechiney, the disclosure and sharing of collective knowledge for Qantas). The two organizations finally escaped ambiguity by employing tacit repertories of knowledge circulation. The path followed by Indosuez also ends in the collective and tacit dimension, but the curve suggests an attempt to 'pull' the dynamics of the organizational knowledge upwards: towards the explicit, towards the formalized. In fact, the collision of the tacit and the explicit here came from the attempt to integrate an organization whose repertories of knowledge were tacit and individual with an organization that privileged formalized collective knowledge. It was finally the host organization, Indosuez, which modified its knowledge repertories, and adopted the organizational settings that were required: a thawing of its knowledge and of its organizational structure. The path followed by Indigo was opposite to that of these two organizations, and the collision of the tacit and explicit dimensions took place at the end of it (see Figure 9.1).

The first observation is linked to the nature of the ambiguity into which the four organizations were plunged. Facing a growing ambiguity, attitudes were at first explicit: people were prepared to involve themselves explicitly, they sought to position themselves, to 'get their bearings'. In a second phase, dispositions towards the situation become less homogenized. Alongside the initial wary attitude, less 'established', less 'readable' attitudes and behaviours begin to appear. The range of behaviour and affective and cognitive predisposition becomes broad. In a third phase behaviours become more instinctive, less verbalized, and more inscribed in a practice in which people do their best to manage the situation while still trying to position themselves. In a fourth and final phase we observe that behaviours and attitudes – and this is true of all four cases – become collective.

The second observation relates to the difference in behavioural reactions or in resultant affective or cognitive predisposition according to whether the ambiguity is intensified or reduced by an external event. The reduction of ambiguity by an external event does not entail many behavioural manifestations or explicit cognitive and affective dispositions. On the contrary, each intensification of ambiguity entails a new attitude or a new behaviour; of which a change in collective attitude is the most frequently observed.

When they were faced with an ambiguous situation, all four organizations tried to introduce processes which involved a greater or smaller number of actors. These processes can contract (actors exit) or expand (actors enter) as the situation develops.

THE LARGER ORGANIZATIONS 'DE-INSTITUTIONALIZE' THEIR KNOWLEDGE The two comparatively large organizations – Qantas and Pechiney – exhibited a tendency to privilege explicit knowledge when the disconcerting situation first emerged. When confronted with the failure of an institutional resolution of the ambiguous situation, successive adjustments were carried out so as to 'draw in' the perimeter of knowledge generation. By drawing this perimeter of action in, these organizations were embodying their knowledge in existent 'communities of practice'; and from then on practical knowledge entered into the legitimate game of problem-solving: it becomes an accepted practice. People decide that knowledge which is less established, more shifting, may be a way to escape the fog in which the company has been enveloped. The phenomenon common to these two cases is that of a 'de-institutionalization' of knowledge; that is, both organizations sought to shift the intervention field from a context that was over-institutionalized to a more flexible and malleable context. In the Qantas case, its communities of practice were the entities which confronted the disconcerting nature of the situation in a coherent manner. For Pechiney, the resolution of ambiguity was based on a tacit agreement established by people with shared experience and local collective knowledge. Long-term abatement of the ambiguity of the situation could not come from a forced dissolution, since this abatement was not linked to any political issues internal to the organization, but was situated in the inter-organizational domain, that is, in Pechiney's relationship with its environment in Guinea.

SMALLER ORGANIZATIONS COPING WITH AMBIGUITY THROUGH SOCIALIZATION Although Indosuez itself is a large organization, the ambiguous situation we looked at was in its New York division – a medium-sized organization. In this sense, the Indigo and Indosuez case studies can be compared. The Drexelites who remained with Indosuez were able to reconstruct a small community of practice within the organization, in which their autonomy was partially preserved as compared to the earlier situation. In this aspect, the Indosuez case is very different from the others. Although the situation deteriorated in the first three phases, it 'came round' and recovered in the last two. Indosuez's objective was either to reach an agreement, or to question the International Capital Markets' purpose. This last observation poses the question of motivation for the resolution of ambiguity in certain cases, and invites us to review our first analyses. In the Indigo case, the ambiguity was virtually resolved by 'adduction' well before the trial, which engaged a fundamental decision. While shortening the decisional horizon, Maurice Botbol widened the organizational perimeter to deal with the ambiguous situation. In other words, throughout the period of his awareness of the situation, Botbol maintained a mode of action that was limited in its temporal dimension but comprehensive in its organizational dimension, and in doing so he was continually shifting from one mode of knowing to another: two variables remained fairly stable (the decisional horizon and the organizational perimeter), whereas one variable (his mode of knowing) pivoted. Botbol had identified knowledge as, in his words, a 'material that must be worked upon, digested, absorbed or turned inside-out'. A set of characteristics common to the four cases can now be established. These common elements are as follows:

- The resolution of the ambiguous situation was inscribed within a community of practice.
- Actors developed an attitude which called for tacit complicity.
- Actors elaborated an informal matrix of relationships with each other.
- Actors employed repertories of actions which were commonly used within the organization.
- Actors referred to and relied upon local collective knowledge.

Two conclusions can be drawn from these shared characteristics. (1) The dialectic between 'fluid knowledge' (knowledge that is not encapsulated within a fossilizing explicitation) and 'fossilized knowledge' (knowledge encapsulated within its explicitation) seems to play a central role in dealing with ambiguous situations. The mobilization of explicit knowledge, if this knowledge is too 'rigid', can frustrate the resolution of ambiguity; whereas the mobilization of knowledge which is more 'versatile' (individual tacit knowledge) and more adductive is an exemplary way to move out of ambiguity. (2) The second conclusion we can draw involves the organizational structure. We find here the same dialectic of the 'frozen' and the 'fluid'. Whereas 'mechanistic' organizations (strongly hierarchic, institutionalized) can constitute an environment that hinders the resolution of ambiguity, 'organic' organizations – if a thawing of structures is accompanied by a thawing of knowledge – provide an environment favouring the resolution of the ambiguous situation.

To present these findings more clearly I have organized them into a table, according to two simple criteria: 'favours resolution of the ambiguous situation' and 'frustrates resolution of the ambiguous situation'. I have listed the possible domains of intervention, and the possible actions. The table includes what we have learnt from both the qualitative and the comparative analyses of the four cases.

We can see in this table the factors that 'freeze' or 'fossilize' knowledge on one side, and the factors that 'fluidify' knowledge on the other. The paradox lies in the necessity of maintaining a sufficient 'density' of knowledge while reducing decisional horizons and perimeters of action. It appears that the management of tacit knowledge does not corroborate Cyert and March's principle of 'bounded rationality' (1963): if actors proceed from a rationality in which solutions are drawn from within the vicinity of the problem, their tacit knowledge draws its resources from the density and the frequency of their socialization. The larger and more diverse these past tacit surroundings, the smaller and more precise the chosen perimeter of action by decision-makers thrown into equivocal settings.

Contemporary industrialized society encourages people to embrace larger and larger problems, and to face continual waves of information: they finish by forming simplistic cognitive models, of very limited validity (Hedberg, 1981; Starbuck, 1983). At the same time, 'these societies advocate rationality, justification, consistency and bureaucratization: people are supposed to see causal links, interdependencies, and logical implications; to integrate their ideas and to extrapolate them beyond immediate experience: to weed out dissonance and disorder' (Starbuck, 1983: 95). This inclination on the part of contemporary society is summarized by the concept of 'hard knowledge': that knowledge which submits to the positivist Cartesian method. If we examine our two groups of factors we find on one side the factors relating to 'soft knowledge' – those which do not submit to the Cartesian method – and on the other side, 'hard knowledge'.

Therefore, learning to deal with ambiguity is based on the establishment of a 'thick' and 'soft' knowledge, whereas organizations encourage the employment of perceptual categories – in their documentation and their standards – which destroy subtlety and lead to reductive visions of reality.[1] Sense-making efforts require knowledge of a certain thickness and texture: a knowledge that is contoured and accepts both imperfections and 'replies in the form of questions'. Our observation of this learning reveals its conjectural nature. In the case studies, we have seen solutions generated in the course of action (Starbuck, 1983); actors proceeding by trial and error or through a process of 'fine-tuning'; and inferences induced from other inferences which themselves rest principally on tacit knowledge.

Table 9.1 *Obstacles and triggers of ambiguity resolution*

	Hinders resolution	Favours resolution
Size	Larger organizations, if the process involves the whole organization	Smaller organizations, as the formation of a collective interpretation is easier
Knowledge	The mobilization of collective and explicit knowledge can frustrate resolution, if it 'fossilizes' knowledge Without systematically frustrating resolution, individual explicit knowledge does not play a determining role in the resolution of ambiguous situations	The mobilization of collective and tacit knowledge accompanies the resolution of ambiguity The versatility of individual tacit knowledge, across all forms of behaviour and attitudes
Attitudes	Adjustments based on the continuation of earlier actions Attitudes that are normative, contradictory or compartmentalizing	'Floating' attention Behaviours inscribed within a community of practice Deliberate ambiguity
Actions	Actions which fossilize knowledge or the structures in which actors circulate knowledge	Web of informal relationships Clandestine management Actions which are dislocating, then re-articulating tacit knowledge
Structures of the organization	A 'mechanistic' organization (hierarchical, institutionalized) The multiplication of structures, measures and procedures is largely ineffectual	An 'organic' organization, if this organic character is synonymous with a dense fabric (favouring socialization) A 'thawing' of structures, if it is accompanied by a 'thawing' of knowledge
Decisional horizon	Long decisional horizons, without inevitably frustrating resolution, do not contribute to easing or resolving the ambiguity	A succession of short-term actions, if their object is to absorb a larger number of stimuli so as to augment actors' tacit knowledge
Perimeter of action	Perimeters of action that are inferior to the concerned or affected perimeter	An encompassing perimeter of action, at least equal to the size of the affected or concerned perimeter
Number of actors involved	The augmentation of the number of actors implicated, if this widening of the process inhibits the socialization necessary for the creation of collective tacit knowledge	The reduction of the number of actors involved in the process, if the remaining actors establish common practice (this is important, but not determinant)

A too distant management of knowledge

The dynamics of organizational knowledge are very often disregarded by corporate executives. When the concept is presented to them they question the nature of the discourse: 'is it sociology?' ask some; 'information?' ask others. In an effort to improve their company's management of its knowledge, these same executives often multiply initiatives – most of the time by creating structures to collect and distribute information – and so the company becomes flooded with information and dies of its need for knowledge.

Knowledge is becoming one of the organization's main sources of competitive advantage; yet, unlike strategic marketing, finance or accountancy, there is as yet no discipline that delimits what is known by an organization and that enables organizations to implement strategic management of their knowledge. It could be argued that the academic discipline of 'management' fulfils this role of the adjustment and development of organizational knowledge; that such educational faculties are themselves 'knowledge organizations'. Yet we must also acknowledge the difficulties met by all organizations today – by businesses and administrations – in encouraging and organizing learning processes.

The first question is to determine whether knowledge management is capable, as is supposed, of encompassing all of an organization's knowledge. In short, when all marketing analyses have been exhausted, when profiles have been put together for all of a company's employees, when all production processes, delegation of authority, and divisions of labour have been optimized . . . has one embraced all of an organization's knowledge?

WHAT IS WRONG WITH CURRENT PRACTICES OF KNOWLEDGE MANAGEMENT Training towards a mastery of knowledge is essentially founded on a conception of expertise as strongly *individual* and *individualizing*. It is individual because it promotes intellect above agency, 'knowledge about' above 'knowledge of', strategic thought above its execution. It is 'individualizing' because its evaluation rests, finally, on only two knowledge creation processes: its formalization and its restitution. It pushes aside those processes which we have seen are critical for organizations when they face difficulties: the quality and the subtlety of socialization, and the ability to articulate knowledge that is neither fossilized nor certain (which is the reverse of the combination of certainties that is often the sole criterion of 'excellence' in management literature). Knowledge is conceived, in our Western societies, as a rigid, tangible and measurable key to fit all locks – and this brings organizations to a terrible confusion between information and knowledge, between determination and comprehension, between description and involvement. As Girin noted, 'ultimately, interpretation is founded on a tacit knowledge base. One can always, and one often should, attempt to bring to light what is behind people's agreements or disagreements on meanings' (1995: 277). Nonetheless, should we really become involved in an explicit engineering of the foundations of meaning in organizations? In other words, by liberating sense-making from its ambiguities, its 'confused mandates', are we not breaking the relationships of trust which develop among people?

Management's responsibility extends beyond simply 'getting things done'. It is also responsible for the reduction of the asymmetry between reflection and action, in both its activities of sense-making and its encouragement of people's commitment to the continual development of their knowledge – a commitment which itself turns on the employees' own activities of sense-making, on the integration of action and meaning. But although a traditional perspective of commitment would want it to conform to three conditions: 'the behaviour is explicit (there is clear evidence that the act has taken place), public (people have seen that the act has taken place), and irrevocable (the action cannot be revoked)' (Weick, 1995: 157), our case studies, and particularly those of Pechiney and Indosuez, reveal that careful observation of organizations does not lead to such conclusions. Pechiney managed to work through its difficulties in Guinea by a commitment to respect an agreement that was not made explicit. Indosuez managed to keep the Drexelites' team not by insisting on the irrevocability of their presence, nor by publicly lecturing them or making the adoption explicit, but by letting them make their own choice: by avoiding collective discussion of the grounds for their decision to remain. Indosuez's CEO gave the Drexelites a week to evaluate their options privately and peacefully. Consequently, regardless of whether it was individual or collective, their commitment cannot be reduced to its explicitation.

CONFUSION BETWEEN SOCIAL RITE AND THE REALITY OF COMMITMENT   It is not difficult to identify the origin of this misunderstanding. Through rites of baptism, communion, bar mitzvah, engagement and marriage, Western society presents images of public and declarative acts of commitment. But the analyses of Georg Simmel or Takeo Doi are closer to the reality of commitment than is a surface reading of the rituals of socialization. The full dimensions of true commitment cannot be explained explicitly: whether it be individual or collective, true commitment rests on tacit foundations. Its explicit expression demonstrates a desire to signify to others that the commitment has been made. It is a 'shared meaning' (Smircich, 1983), and not an imposition of commitment by the collectivity.

Simmel, at the beginning of this century, and Doi more recently, have formulated a sequence that is similar to that of commitment and detachment. For both of these researchers explicitation kills a relationship, because it takes away its freedom of action, its hope and its elevation. When two people enter into conflict, the only escape route is upwards: towards a renewal of trust, with ever higher stakes, a renewed shared *purpose*. If two people no longer hold any mystery for each other – if they become predictable to each other – the conflict cannot be resolved with a renewal of trust: because there is no longer anything that is unknown, anything that is tacit. When the relationship moves into the territory of resentment, the rupture is consummate; tacit knowledge pursues its own dynamics, independently of the relationship's explicit aspects.

TACIT KNOWLEDGE: TOOL FOR LIBERATION OR WILE?   Industries too have their share of emotion. Constrained to exist without commitment, reduced to the execution of tasks that do not correspond to their aspirations, people will often prefer to lie to themselves rather than opt for resentment: self-deception at least helps to maintain self-respect (Fingarette, 1969). In sectors with strong industrial traditions the older generation regards young arrivals with curiosity. While these older employees have accepted moral agreements, relationships based on mutual trust, younger newcomers now prefer a formal and contractual relationship. In place of an interaction based on a tacit agreement between executives we find this newer generation of managers taking refuge in a codified and ruled relationship, finding it difficult to have confidence in an agreement without this written bedrock. Older employees are in turn uncomfortable with relationships reduced to such formal expression. For entrepreneurs, the tacit can be a source of trust, of recognition of the quality of their relationships with employees, but for administrators it is a sign of the uncertainty of the relationship. While entrepreneurs reproach administrators for dehumanizing the workplace, administrators reproach management for refusing to establish workplace relationships clearly (see, e.g., Ibert, 1996).

Tacit knowledge can act either to liberate or to work mischief. It can free managers to adjust their interpretation of a situation, and to tolerate incertitude, their actions then becoming limited only by their determination or irresolution to believe in the limits to their knowledge: 'If I believe what he thinks I believe . . . .' This freedom creates dependence on a knowledge which is not as yet entirely revealed: 'The quality of the knowledge that so develops only reveals itself after the fact, that is, when all the cards have been played' (Dumez and Jeunemaître, 1995: 31). Tacit knowledge can be used by cunning managers to avoid explicit contingencies that are in conflict with their goals, by allowing them to anticipate what their counterparts' final positions will be once the explicit figuration of their knowledge is obsolete. This is primarily a case of transgressing the rules of socialization, without putting these rules into question: lying without lying. Collective tacit knowledge is thus employed to meet specific tactical needs. If the presumed, and non-expressed, rules of the transaction turn out not to be accurate *ex post*, the malicious intentions may be perceived as treachery, marking the end of an actor's membership of a community: the actor may be accused of not respecting 'the rules of the game'.

The Taylorization of knowledge

'The confrontation of individual knowledge bases is an activity which has a great wealth of relational models: it shows up potential associations with other systems of knowledge, other expertise, it highlights different or common objects and unveils inconsistencies or unsuspected lacunae' (Hatchuel and Weil, 1995: 146). In other words, an industrial culture that sees itself as an element that rationalizes knowledge is today a culture that is no longer accurate.

Confrontations between employees of longer standing (for example the 'old boys' at Qantas) and younger arrivals illustrate this quandary. The systematic application of management methods to the life of an organization pushes the organization to cut back, not only its relational modes, but equally the knowledge circulated within these relationships. The implementation of a rationalization of activities creates a gap between those who innovate, who generate new knowledge, and those who exploit this knowledge.

A large part of organizational knowledge escapes discourse, standardization and generalization. Organizations tend to privilege formalization and combination, whereas their critical resources rest upon the versatility and renewal of their collective tacit knowledge.

This separation is often accompanied by a mechanism which distinguishes the transmitters of knowledge from the receivers of this same knowledge. We often hear managers complaining that although they aim to offer their clients service of the highest quality, standardizing performance is not easy. They point out the difficulty of expecting people from Chicago to behave in the same manner as people from Los Angeles, and that moreover these people have no desire to be alike; in any case, the bottom line is that each group of people believes its system to be superior. These difficulties stem from the fact that people, to identify themselves with the roles they play in the organization, need to take on the knowledge that they have to use and convey; they stem equally from the assumption that standardization must be approached from a 'top-down' perspective – in other words, by imposing a priori, as the model of what is 'correct', staff training that in the end calls for this standardization.

THE QUEST TO ECONOMIZE ON COORDINATION COSTS: AND THE LOSS OF CURIOSITY The problem of specialization and the standardization of knowledge acts as a bottleneck for many organizations. Organizations tend to optimize the codification of their knowledge through routines in order to reduce codification and transaction costs between their members. Doing so, they increase the gap between a more and more autonomous tacit knowledge base, and a poorer explicit know-how. Employees perceive learning a routine combination process. In the services industry, extensive codification of franchisees' knowledge is accordingly a lever for overall margin of operations, but at the same time, it impedes the firm's ability to re-orientate.

For instance, a firm like McDonald's is able to reach a high degree of codification by way of training that instils behavioural reflexes: codification enables it to guarantee that every consumer will receive the same quality of service in each and every McDonald's outlet. The routine aspect of the knowledge mobilized at McDonald's allows this codification to be pushed to the extreme. Yet, while a certain level of homogeneity is essential for any organization – as the more homogenized their knowledge, the easier its circulation becomes, and the lower their costs of coordination and transmission – in many organizations this type of automatic response can threaten the quality of the service offered. When routinization is a menace to quality maintenance – when tacit knowledge of the commercial realm is crucial to its success – the firm is faced with resistance to the standardization of both management and of the transmission of knowledge.

In an effort to objectify their collective knowledge, organizations ground their homogeneity in the definition of norms and procedures relating to the processing of this knowledge. This may include formats for the documentation of events, criteria on which employees are to be judged, or even standardization of the distribution of knowledge. For example, an organization may have found it difficult to gain a reliable perception of its financial position, and so will institute a system of management control under which people will be required to communicate a codification of their situation. Persuaded that this 'codification' is as much a means of sanction as a means of knowledge, people will try to outwit it by trying to circumvent it, or to profit from its fuzzy zones by employing a free interpretation of recommended stocktaking methods; playing with contingency reserves; delaying the payment of accounts; or eventually creating a new account to escape organizational scrutiny, as occurred in the Baring's financial disaster. People will limit themselves to criteria on which they feel themselves to be judged, and throw themselves into the codification which has been imposed upon them, thus realizing self-fulfilling prophecies.

Such an organizational device becomes pernicious when standards of codification are applied to a community of practice whose success lies in a core of tacit knowledge. In this case, the imposition of codification will interfere with the community of practice's normal process of fine-tuning, to such a point that the community's emergent and non-codified regulation will be supplanted by a codified and mechanistic coordination (see Figure 9.2).

Individual knowledge   **Collective knowledge**

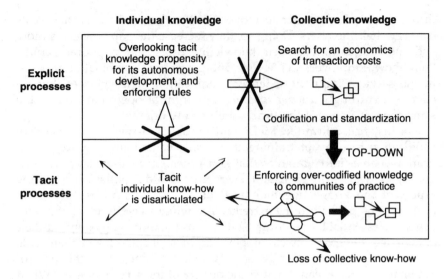

Figure 9.2 *How organizations dismantle valuable tacit knowledge*

EVOLUTION OF ROLES AND EVOLUTION OF KNOWLEDGE   From then on, the community ceases to capitalize on its collective learning. It becomes victim to a regulation of its processes that is detrimental to the socialization and the collective memory through which its collective tacit knowledge has been maintained: it replaces its RAM with ROM.

This belittling of socialization, its dissolution through an interference of the codified with a dynamic whose equilibrium lies in its non-codifiable character, is resented at the individual level – 'Things used to work smoothly, we didn't have to justify everything we did' – a resentment that provokes lethargy and a freezing of managers' individual expression. The game-rules have been broken, socialization has been violated, and their personal contribution to an explicit collective knowledge has lost its meaning (see Figure 9.1, p. 198).

By establishing rules about the manner in which learning should occur, organizations ultimately risk being more Taylorist than Taylor intended them to be. In standardizing their knowledge, organizations achieve a security that is superficial: the assurance that the codified is codified throughout in the same manner. What they risk, however, is the loss of their 'thick' knowledge; that which is born of 'a multiplicity of complex conceptual structures, many of which are superimposed or bound together, and which are simultaneously strange, irregular, and inexplicable' (Geertz, 1973: 10).

Organizations often attempt to replenish their knowledge by replenishing or renewing their teams: they learn from their new members, who bring with them new expertise; the new members too learn from the organization (primarily via socialization); values, beliefs and practices within which they will exercise their cognitive activity. Indosuez did try to do this. Such acceptance that changes to their teams will replenish their knowledge should entail a conception of careers as tools of knowledge management; a risk that becomes all the more salient as the economy destabilizes. Organizational and human competition organizes itself today around knowledge 'poles': but are organizations taking this into account in the management of their human resources?

The reply is for some unequivocal: 'The element lacking in traditional career definitions is found in the information and knowledge acquired through a sequence of professional experience. . . . Careers are accumulations of information and knowledge that assert themselves as talents, expertise, and networks of relationships' (Bird, 1994: 4). Nonaka and Takeuchi also take up this idea: 'One of the unique characteristics of Japanese companies comes from the fact that no department or group of experts has exclusive responsibility for the creation of new knowledge. Employees from ground floor level through to management and decision-makers all have their role to play' (1995: 15). Tacit knowledge is particularly crucial in this dynamic. As the Indigo case suggests, a high level of competitiveness does not automatically rest upon the sophistication of organizational knowledge codification. On the contrary, knowledge intensity is not measured by the density of formalized process, but rather leverage ration between the knowledge output and the codification needed to produce it. The less codification is required to produce the same knowledge, the more intense is the knowledge of the organization. Experienced managers in our case studies are less preoccupied with the formalization and codification of their cognitive activities.

Accordingly, lack of experience is above all lack of the aptitude to translate practical information into knowledge. On the one hand, market signals are often vague and ambiguous. On the other hand, employees can be prisoners of their own reductive schemas, and lose sight of a wider perspective: what is perceived to be so in one context may be altered or even lose all meaning in another. From then on, there is a continual confusion insofar as the new knowledge is distributed within the organization. In fact, it is primarily to middle management that the creation of a context favourable to experience belongs. It is up to them, then, to orient and to crystallize the sometimes chaotic knowledge that is derived from action. And this crystallization poses a crucial challenge for organizations: that of the creation and the protection of communities of practice.

Developing and protecting communities of practice

Lave and Wenger define 'communities of practice' as communities of practitioners within which situational learning develops and is legitimized: 'the mastery of knowledge and skill requires newcomers to move toward full participation in the sociocultural practices of a community' (1991: 29). Thus, a community of practice is: 'a system of relationships between people, activities, and the world; developing with time, and in relation to other tangential and overlapping communities of practice. A community of practice is an intrinsic condition of the existence of knowledge' (1991: 98).

COMMUNITIES OF PRACTICE AND REDUCED COORDINATION COSTS
In the different cases presented – notably in the Qantas case – we have seen how communities of practice enable puzzled or disconcerted organizations to resist the dissolution of their socialization, and to direct themselves towards strategic re-establishment. This is achieved through two characteristics of such communities: the indivisibility of their collective commitment, which therefore serves to avoid ruptures; and their coordination – tacit – which does not necessitate managerial intervention, and so allows them to avoid explicitation (only too often a source of conflict).

Another characteristic of communities of practice is to be found in their capacity to contain and to maintain expertise – and therefore a certain form of specialization – without resorting to an irreversible division of labour. While 'an elevated degree of specialization generally favours learning, both in its tacit and its formalized dimension', at the same time it 'generally complicates the exploration of new ideas and the implementation of pre-established plans; as the absence of redundancy in the structure works against the diffusion of tacit knowledge indispensable to the exploration of new possibilities' (Reix, 1995: 25). Communities of practice are learning communities. They couple a capacity to explore and transmit knowledge with an aptitude for specialization. For example, Qantas's 'operations' community both experiments with new processes and applies a very codified knowledge to ensure highly reliable operations.

JUST HOW DURABLE ARE COMMUNITIES OF PRACTICE?   Why then are all organizations not organized in the form of communities of practice? On the one hand, procedural specificity of communities of practice limits their growth. They are created and maintained under the *sine qua non* condition of shared practice. This sharing must be unequivocal and continuous. Consequently strained, temporary or discontinuous relationships do not provide good conditions for the emergence of a community of practice. On the other hand, organizations are not crucibles of stability and uniformity: their regulation is by way of ruptures, introductions of brutal changes, unilateral decisions to which communities of practice may adapt badly. Here lies the fragility of such communities: they are subject to ageing and mortality – because their performance depends upon the quality of socialization that takes place in their midst.

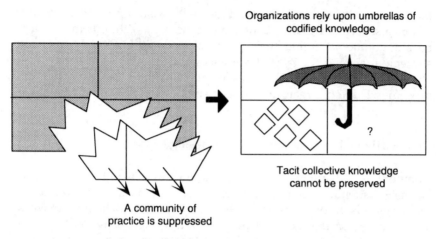

Figure 9.3   *The effects of the disappearance of a community of practice*

The loss of a key actor from a community of practice is enough to disrupt it, and damage the connections between its members. If these communities preserve the organization's tacit knowledge, they do so by permanently renewing it; the suppression of a community of practice thus has weighty consequences for an organization, as the case of the small community of Drexelites suggests. For want of its socialization, which had been frustrated by the mother organization, the small community was no longer a harmonious body of mutual adjustments and became no more than a sum of individual tacit knowledge, which the organization tried to cover with an umbrella of codified knowledge (see Figure 9.3).

The third impediment is provided by the fact that such communities of practice are anchored by a strong identification with practice. Learning processes and cycles can isolate executives from the rest of the organization by creating the phenomenon of identity associated with practice. This was the case with the Drexelites and their experience with derivatives, and similarly with Qantas's 'old boys' and their understanding of piloting and operations management. The paradox of these communities comes from both their dependence on a core of tacit understanding, and from the distinction they seek of their members in the form of initiation rites and a mastery of specialist learning. They know more than they can express, but they are aware that they know it. They possess knowledge that they know neither how to individualize nor to make collectively explicit, yet this in no way diminishes their confidence in its possession. They could not define their own boundaries, nor clearly say why one particular member belongs to their community, yet they know who doesn't belong.

In other words, while communities of practice may appear to be adequate organizational forms for the management of tacit knowledge, their propensity to combine durability with a strong sense of identity can be a source of rigidity. Knowledge generated within them may then be autonomous, limiting their potential as tools for a deliberate and strategic management of tacit knowledge, as much as they may seem obvious for such a role. The question remains: how can we exploit the tacit knowledge of organizations as a source of competitive advantage?

Competitive advantage and tacit knowledge

Competitive advantage from tacit knowledge has recently drawn extensive attention from researchers (e.g. Baumard, 1995; Moingeon and Edmondson, 1996; Spender, 1993; Winter, 1987). Most of these works are premised on the idea that practical knowledge, common to groups and communities, is a strategic resource that organizations tend to ignore or reject. To acknowledge that tacit knowledge is a key resource to organizations is however not excessively counter-intuitive. The issue is to translate such an observation into new managerial practice, i.e. to unlearn current strategic practices. Strategic management acknowledges the importance of tacit knowledge in developing and preserving rents, or in the protection of organization core capabilities from competitors' covetousness. Yet, in this perspective, knowledge is undertaken as a merely static shock of resources, whereas the strategic role of tacit knowledge relies more on competitive dynamics. As the case studies suggest, building competitive advantage rests more upon skills of knowledge transformation, rather than capabilities of reproduction and preservation.

The contingency of tacit knowledge

The question of competitive advantage founded on tacit knowledge comes up against two major obstacles: firstly, tacit knowledge is 'live' knowledge – that is to say, it would not survive outside the human system through which its dynamics is sustained; secondly, tacit knowledge is singular – it very often proves unable to adapt to different places, other conditions, other cultural and social contexts. It is these two characteristics that detract from tacit knowledge's applicability as a strategic instrument. This is what we could label the 'contingency' of tacit knowledge.

STRATEGISTS OF THE TACIT LOST IN ANOTHER TACIT WORLD   This contingency of tacit knowledge expresses itself in the socially constructed character of reality (Berger and Luckmann, 1966). The reality of Indigo's tacit knowledge was inherent to a different symbolic universe than that which underlay the reality of Pechiney's tacit knowledge. The language of the mining engineers, and the tacit knowledge of the aluminium trade, would most certainly prevent Maurice Botbol from

being such an effective 'articulator' of tacit knowledge if he was transported to the context of Guinea's self-determination in 1955. Vice versa,
one would have to belong to the community of practice of those familiar
with Indigo's secretive environments to be able to decipher their tacit
content. We can only speak of competitive advantage founded on tacit
knowledge within a specific social reality: an industrial family, a sector,
a corporation at the macro-economic level, a community of practice, a
family at the microsociological level. The learning curve of the tacit is
itself, in all likelihood, strongly singular and specific to the sector,
the path or the social system in which it takes form: that is to say, the
combinatives of the aluminium industry are probably ineffective in
the confidential letter industry. Generic strategies applied to the tacit
knowledge to be found in the aluminium industry would certainly
appear ineffective in another industry. Industries are idiosyncratic
bodies: their recipes are difficult to transfer to other industries because
they are constituted of a basis of knowledge that is peculiar to themselves (Spender, 1989).

We must therefore admit to an important limit to the power of tacit
knowledge: it is very strongly dependent on those places and human
systems that precede or induce its generation. It is, however, the systematic overestimation of this obstacle that leads organizations to
neglect tacit knowledge; only to realize once it is too late that it hides
within it the solution to their disconcerting situation.

The non-capitalization of tacit knowledge

It is in the exploration of new markets, and in the internationalization of
their activities, that – paradoxically – tacit knowledge plays a particularly determining role in organizations. Paradoxically, because the
globalization of organizations' activities would suggest a desire to economize on coordination costs, and therefore to standardize procedures
and knowledge.

General Motors' experience with the joint-venture Nummi illustrates
this effect of the widening of organizations' activities: 'When it became
apparent to General Motors that the Nummi factory in Fremont,
California, was effective thanks to cooperative management techniques
introduced by Toyota, managers and workers from the Van Nuys factory
some hundred miles further south were sent to Nummi to learn these
techniques. Although the Fremont factory managers were willing and
able to teach them these new techniques, the Van Nuys employees could
only stay for two weeks. This short period of time proved to be
insufficient for them to absorb and assimilate what they were taught.
When they returned to Van Nuys, very few among them were capable of
applying what they had learnt' (Bird, 1994: 24).

Field experience generally provides a more nuanced image of the competitiveness of strongly internationalized organizations. In the Pechiney

case, which unfolded in a pioneer period of internationalization for French companies, we note the importance of the tacit articulation of knowledge to the resolution of the crisis. This articulation necessitated the frequent displacement of executives who were normally based at the organization's central office in Paris, as well as their commitment to a difficult, but necessary, socialization.

MANAGING KNOWLEDGE INTERNATIONALLY   Two things particularly threaten internationalized organizations: the possibility of losing knowledge, of a knowledge 'breakdown' (as a result of a process that is non-dynamic); and the possibility of non-capitalization of experience (as a result of a process that is non-cumulative). For example, an organization may commission managers to clear the way for a new market: they are to assess the available knowledge of this market and to incorporate this into their strategies, so as to decide on what policy to follow. A team is composed of experts from within the organization who, if not explicitly, then implicitly, are retained because of their field experience. This type of operation can be very expensive, the 'scouts' often staying a few months on the field to 'socialize' with local partners. In this kind of assignment companies consider they are 'testing the temperature' of the market. But what happens if, a few months later, the idea of entering into the market is abandoned, or if a competitor gets in ahead?

The 'scouts' will return to the head office they came from, and the tacit knowledge they have accumulated will be lost. In other words, the experience will not have been *conceptualized*, it will not have been introduced into the organization's collective memory – there is a knowledge breakdown. If later a second opportunity presents itself on the same market, many organizations will reconstruct, or 're-improvise', a form of approach. Instead of investing in knowledge and in the capitalization of this knowledge, efforts will have been diluted within the system: rather than being economical the system is profligate. This is the phenomenon of *non-capitalization of a community of practice*. The absence of dialogue, during and *about* the process, and the absence of a collective knowledge culture, transform what could have been a true learning dynamic into a sum of singular experiences.

Such are the effects of the dysfunction of an emergent and spontaneous management of knowledge. This example demonstrates, if it needs to be demonstrated, the importance of knowledge in the phenomenon of competition between organizations. In fact, as we will see, knowledge is ubiquitous in organizations' interrelations with their partners.

The tacit and the explicit in the relational triptych

Relational policies refers to all of the different modes of interaction offered to organizations to enter into relations with other organizations in their strategic universe. These relational policies fit into a triptych of confrontation, avoidance and cooperation.

The tacit and the explicit are at the heart of the relational triptych, as industrialists operating in markets with a weak price elasticity of demand well know. When the reduction of prices has no positive effect on the volume of demand, a reduction in tariffs is particularly unattractive. This shared knowledge of the sector's functioning pushes executives into agreement. So long as the products concerned have no real substitutes, the interest of each manufacturer converges with the collective interest, without this needing to be discussed collectively. Each knows that the other knows that nothing is to be gained by embarking on a price war that would be damaging for the whole sector. Managers eventually intuitively anticipate their competitors' reactions. The agreement is neither formal, nor explicit; it can be tacit.

Dumez and Jeunemaître offer a similar analysis, of the cements sector: 'firms independently compile a body of knowledge about their market and possible strategies', while being 'aware of the profound uncertainty that this knowledge conceals' (1995: 30). They use this knowledge to seek indications of competitors' capacities, their intentions and their plans. But this accumulation of explicit knowledge is accompanied by an emergent regulation of relationships within the sector, based on a tacit and collective knowledge of it. 'In the absence of any possibility of communication, something is perceived by both parties, and this perception seems to persist, even in a diluted form, when communication becomes possible (Schelling, 1960: 98). Suggestion takes the place of information, and tacit knowledge takes the place of codified knowledge.

And so there are different degrees of codification of conflict, cooperation and avoidance. They may be either more or less tacit or explicit, according to how much leeway the interrelation necessitates – the more vague, the 'fuzzier' the interrelation, the more ambiguity there is and the less codification; if the scope to manoeuvre is less, there is less fuzziness, less ambiguity and more codification.

This double distinction allows us to establish a cartography of the explicit and the tacit in relational modes (Figure 9.4). Findings from the four cases studied suggest that both coupling and trust play a central role in facilitating either conflictual or cooperative knowledge in the interfirm. Loose coupling fosters equivocations that allow knowledge to undergo autonomous and tacit adjustments, while tight couplings force managers to make common knowledge more explicit. For example, in the Indosuez case, the desire to tighten coupling between ICM and Indosuez turned what was a tacit avoidance into an explicit one. It worsened the situation, as the Drexelites would eventually overemphasize their difference when asked to codify their knowledge. Difficulties in articulating tacit knowledge between partners can turn a potentially,

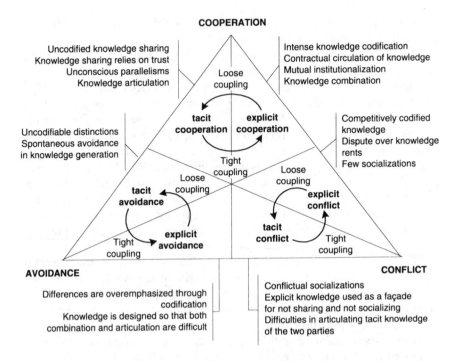

Figure 9.4   *Explicit and tacit processes in inter-organizational relations*

yet tacit, conflictual situation into a real one. Tight coupling can foster disputes over knowledge rents, force people to leave equivocal boundaries to settle harshly guarded cognitive territories through competitively codified knowledge. For example, to the extent that their esoteric expertise was loosely coupled with Indosuez, the Drexelites wouldn't move into explicit conflict. But as soon as Indosuez tried to enforce a reasonable codification on how this 'know-how' is being processed, a crisis crystallized.

Hence, the Indosuez case illustrates the role of knowledge in a situation that permanently shifts from conflict to avoidance (see Figure 9.4). The role of the Chief Executive Officer in tightening or loosening the coupling between Indosuez and the absorbed organization was effectively crucial to the crisis resolution. A more cooperative handling of the situation is found in Pierre Jouven's management of the Guinean crisis. Yet the role of tight or loose coupling is very similar. Loose coupling allows a shift from unsuccessful and enforced explicit cooperation, to smoother and somewhat more successful tacit cooperation. On one side, Pechiney's desire to tighten and enforce the local coupling forced the Guinean government into an undesired explicit cooperation that made them lose face and credibility with the local population. On the other side, the commitment to over-codified knowledge of the situ-

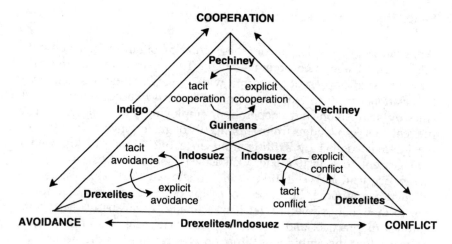

Figure 9.5 Coupling, knowledge and relationships in three case studies

ation blinded Pechiney's managers to the real threat of this situation. Pechiney had to move to less codified knowledge management – which it somehow did by loosening its local coupling – to foster a more cooperative atmosphere (see Figure 9.5).

Hence, to a codified knowledge and a codified confrontation there are corresponding explicit conflicts. To a non-codifiable knowledge and to a quest for an intangible (interpretational) result there is a corresponding tacit conflict. To a deliberate and codified division corresponds explicit cooperation, whereas a non-codifiable division will provoke intuitive anticipation and tacit cooperation. To a codifiable distinction will correspond an explicit avoidance, while to a non-codifiable distinction will correspond a tacit avoidance. The degree of completeness or incompleteness conditions the organization's choice of relational mode. The puzzled organization is that which cannot find the foundations of choice in either its codified nor its non-codifiable knowledge: to cooperate or to confront, to avoid or to accept; for it, these options are ambiguous alternatives. Shifting back and forth from tacit to explicit knowledge, Pechiney shifts from cooperation to conflict; whereas Indosuez travels along the avoidance–conflict continuum. Until Indigo is pushed into explication by the Court of Justice, it remains smoothly out of reach of any conflictual relationships or coupling with external bodies that might threaten its peaceful work. While Indosuez and Pechiney are exemplars of firms learning to manage tacit knowledge through a painful and unsteady approach, Indigo really stands, as our findings corroborated, as an organization skilled in the management of tacit knowledge. It should be noted that Indigo travels on a continuum that never leaves the arena of tacit cooperation or tacit avoidance. Would this be the key to its success?

Strategists and tacit knowledge management

What can we, finally, learn from these 'puzzled organizations' about the role of knowledge in corporate strategy? The lessons are manifold. The four case studies present us with a wide range of situations that cover the relational triptych fairly well. Indosuez tried to acquire new knowledge by acquisition and cooperation, employing a tacit agreement to prevent this knowledge from slipping through its fingers. It managed the internal conflict by shifting from an explicit mode of knowledge management to a tacit mode. Qantas was shaken by two successive merger-acquisitions. The first, with Australian Airlines, resulted in different communities of practice overlapping, and not always adapting well to their new situation; yet it was finally by means of these communities of practice, and not through explicit measures taken by the company, that the ambiguous situation was resolved. Indigo sought to understand its environment by favouring socialization, and by avoiding at all costs the 'fossilization' of its knowledge. Pechiney eventually understood that the discordant situation it found itself in was not to be resolved by means of its collective explicitation. What is the precise role of knowledge at the heart of each relational mode? What knowledge is the most useful and the most intense during conflict? During cooperation? During avoidance?

Knowledge and competitive strategies

Knowledge, as it becomes more codified and increasingly transportable (with the advent of information digitization), is also becoming the object of increasingly radical competitive tactics. But though it is relatively easy to misappropriate knowledge whose codification norms are standardized – such as software prototypes, for example – most technology and know-how are less easy to plunder.

Companies usually seek to protect themselves from these attacks on their codified knowledge. If it is not possible for them to 'recombine' their codified knowledge – to break it up and render it less imitable – they can have recourse to a culture of secrecy (in which knowledge is contained in socialization), as a judicial protection of their knowledge. But the most efficient protection is still to increase the difficulty of accessing their codified knowledge. One of the strongest barriers is thus found in the ambiguity concerning connections between the company's observable actions and the results it obtains. This causal ambiguity blocks the process of competitor imitation and so maintains the initial advantage. One finds this system of knowledge protection in industries that depend strongly on their technological advantage. In the pneumatics industry for example, companies like Michelin add to a culture of secrecy (learned through a socialization that protects the organization's knowledge) sophisticated systems for the protection of their

	Individual knowledge	Collective knowledge
Explicit	Formalization of interpersonal relations; confidentiality clauses Head hunting key experts from competitors (Indosuez)	Reverse engineering Cost domination with systematic adjustment to competitors' codified knowledge Equivocal combinations (Michelin) Takeover (Indosuez) Recombination of existing knowledge
Tacit	Purposefully uncodified expertise: individual tacit knowledge blocks substitution or imitation Coalition around individual idiosyncratic knowledge (Drexelites) Refusing socializations (Drexelites)	Merger and fusion (Qantas) Barriers to entry to a community of practice Ambiguous causal relationships Culture of secrecy

Figure 9.6   *Acquiring and defending knowledge in competitive strategies*

codified knowledge. For example, the company has adopted a policy of purchasing sample materials every year in the same quantity. This organizational precaution – the standardization of codified information accessible to third parties – prevents curious competitors from evaluating what possible combinations the organization may be studying. Michelin has made its codified knowledge equivocal so that no one combination overcomes another one. By precluding the possibility of combination, the company precludes access to its strategic knowledge.

Conflict means the end of a relationship: the end of the unspoken, the end of the implicit. 'In focusing itself on its objects, competition conceals this cruelty that is part of all forms of objectivity: not by taking pleasure in the suffering of others, but precisely by eliminating any subjective factors from their calculations. This indifference to what is subjective, which also characterizes logic, law, and finance, leads people who are by no means cruel themselves to engage in the full brutality of competition' (Simmel, 1955: 109). In fact, explicit and collective knowledge play an important role in conflicts, whether through their systematic alignment, their recombination, or their protection (see Figure 9.6).

But the conflict could not be resolved by a simple explicit confrontation. In the Indosuez case for example, the Drexelites' strong rapport was based on the non-codifiable, and therefore non-transferable, character of their knowledge – on the fact that their knowledge, while indivisible and tacit, constituted a supplementary potential for aggression. The game of the conflict then consisted of refusing all socialization: not attending meetings, playing only walk-on parts, segregating themselves within their own offices, refusing to make their expertise explicit, requesting a separate institutional entity. Their collective and tacit knowledge supported this conflict strategy: the community of practice that was the Drexelites constituted a barrier to entry into their area of competence. The mode of regulation they used, together with the asymmetry of the tacit knowledge which characterized them collectively, increased their resistance within the larger organization.

From all the evidence, tacit knowledge is a strategic lever in conflict situations. It enables an insurmountable barrier to be erected against an adversary: that of the impossibility of its substitution or imitation, or at least of the high cost of doing so. Organizations that privilege a culture of secrecy over legalistic protection of their knowledge follow this precept.

Knowledge and avoidance strategies

Of the four cases studied, Indigo furnished the clearest example of management by avoidance, founded on a management of knowledge; but forms of avoidance are also to be found in the Indosuez case. In the Indigo case, avoidance was realized through a toning-down of individual explicit knowledge: through a modest attitude towards Indigo's own competencies. This enabled its editors, firstly, to avoid positioning themselves in opposition to their interlocutors and, secondly, to avoid any explicit clarification of their area of expertise. The personalization of knowledge is equally a form of avoidance: it allows relations that are in conflict to be managed through understandings between people, and so avoiding confrontation between organizations. This was the role Pierre Jouven played in the denouement of the Guinean affair, and Jean-Claude Gruffat in his negotiations with the group of Drexelites. On the contrary, the status quo can be maintained by refusing the socialization or the explicitation of tacit and personal knowledge. This is regulation by silence (see Figure 9.7).

Avoidance can also be achieved by the maintenance of rules within a sector that are only barely codified or otherwise made explicit. Frequent socializations allow managers to manage disagreements about positioning without entering into direct conflict: 'To arrive at an agreement in spite of a lack of communication or deficiencies in its quality, negotiators have to be attentive to constraints introduced by the structure of the situation itself, which will have an influence on the final choice' (Schelling, 1960: 103). The possible consequences or outcomes of a situation are taken into account by the parties involved: managers all know what will happen to the collectivity in the event of a conflict, but nobody can really express it. In this way each actor individually acts upon their own choice to avoid competition.

	Individual knowledge	Collective knowledge
Explicit	Specialization of individual expertise Use of equivocal explicitations to avoid conflict between expertises (Indigo) Systematically avoiding clear-cut explicitation (Indigo)	Overemphasizing distinctions and institutionalizing parochialism during mergers and absorptions (Indosuez) Disseminating knowledge on a 'need to know' basis (Pechiney) Geographical separations (Indosuez)
Tacit	Avoiding being inquisitive about foundations of personal expertise (Indosuez) Avoiding socializations that would force explicitation of personal knowledge (Drexelites) Ambiguous talk (Indigo)	Leaving polemics undisclosed Isolating a body of tacit knowledge into a new entity (Indosuez) Relying on tacit coordination to prevent confrontations (oligopolistic industries) Valuing and rewarding collective know-how without asking for explanations (Indigo)

Figure 9.7   *Knowledge and avoidance strategies*

Communities of practice, by refusing the conceptualization of their knowledge, can similarly practise avoidance: thus they preserve their singular distinction which separates them off naturally within a tacitly reserved area.

Knowledge and collective strategies

When a collectivity has succeeded in producing a certain solidarity, 'it is relatively easy to rectify wrongs caused here and there by hostile confrontations . . . the elements of this solidarity give the collectivity enough strength or confidence to enable it to accord a certain liberty to isolated individuals, even to indulge in antagonisms, because it is assured that the effort expended on this could have just as easily been compensated. This is why very well-organized collectivities can support more ruptures and friction than more mechanical conglomerates, without internal cohesion' (Simmel, 1955: 85). Here we find the fundamentals of the maintenance of communities of practice. In fact, tacit knowledge also plays an essential role in this third relational mode (see Figure 9.8).

In an alliance, tacit knowledge primarily acts as a guarantee of the relationship's security. If this knowledge necessitates specific aspects of socialization the alliance is even more difficult to break. This was the advantage Drexel had during their negotiations with Indosuez. At the same time, the mutual advantages of cooperation can be assured

	Individual knowledge	Collective knowledge
Explicit	Mapping the organizational individual know-how into databases Bringing in consultants to interact with managers	Standardizing rules for combination to allow easy combinations Implementing efficient communication devices (e.g. Intranet)
Tacit	Favouring informal and interpersonal relations instead of procedures (Jouven, Gruffat) Experimental socializations (Indigo) Modes attitude (Indigo)	Mixing managers from parent companies into the new merged entity to favour socialization and fusion of communities of practice (Qantas) Preservation is embodied in a collaborative and practice-sharing organizational culture (Qantas)

Figure 9.8 *Managing collective knowledge*

only if all parties involved are able to benefit from identical conditions of socialization, at least as far as this shared knowledge is involved. In the Indosuez case, the company purposefully committed itself to learning, but the organizational conditions did not permit it to profit from this as it had expected to.

Knowledge is then an ambiguous and contradictory material, as the case studies make abundantly clear. When people or groups cooperate they ask for clarification of each other's knowledge – and so for its explicitation. But by the very act of clarification firms render themselves imitable, and introduce the risk of diverting or corrupting the alliance. Knowledge sharing is ultimately based on trust: ultimately we must believe not only in the truth of the proposed codified combination, but also in the faltering perception we have of non-codifiable knowledge which we hope will correspond to our expectations.

A different reading of organizations

While organizational forms often go through profound changes, those organizations that reject such change risk believing that their knowledge management does not have to change either. Large organizations often engage in downsizing, and are increasingly able to externalize their human resources, often employing as consultants executives who have left the company. Dispersed organizations, held together by tenuous threads of information, are making their appearance. Organizations in networks, who share resources or marketing platforms, are now employing the same bureaucratic and mechanistic models that for eight decades have characterized only the very largest organizations. In the torments of these great changes, what happens to organizational knowledge? Should we reconsider the organization, and view it through the prism of the dynamics of its knowledge?

To enable tacit knowledge to develop autonomously, without impeding the organization's dynamics of performance and durability, calls for a new organizational architecture. This new architecture has to be able to privilege the formation of tacit knowledge, and its articulation as close as possible to the organization's strategic preoccupations. We can visualize a flexible, decentralized organization, encouraging horizontal and vertical socialization. The question of capitalization of organizational knowledge, however, cannot be resolved simply by according knowledge generation a supplementary degree of liberty: to a certain extent, to make knowledge explicit is to seek security through stabilization and regularity, whereas to privilege tacit knowledge is to gain pertinence through irregularities.

If knowledge is to be used as a strategic lever of the organization, we must be able to ensure both its stability and its exhaustion, its generation and its discontinuation. In this study we have seen it taking the most varied forms: tacit or explicit, individual or collective, encapsulated in structures or abstract. Knowledge cuts across all organizational relational modes; it authorizes redefinition of a career as a process of knowledge accumulation and valorization, and it calls for the development and the protection of communities of practice within organizations.

In sum, knowledge calls for a strategic management that ensures, as does the organization, the conditions necessary for its development, its preservation, and its renewal. However, too much preservation is detrimental to its diffusion. Too much generation is detrimental to its discontinuation. Like organizations, communities and individuals have to be able to learn as well as unlearn – they must be able to generate and to dissolve, to preserve and to sacrifice, to diffuse and to retain the organization's knowledge.

Note

1 For 'thick' vs. 'soft' knowledge, see Geertz (1983). For a dicussion of the reductive consequences of perceptual categories, particularly within political organizations, see Axelford (1976).

Conclusion

With relief,
with humiliation, with terror,
it understood that it also was an appearance,
that another was in the process of dreaming it.

Jorge Luis Borges
Fictions, 1956
'Circular Ruins'

There is nothing more perplexing than human knowledge. Most of its resources are mobilized to resolve its own contradictions. Hardly do we reach a likely representation of it than it reveals the distortions of which it is the fruit (Milliken and Starbuck, 1988). Like the frog who, when placed in a jar of cold water, does not realize that the water which is gradually heating up – in which it swims, to which it acclimatizes – will soon reach boiling point, and will soon scald it, people are accustomed to their knowledge, which soon will betray them. 'If there is no separation, then there is no longer either subject nor object of knowledge; there is no longer either an internal usefulness in knowing nor an external reality to know' (Morin, 1986: 205). It is all a question of *inherence*. We must understand that we belong to the same world, to understand that this world has limits. As with the batrachian who cannot imagine that the jar's function is to maintain the heat of which it will soon be the victim, it is difficult for us to conceive our own knowledge, to feel the walls that close us off, to distinguish just what part of 'what we know without being able to express' is critical to know. Words are our refuge, yet words are misleading. As Morin continues: 'The subject who wants self-knowledge must, in some way, distance himself from himself to become his own object of knowledge.'

Indigo, a small organization only ten years old, managed to do this. While the ambiguous situation enveloped it in interpretative meanders, Indigo refused to acclimatize. It refused to fine-tune itself, to make any statements that might have been rash or untimely, too tangible or too stable. Its management used a reflexive practice to critically analyse their actions, in order to improve them.

Observation corroborates this 'commitment that requires that individuals adopt the position of an external observer to identify the postulates and emotions that affect their practice' (Imel, 1992). This reflexive practice represents deliberate learning. Indigo's founder continually questioned his role, his approach, which he deliberately made open and mutable.

At the organizational level, this conscious management of knowledge was translated into a certain latitude enjoyed by its members, the possibility of exchanging roles, and an organic development of its structures. At the strategic level, Maurice Botbol was an 'articulator'. His favourite dimension was the tacit. His knowledge was organic, in the same way as the impetuses he gave to his organization were. Botbol wanted to be a 'reflexive practitioner' (Schön, 1983), of whom 'the action of knowing is inscribed in action' (Schön, 1988). On the knowledge matrix, the path taken begins in the individual and tacit dimension. At first its articulations are endogenous. They take place in the realm of thought, reducing externalities to a minimum. Then they enter a phase of socialization; they mix creatively with the stimuli offered by the environment, feed themselves, articulate themselves anew with collective and tacit elements of others' knowledge. But the small organization encountered a difficult transition. Although their policy normally was to wait until they had 'a convergence of concordant elements', they moved on to the tangible dimension, and wrote and published what remained in a precarious balance of blurred articulations.

Two worlds entered in collision as Indigo was confronted by the legal challenge. The legal world relied on tangible facts, on the veracity of the evidence presented, on that 'which can be expressed formally and without ambiguity'. On one hand, it required an explicitation that could not be put off; on the other hand the disorientation of having to 'counter-articulate', to unpack a whole body of knowledge that had been progressively assembled over a number of years.

This collision of the tacit and the explicit worlds was also found in Indosuez's New York offices. This time we saw an organization wanting to apply deliberate learning. I chose to follow the small group of experts from the Drexel-Lambert company, whom Indosuez had introduced into the company in the hope of procuring their knowledge of derivatives and the North American market. But this knowledge was intangible. There were no recipes, no rules, no imitable knowledge but, in the way that a technician's knowledge is based on experience, on know-how that is intuitive but not very imitable, the Drexelites' knowledge was organic, indissociable from the body in which it was lodged. The environment into which this knowledge was to be filtered was institutionalized and rigid, and the organization that received it tried to chain this knowledge down, where simple ties were all that were necessary. The experts' individual and tacit knowledge could not be articulated in a rigid knowledge dynamics. The organization reinforced its rules, surrounding this new organic element with a hedge of procedures and combinations that it didn't adopt. On their side, the new arrivals were rebellious about the combination of their activities with those of the group. They didn't speak the same language. Understanding perhaps that 'individuals with different cognitive styles, different tolerances to ambiguity, and different emotional flexibilities produce very different representations of the same reality' (Hedberg, 1981: 22), Indosuez's director undertook to resume the dialogue. But some things cannot be brought out into the open, because they are inscribed in a community of practice that cannot tolerate them, because intuitively, perhaps unconsciously, this was how the emergent challenge was raised. In fact, we found that the director gradually integrated, or absorbed, his interlocutors' tacit repertories. He too, like Indigo's founder, was an 'articulator' of the tacit. As an intangible matrix of relations between the two conflicting parties developed, the ambiguity was assuaged. The intangible dimension becomes a mirror of the tangible, acting as an antithetical process that stabilizes the collectivity.

We came across a third collision of the tacit and the explicit worlds in Australia, at Qantas Airways. This time it was not particularly managers, but an entire collectivity which revealed its inherence. We can, however, distinguish here between two forms of *invisible knowledge*: that of 'we don't know that we know', and that of 'we no longer know what we know' – present and reminiscent. Here, the trajectory taken by organizational knowledge dives into a tacit dimension that very quickly appears familiar to it. The conscious inherence concealed an unconscious inherence, that of culture and organizational history, those repertories of action learnt without people being aware they have learnt them (Thorndike and Rock, 1934). The organization, facing a turbulent environment and a globalization whose rhythm was exceeding all its estimates, first merged with Australian Airlines (Australia's domestic airline), and then with British Airways. But these organizational changes had very little effect 'below the organizational surface' (Moullet, 1992) – the inertia acquired by knowledge. Organizations think in terms of 'strategies and structures', responding anxiously to a paradigm of which the evidence is only too well established, and abandoning the renewal or regeneration of their knowledge dynamics. The combination of explicit knowledge that is imposed on a founding articulation of the company's tacit knowledge fails and little by little, knowledge returns to the paths it has never forgotten, those of communities of practice, of clans, tribes and shared histories, that make up the invisible fabric of all organizational knowledge. Once again, the ambiguity was assuaged.

The fourth and last collision of the tacit and explicit worlds was that encountered by Pechiney in Guinea at the end of the 1950s. This time we were able to observe the full course of the phenomenon, not as the events took place, but with the benefit of hindsight which history offers. As with Indigo, the ambiguity stemmed from an emergent challenge. Pechiney went to Guinea to seek bauxite in response to the demands of a combinative technique. The paradigm in which it set itself up, step by step and by trial and error, in the years immediately following the Second World War, was that of formal statements, topographic maps and geological reports. These explicit elements were bound together – combined and prescribed – by a succession of agendas and plans. Operations began fairly soon after, as did Guinea's demand for independence. Pechiney's employees in Guinea knew things were changing; at least, they knew 'more than they could express' (Polanyi, 1966a). And here we came across another 'articulator': an emissary sent by Paris to see and to understand, and to propose solutions. He was a translator of the tacit, a reader of this knowledge that is invisible to some and visible to others. His behaviour, his reports, enable us to establish a new distinction between two forms of invisible knowledge: the permanent and the transitory. This transitory tacit knowledge provides 'islands of respite' as actors make efforts at sense-making. They allow actors to take an 'option on time', to temporarily suspend their decisions, to avoid 'fossilizing' their knowledge – the constant concern of Indigo's founder – and to proceed to new articulations. It is these reservoirs of knowledge that enable us to avoid questions of what is true or false. Through them we enter into 'the game of ruse, concealment, illusion; of tricks that we indulge in between our different selves . . . in the multiplicity of a knowing being' (Morin, 1986: 225). This is our live memory, our RAM, our backup, which we can dip into but cannot rely on. Hence, tacit knowledge does not need to be verbalized to be acted, any more than the imaginations of organizations need to be awakened and made explicit to be put into practice. Contrary to action-research suggestions on change, tacit resources are more effective when left aside from the explicitation processes of organizations. Yet, their embodiment in socialization needs attentive care. It responds to a logic of mobility, of mutation, and does not outlive these metamorphoses. Tacit resources enabled Pechiney to stick to its schedule, to obtain, by successive articulations, tacit agreement for the continuation of its project.

Changing knowledge modes

When faced with disconcerting situations, the four organizations that we have studied adopt dominant modes of knowledge, but it is in their ability to change these rapidly at the appropriate moment that their success lies. These transitions are not easy, however. They are expensive. They require that organizations engage in processes that will allow them to 'learn to unlearn and relearn' (Hedberg, 1981: 23).

This 'agility', that allows us to slip from one knowledge mode to another, depends on several factors. The vehicles must correspond to the transition being undertaken. These vehicles can be an individual – an 'articulator' like Indigo's founder, Pechiney's emissary, and Indosuez's leader. But this operator can equally be a collectivity, as in the Qantas case, where the collectivity spontaneously re-adopted a tacit knowledge dynamics to confront the ambiguity. On the other hand, this transition presupposes an organizational configuration to facilitate it. Here we find the link between the behavioural and the cognitive. If it is imperative to thaw knowledge to facilitate its re-articulation in the intangible, the organization itself has to be able to be 'thawed' to liberate the phenomenon from it. The organizations studied drew lessons from these disconcerting periods. Qantas adopted informal consultation over the telephone for its new decision-making; Indosuez preserved a matrix functioning by linking its directors to the trading room; Pechiney tried to reform its information system by establishing periodic meetings to discuss its prospects. We finally uncover a principle of the inherence of knowledge to the organization, and vice versa, of the organization to its knowledge. And so it appears essential that organizations learn to move their knowledge, when they themselves begin to move.

To foster unlearning, Indigo's founder refused to fossilize his knowledge into extensive archives. He preferred a dynamic fog to a reassuring cemetery. It is not only one but an entire series, indeterminate and incomplete, of 'secondary socializations' (Berger and Luckmann, 1966: 138) which are implemented according to roles that the organization must 'absorb' if it is to achieve its goals. Tacit knowledge is here *instrumental*. This is not the instrumentality of an automatism – which enables one to accomplish a task unconsciously, by liberating the capacity to undertake another – but an instrumentality consciously conferred upon knowledge that is by nature unconscious.

Strategy sometimes consists in establishing *temporary articulations* to avoid fossilizing knowledge into restrictive statements, and so as to take tactical advantage of their unfinished or mutable character. Strategy sometimes consists in stimulating a *permanent articulation* aimed at leaving a situation in a state of equilibrium that is precarious in nature but durable over time (the tacit collective agreement in Guinea). We have had to correct the notion of articulation introduced by Nonaka. Direct observation shows that not all articulation is systematically for the purpose of constituting explicit knowledge. Two tacit knowledge forms articulated together can endure either in the tacit dimension or in a hybrid state. These strategies are implemented by bending the organizational knowledge: actors capable of changing cognitive styles, of modifying their absorption of the world in which they evolve, according to whether they require visibility or invisibility, tangibility or intangibility, collective or individual processes; seasoned navigators of the dimensions of knowledge.

Vertiginous matter, essential to the competitiveness of organizations

'Complexity renders us sensitive to dormant evidence: to the impossibility of detouring knowledge's uncertainty . . . it exhumes and reanimates the innocent questions that we have been trained to forget and to despise' (Morin, 1986: 383) – because nothing exhausts knowledge, and nothing is exhausted by it. 'In every case, no matter how it is done, knowledge establishes a compromise – based on mutual concessions and reciprocal renunciations – with reality' (Morin, 1986: 221). On one hand we have organizations that are fond of the visible; on the other are those that are fond of the invisible. Nevertheless, what these organizations have in common are numerous and dense connections, close to Geertz's 'thick descriptions' (1984, 1986), that do not allow any detail, any meaning, to escape them. Their preoccupation with making links between their knowledge is constant: *mechanical* and *combinative* for organizations fond of the visible, *organic* and *articulatory* for organizations fond of the invisible. The organizations studied escape ambiguity when they cease concentrating on the *reduction* of complexity, but, on the contrary, direct their efforts towards its *penetration*. The comprehension and management of organizational knowledge is a complex task. This book has attempted to observe this knowledge in motion in the hope of promoting the study of puzzled, or disconcerted, organizations. While being investigated, these organizations were invited to continually associate cognitive ideas with structural; to include – in all of its dimensions – knowledge as both object and subject of the formulation, the implementation and the control of their strategies.

Like the Borges character wandering in the 'Circular Ruins', we cannot but observe how much 'the enterprise of modeling the incoherent and vertiginous matter [of which the unconscious is composed] is the most arduous that a man could tackle, even if he penetrates all its enigmas of higher and lower orders: a lot more arduous than to weave a cord of sand or to sell a faceless wind' (Borges, 1974: 56). The unconscious dimension of knowledge still resists us, as it resists the scientist who attempts to elucidate the brain's functioning (Morin, 1986), or the philosopher who cannot solve the problem of the knowing and the knowable subject (Reber, 1993: 147–50), or organizational sciences that try to penetrate 'the thinking organization' (Sandelands and Stablein, 1987).

The main point of this book is to resist prescriptions which force tacit knowledge into destructive explicitations. Yet our findings do not escape imperfection. Some of the links drawn between the organization and its knowledge are perhaps only 'cords of sand'. *Unintentional cognition* can be compared to a grain of sand detached from one of its ephemeral bonds, and able at any given time to block a complex machines. It escapes tools, observable categories, the reflexive practice of actors. A lot of cognitive processes 'work' far beyond normative notions of rationality and logic, and entirely outside the field of the conscious. The dialectic is one of rigidity and fluidity, as much in organizational dispositions as in the dynamics of knowledge.

In attempting to penetrate organizational knowledge, I have encountered organizations that are unequal in the face of ambiguity. Successfully commingling complex organizational and cognitive dispositions, some flourish in the intangible while others labour to institute the processes that could enable them to learn and to unlearn. The ambiguity lies, ultimately, in this collision of the tacit and the explicit, which some handle swiftly by shifting their knowing mode, whereas others suffer until they realize how much they misunderstand the knowable.

Bibliography

Aguilar, F. (1967) *Scanning the Business Environment*, New York: Macmillan.

Alesina, A. and Cukierman, A. (1990) 'The politics of ambiguity', *Quarterly Journal of Economics*, 105: 829–850.

Alvesson, M. (1993) 'Organizations as rhetoric: knowledge-intensive firms and the struggle with ambiguity', *Journal of Management Studies*, 30: 997–1015.

Ames, E. and Reiter, S. (1961) 'Distributions of correlation coefficients in economic time series', *Journal of the American Statistical Association*, 56: 637–656.

Anderson, J.R. (1976) *Language, Memory and Thought*, Hillsdale, NJ: Erlbaum.

Anderson, J.R. (1983) *The Architecture of Cognition*, Cambridge, MA: Harvard University Press.

Argyris, C. and Schön, D.A. (1978) *Organizational Learning: A Theory of Action Perspective*, Reading, MA: Addison-Wesley.

Argyros, A.J. (1993) 'Chaos versus contingency theory: epistemological issues in Orwell's *1984*', *Mosaic*, 26 (1): 109 ff.

Ashby, W.R. (1970) 'Analysis of the system to be modeled', in R.M. Stodgill (ed.), *The Process of Model Building in the Behavioural Sciences*, London: Norton. Chapter 6.

Astley, W.G. (1985) 'Administrative science as socially constructed truth', *Administrative Science Quarterly*, 30: 497–513.

Astley, W.G. and Van de Ven, A.H. (1983) 'Central perspectives and debates in organization theory', *Administrative Science Quarterly*, 28: 245–273.

Axelford, R.M. (ed.) (1976) *Structure of Decision: The Cognitive Maps of Political Elites*, Princeton, NJ: Princeton University Press.

Baars, B.J. (1986) *The Cognitive Revolution in Psychology*, New York: Guilford.

Bachelard, G. (1989) *La Formation de l'esprit scientifique: contribution à une psychanalyse de la connaissance objective*, Paris: Librairie Philosophique J. Vrin.

Baden-Fuller, C. and Stopford, J. (1990) 'Corporate rejuvenation', *Journal of Management Studies*, 27 (4): 399–415.

Baden-Fuller, C. and Stopford, J.M. (1994) *Rejuvenating the Mature Business. The Competitive Challenge*, Boston, MA: Harvard Business School Press.

Bailyn, L. (1993) 'Patterned chaos in human resource management', *Sloan Management Review*, 34: 77–83.

Bantel, K.A. and Jackson, S.E. (1989) 'Top management team and innovations in banking: does the composition of the top team make a difference?', *Strategic Management Journal*, 10: 107–124.

Bargh, J.A. and Uleman, J.S. (1989) *Unintended Thought*, New York: Guilford.

Barnard, C.I. (1938) *The Functions of the Executive*, 2nd edn, Cambridge, MA: Harvard University Press.

Barney, J.B. (1985) 'Dimensions of informal social network structure: toward a contingency theory of informal relations in organizations', *Social Networks*, 7: 1–46.

Barrand, P., Gadeau, R. et al. (1964) *L'Aluminium*, 2 vols, Paris: Eyrolles.

Barry, D. (1994) 'Making the invisible visible: using analogically-based methods to surface the organizational unconscious', *Academy of Management Proceedings*, Dallas, Texas, 14–17 August, pp. 192–196.

Barthes, R. (1972) *Mythologies*, trans. A. Lavers, London: J. Cape.

Bartlett, F.C. (1954) *Remembering: A Study in Experimental and Social Psychology*, Cambridge, MA: Harvard University Press.

Barton, A.H. (1969) *Communities in Disaster: A Sociological Analysis of Collective Stress Situations*, Garden City, NY: Doubleday.

Barton, S. (1994) 'Chaos, self-organization, and psychology', *The American Psychologist*, 49 (1): 5.

Bartunek, J.M. and Moch, M.K. (1987) 'First order, second order, and third-order change and organization development interventions: a cognitive approach', *Journal of Applied Behavioral Science*, 23 (4): 483–500.

Baumard, Ph. (1991a) 'Must one see without being seen?', *Social Intelligence*, 1 (2).

Baumard, Ph. (1991b) *Stratégie et surveillance des environnements concurrentiels*, Paris: Masson.

Baumard, Ph. (1992) 'Concertation et culture collective de l'information', in *Annales des mines*, Paris: Eska.

Baumard, Ph. (1994a) *Oblique Knowledge: The Clandestine Work of Organizations* (research paper, DMSP 228), Paris: Université de Paris-Dauphine.

Baumard, Ph. (1994b) 'From noticing to making sense: using intelligence to develop strategy', *International Journal of Intelligence and Counterintelligence*, 7 (1). New York: Intel.

Baumard, Ph. (1994c) 'Disconcerted organizations: the dynamics of knowledge of organizations facing ambiguity'. Paper presented at the Society of Advanced Socio-Economics Annual Meeting, Paris.

Baumard, Ph. (1995) 'Des Organisations apprenantes? Les dangers de la consensualité', *Revue Française de Gestion*, 105: 49–57.

Baumard, Ph. (1996a) 'Organizations in the fog: an investigation into the dynamics of knowledge', in B. Moingeon and A. Edmondson (eds), *Organizational Learning and Competitive Advantage*, London: Sage Publications.

Baumard, Ph. (1996b) *Prospective à l'usage du manager*, Paris: Litec.

Baumard, Ph. and Spender, J.C. (1995) 'Turning troubled firms around: case-evidence for a Penrosian view of strategic recovery'. Paper presented at the Academy of Management Annual Meeting, Vancouver.

Baumol, W.J. and Benhabib, J. (1989) 'Chaos: significance, mechanism, and economic applications', *Journal of Economic Perspectives*, 3 (1) (winter): 77–105.

Berger, P.L. and Luckmann, T. (1966) *The Social Construction of Reality*, Garden City, NY: Doubleday.

Berry, M. (1983) *Une Technologie invisible? L'impact des instruments de gestion sur l'évolution des systèmes humains*, Paris: Centre de recherche en gestion de l'École Polytechnique.

Bird, A. (1994) *Careers as Repositories of Knowledge: A New Perspective on Boundaryless Careers*, New York University, Working Paper Mgmt 94:9.

Blaug, M. (1980) *The Methodology of Economics*, New York: Cambridge University Press.

Blumer, H. (1939) *Appraisal of Thomas and Znaniecki's 'The Polish Peasant in Europe and America'*, New York: Social Science Research Council.

Blumer, H. (1940) 'The problem of the concept in social psychology', *American Journal of Sociology*, 1: 707–719.

Bocquentin, J. (1994–95) 'Problèmes de relations entre Européens et Africains sur le chantier de Fria (1957–60)', *Cahiers d'Histoire de l'Aluminium*, winter: 78–117.

Bogdan, R.C. and Biklen, S.K. (1982) *Qualitative Research in Education*, Boston: Allyn & Bacon.

Boiney, L.G. (1993) 'The effects of skewed probability on decision making under ambiguity', *Organizational Behavior and Human Decision Processes*, 56: 134–148.

Boland, R.J. and Greenberg, R.H. (1987) *Method and Metaphor in Information Analysis*, Research Paper, Dept. of Accountancy, University of Illinois at Urbana-Champaign.

Borges, J.L. (1974) *Fictions*, London: Calder and Boyars.

Boudon, R. (1989) *The Analysis of Ideology*, trans. M. Slater, Chicago: University of Chicago Press.

Bougon, M.G. (1983) 'Uncovering cognitive maps', in G. Morgan (ed.), *Beyond Method: a Study of Organizational Research Strategies*, Thousand Oaks: Sage.

Bourdieu, P. (1998) *Practical Reasons: on the Theory of Action*, Stanford, CA: Stanford University Press.

Bourgeois, L.J. (1979) 'Toward a method of middle-range theorizing', *Academy of Management Review*, 4: 443–447.

Bowman, E.H. and Kunreuther, H. (1988) 'Post-Bophal behavior at a chemical company', *Journal of Management Studies*, 25 (4): 387–402.

Brewer, W.F. (1974) 'There is no convincing evidence for operant or classical conditions in adult humans', in W.B. Weimer and D.S. Palermo (eds), *Cognition and the Symbolic Processes*, Hillsdale, NJ: Erlbaum. pp. 1–42.

Brooks, L.R. (1978) 'Nonanalytic concept formation and memory for instances', in E. Rosch and B.B. Lloyd (eds), *Cognition and Categorization*, New York: Wiley.

Brown, J.S. and Duguid, P. (1991) 'Organizational learning and communities of practice: toward a unified view of working, learning and innovation', *Organization Science*, 2 (1): 40–57.

Brown, M. and Webb, J.N. (1941) *Seven Stranded Coal Towns*, Washington, DC: Federal Works Agency, Works Progress Administration, Research Monograph 23.

Brun, W. and Teigen, K.H. (1988) 'Verbal probabilities: ambiguous, context-dependent, or both?', *Organizational Behavior and Human Decision Processes*, 41: 390–404.

Buckley, P.J. and Casson, M. (1988) 'A theory of cooperation in international business', *Management International Review*, special issue: 19–38.

Bulwer-Lytton, E. (1829) *The Disowned*, in *The Complete Works*, Vol. II, New York: Thomas Crowell.

Burke, W.W. and Church, A.H. (1992) 'Managing change, leadership style, and intolerance to ambiguity: a survey of organization development practitioners', *Human Resource Management*, 31: 301–318.

Bygrave, W.D. (1993) 'Theory building in the entrepreneurship paradigm', *Journal of Business Venturing*, 8 (3): 255 ff.

Camara, S-S. (1976) *La Guinée sans la France*, Paris: Presses de la Fondation Nationale des Sciences Politiques.

Carney, C. (1993) 'Community and organisation capacity: the key to disaster response and recovery: Des Moines marshalled its resources to cope with flood', *Public Management*, 75: 11–14.

Carrier, D. (1992) 'A methodology for pattern modeling nonlinear macro-economic dynamics', *Journal of Economic Issues*, 26 (March): 221–242.

Castaneda, C. (1968) *The Teachings of Don Juan: a Yaqui Way of Knowledge*, Los Angeles: University of California Press.

Castaneda, C. (1974) *Le Voyage a Ixtlan: les leçons de Don Juan*, Paris: Gallimard, Collection Témoins.

Céline, L.-F. (1980) *Journey to the End of the Night*, trans. R. Manheim, London: J. Calder.

Charue-Duboc, F. (ed.) (1995) *Des Savoirs en action. Contribution de la recherche en gestion*, Paris: L'Harmattan.

Coase, R.H. (1937/1987) 'The nature of the firm', *Economica*, 4 (1937), pp. 386–405; French translation in *Revue Française d'Economie*, 2 (1) (winter 1987): 133–157.

Coats, D.W. (1985) *Natural Phenomena Hazards Modeling Project: Extreme Wind/ Tornado Hazard Models for Department of Energy Sites*, Livermore, CA and Springfield, VA: Lawrence Livermore Laboratory, University of California.

Cohen, J. (1960) 'A coefficient of agreement for normal scales', *Educational & Psychological Measurement*, 20 (1): 37–46.

Crozier, M. and Friedberg, E. (1980) *Actors and Systems: the Politics of Collective Action*, trans. A. Goldhammer, Chicago: University of Chicago Press.

Crutchfield, J.P. and McNamara, B.S. (1987) 'Equations of motions from a data series', *Complex Systems*, 1: 417–452.

Curle, A. (1972) *Mystics and Militants: A Study of Awareness, Identity and Social Action*, London: Tavistock.

Curley, S.P., Yates, J.F. and Abrams, R.A. (1986) 'Psychological sources of ambiguity avoidance', *Organizational Behavior and Human Decision Processes*, 38: 230–256.

Cyert, R.M. and March, J.G. (1963) *A Behavioral Theory of the Firm*, Englewood Cliffs, NJ: Prentice-Hall.

Dacey, R. (1976) *The Role of Ambiguity in the Manipulation of Voter Behaviour, Theory and Decision*, 10 (4): 265–279.

Daft, R.L. and Weick, K.E. (1984) 'Toward a model of organizations as interpretation systems', *Academy of Management Review*, 9 (2): 284–295.

De Groot, A.D. (1965) *Thought and Choice in Chess*, The Hague: Mouton.

De Groot, A.D. (1966) 'Perception and memory versus thinking', in B. Kleinmuntz (ed.), *Problem Solving*, New York: Wiley.

Dedijer, S. (1975) *Social Intelligence: A Comparative Social Sciences Approach to an Emerging Social Problem*, Darmouth, NH, cahier de recherche.

Dedijer, S. (1989) *Self-Deception in Government and Management*, Lund Institutet för Ekonomisk Forskning, Research Paper.

Demos, R. (1960) 'Lying to oneself', *Journal of Philosophy*, 57: 5–32.

Denton, T.A., Diamond, G.A., Helfant, R.H., Khan, S. and Karagueuzian, H. (1990) 'Fascinating rhythm: a primer on chaos theory and its application to cardiology', *American Heart Journal*, 120 (6): 1419 ff.

Détienne, M. and Vernant, J.P. (1978) *Cunning Intelligence in Greek Culture and Society*, trans. J. Lloyd, Hassocks: Harvester Press.

Dewey, J. (1922) *Human Conduct and Nature: An Introduction to Social Psychology*, London: George Allen & Unwin.

Dilman, I. (1972) 'Self-deception', in I. Dilman and D.Z. Phillips (eds), *Sense and Delusion*, London: Routledge & Kegan Paul. pp. 62–92.

DiMaggio, P.J. and Powell, W.W. (1983) 'The iron cage revisited: Institutional isomorphism and collective rationality in organizational fields', *American Sociological Review*, 48: 147–160.

Doi, T. (1985) *The Anatomy of Self*, Tokyo: Kodansha.

Donovan, G.M. (1986) 'Evidence, intelligence and the Soviet threat', *International Journal of Intelligence and Counter Intelligence*, 1 (2): 1–28. New York: Intel Publishing Group.

Dretske, F. (1981) *Knowledge and the Flow of Information*, Cambridge, MA: MIT Press.

Drummond, H. (1992) 'Triumph or disaster: what is reality?', *Management Decision*, 30 (8): 29–33.

Dumez, H. and Jeunemaître, A. (1995) 'Savoirs et décisions: réflexions sur le mimétisme stratégique', in F. Charue-Duboc (ed.), *Des Savoirs en action. Contribution de la recherche en gestion*, Paris: L'Harmattan.

Duncan, R.B. and Weiss, A. (1979) 'Organizational learning: implications for organizational design', in B. Staw (ed.), *Research in Organizational Behavior*, Vol. I, Greenwich, CT: JAI Press. pp. 75–123.

Eco, U. (1990) *The Limits of Interpretation*, Bloomington: Indiana University Press.

Edelman, M. (1988) *Political Language: Words That Succeed and Policies That Fail*, New York: Academic Press.

Einhorn, H.J. and Hogarth, R.M. (1986) 'Decision making under ambiguity', *Journal of Business* (Chicago, IL), 59 (2): 225–250.

Eisenhardt, K.M. (1989) 'Building theories from case study research', *Academy of Management Review*, 14 (4): 532–550.

Eisenhardt, K.M. and Bourgeois, L.J. (1988) 'Politics of strategic decision making in high-velocity environments: toward a midrange theory', *Academy of Management Journal*, 31 (4): 737–770.

Ekman, P. (1985) *Telling Lies: Clues to Deceit in the Marketplace, Politics and Marriage*, New York: Norton.

Ekstedt, E. (1989) *Knowledge Renewal and Knowledge Companies* (Research Report 22), Uppsala: Uppsala Papers in Economic History, Uppsala University.

Engle, S.L. (1994) 'Social networks and Barnard's informal organizations'. Paper presented at the Academy of Management Annual Meeting, Dallas, 11–16 August.

Eriksen, C.W. (1958) 'Unconscious processes', in M.R. Jones (ed.), *Nebraska Symposium on Motivation*, Lincoln: University of Nebraska Press. pp. 169–278.

Fagre, N. and Wells, Jr., L.T. (1982) 'Bargaining power of multinationals and host governments', *Journal of International Business Studies*, 3: 9–23.

Fahey, L. and King, W.R. (1977) 'Environmental scanning for corporate planning', *Business Horizons*, 20 (4): 61–71.

Farmer, J.D. and Sidorowitch, J.J. (1988) 'Exploiting chaos to predict the future and reduce noise', in Y.C. Lee (ed.), *Evolution, Learning and Cognition*, New York: World Cognition.

Feyerabend, P. (1979) *Contre la méthode: esquisse d'une théorie anarchiste de la connaissance*, Paris: Editions du Seuil.

Fineman, S. (ed.) (1993) *Emotion in Organizations*, London: Sage Publications.

Fingarette, H. (1969) *Self-Deception*, London: Routledge & Kegan Paul.

Fischer, H.W. (1992) *The Impact of Media Blame Assignation on the EOC Response to Disaster: a Case Study of the Response to the April 26, 1991 Andover (Kansas) Tornado*, Boulder, CO: Natural Hazards Research & Applications Information Center, University of Colorado.

Fischhoff, B. (1982) 'For those condemned to study the past: heuristics and biases in hindsight', in D. Kahneman, A. Tversky and P. Slovic (eds), *Judgment under Uncertainty: Heuristics and Biases*, Cambridge: Cambridge University Press. p. 343.

Fishbein, M. and Ajzen, I. (1975) *Belief, Attitude, Intention and Behavior*, Reading, MA: Addison-Wesley.

Fiske, S.T. and Linville, P.W. (1980) 'What does the schema concept buy us?', *Personal Psychology and Social Psychology Bulletin*, 6: 543–557.

Fombrun, C. (1992) *Turning Points. Creating Strategic Change in Corporations*, New York: McGraw-Hill.

Forbes, G.S. (1978) *The Cabot, Arkansas Tornado of March 29, 1978*, Chicago: Satellite & Mesometeorology Research Project, Dept. of the Geophysical Sciences, University of Chicago.

Forbes, G.S. (1979) *Observations of Relationships between Tornado Structure, Underlying Surface, and Tornado Appearance*, Boston: American Meteorological Society.

Foucault, M. (1972) *The Archaeology of Knowledge*, New York: Pantheon Books.

Foucault, M. (1977) *Discipline and Punish: the Birth of the Prison*, New York: Pantheon Books.

Fredrickson, J.W. (1983) 'Strategic process research: questions and recommendations', *Academy of Management Review*, 8 (4): 565–575.

Freedman, D.H. (1992) 'Is management still a science?', *Harvard Business Review*, 70 (6): 26–39.

Freud, S. (1960) *Jokes and their Relation to the Unconscious* (1905), trans. J. Strachey, London: Routledge & Kegan Paul.

Fritz, C.E. and Marks, E.S. (1954) *Human Reactions in Disaster Situations*, National Opinion Research Center, University of Chicago.

Gardner, H. (1993) *Multiple Intelligences: The Theory in Practice*, New York: Basic Books.

Geertz, C. (1972) *Deep Play: Notes on the Balinese Cockfight*, Indianapolis: Bobbs-Merrill.

Geertz, C. (1973) *The Interpretation of Cultures*, New York: Basic Books.

Geertz, C. (1983) *Local Knowledge: Further Essays in Interpretive Anthropology*, New York: Basic Books.

Geertz, C. (1984) 'Distinguished lecture: anti anti-relativism', *American Anthropologist*, 86: 263–278.

Gergen, K.J. (1986) 'Correspondence versus autonomy in the language of understanding human action', in D.W. Fiske and R.A. Shweder (eds), *Metatheory in Social Science*, Chicago: University of Chicago Press. pp. 136–162.

Gibson, E.J. (1969) *Perceptual Learning and Development*, New York: Appleton-Century-Crofts.

Gibson, J.J. (1979) *The Ecological Approach to Visual Perception*, Boston: Houghton Mifflin.

Gide, A. (1955) *Journal of the Counterfeiters*, New York: Modern Library.

Gignoux, C-J. (1955) *Histoire d'une entreprise française*, Paris: Hachette.

Gioia, D.A. and Poole, P.P. (1984) 'Scripts in organizational behavior', *Academy of Management Review*, 9 (3): 449–459.

Girin, J. (1995) 'Les Agencements organisationnels', in F. Charue-Duboc (ed.), *Des Savoirs en action. Contribution de la recherche en gestion*, Paris: L'Harmattan.

Glaser, B.E. and Strauss, A.L. (1967) *The Discovery of Grounded Theory: Strategies for Qualitative Research*, New York: Aldine de Gruyter.

Glaser, R. (1990) 'The reemergence of learning theory with instructional research', *American Psychologist*, 45: 29–39.

Goleman, D. (1985) *Vital Lies, Simple Truths: The Psychology of Self-Deception*, New York: Simon & Schuster.

Gordon, P.C. and Holoyak, K.J. (1983) 'Implicit learning and generalization of the "mere exposure" effect', *Journal of Personality and Social Psychology*, 45: 492–500.

Graham, A.C. (1989) *Disputes of the Tao: Philosophical Arguments in Ancient China*, LaSalle, IL: Open Court.

Gray, B., Bougon, M. and Donnellon, A. (1985) 'Organizations as constructions and deconstructions of meaning', *Journal of Management*, 11 (2): 185–211.

Greenspoon, J. (1955) 'The reinforcing effects of two spoken sounds on the frequency of two responses', *American Journal of Psychology*, 68: 409–416.

Gregory, R.L. (1988) 'Ambiguities of sense and non-sense', *Perception*, 17 (4): 423–428.

Griffin, D.R. (1982) *Animal Mind, Human Mind*, New York: Springer-Verlag.

Griffin, D.R. (1984) *Animal Thinking*, Cambridge, MA: Harvard University Press.

Griffith, V. and Southworth, H. (1990) 'Chaos theory', *The Banker*, 140: 51 ff.

Griney, P.H. and Norburn, D. (1975) 'Planning for existing markets: perceptions of executives and financial performance', *Journal of the Royal Statistical Society*, Series A, 138: 336–372.

Hagemeyer, B.C. (1994) *Peninsular Florida Tornado Outbreaks (1950–1993)*, Fort Worth, TX: US Dept. of Commerce, National Oceanic and Atmospheric Administration, National Weather Service, Scientific Services Division, Southern Region.

Hamel, G. and Prahalad, K. (1989) 'Strategic Intent', *Harvard Business Review*, May–June: 63–76.

Harbulot, C., Clerc, Ph. and Baumard, Ph. (1994) *Intelligence economique et stratégie des entreprises*, Rapport du Commissariat Général au Plan, sous la Présidence de M. Henri Martre, Paris: Documentation Française.

Harrigan, K.R. (1988) 'Strategic alliances and partner asymmetries', in J.F. Contractor and P. Lorange (eds), *Cooperative Strategies in International Business*, Cambridge, MA: Lexington Books.

Harris, S. and Sutton, R. (1986) 'Functions of parting ceremonies in dying organizations', *Academy of Management Journal*, 29: 5–30.

Hasher, L. and Chromiak, W. (1977) 'The processing of frequency information: an automatic mechanism?', *Journal of Verbal Learning and Verbal Behavior*, 16: 173–184.

Hasher, L. and Zacks, R.T. (1984) 'Automatic processing of fundamental information', *American Psychologist*, 48: 1372–1388.

Hatchuel, A. and Weil, B. (1995) *Experts in Organisations: a Knowledge-Based Perspective on Organisational Change*, trans. L. Libbrecht, Berlin: Walter de Gruyter.

Hedberg, B. (1981) 'How organizations learn and unlearn', in P. Nystrom and W. Starbuck (eds), *Handbook of Organizational Design*, New York: Oxford University Press. pp. 3–27.

Hedberg, B., Nystrom, P.C. and Starbuck, W.H. (1976) 'Camping on seesaws: prescriptions for a self-designing organization', *Administrative Science Quarterly*, 21: 41–65.

Helmholtz, H. (1962) *Treatise on Physiological Optics* (1867), Vol. III, trans. and ed. J.P.C. Southall, New York: Dover.

Henschel, R.L. (1971) 'Sociology and prediction', *American Sociologist*, 6: 213–220.

Herzberg, F. (1987) 'Innovation: where is the relish?', *Journal of Creative Behavior*, 21 (3): 179–192.

Hirsch, F. (1977) *Social Limits to Growth*, London: Routledge & Kegan Paul.

Hofstadter, R. (1955) *Social Darwinism in American Thought*, Boston, MA: Beacon Press.

Hölderlin, F. (1973) *L'Unique*, Paris: Maeght Editeur.

Hölderlin, F. (1987) *La Mort d'Empedocle: texte de la première version de Der Tod des Empedokles* (1798), Toulouse: Ombres.

Holland, J.H., Holoyak, K.J., Nisbett, R.E. and Thagard, P.R. (1986) *Induction: Processes of Inference, Learning and Discovery*, Cambridge, MA: MIT Press.

Hollis, M. (1987) *The Cunning of Reason*, Cambridge: Cambridge University Press.

Huber, G.P. (1984) 'The nature and design of post-industrial organizations', *Management Science*, 30 (8): 928–951.

Huber, G.P. (1991) 'Organizational learning: the contributing processes and the literature', *Organization Science*, 2 (1): 88–115.

Hughes, R.N. and Jefferson, R.C. (1993) *The Tornado: its Structure, Dynamics, Prediction, and Hazards*, Washington, DC: American Geophysical Union.

Hume, D. (1955) *Inquiry concerning Human Understanding* (1894), ed. R. Wilborn, New York: Liberal Art Press.

Husserl, E. (1968) *The Ideas of Phenomenology*, La Hague: Nijhoff.

Ibert, J. (1996) 'Articulation et dynamique des politiques relationnelles entre firmes concurrentes'. Paper presented to the International Association of Strategic Management.

Imel, S. (1992) 'Reflective practice in adult education', *ERIC Digest* 122, ERIC Clearinghouse on Adult, Career and Vocational Education, Columbus, OH, sponsored by the Office of Educational Research and Improvement, Washington, DC, Report no. EDO–CE–92–122.

Isaacs, N. (1950) *The Foundations of Common Sense*, New York: Roy Publishers.

Isenberg, D.J. (1988) 'How senior managers think', in D.E. Bell, H. Raiffa and A. Tversky (eds), *Decision Making: Descriptive, Normative and Prescriptive Interactions*, Cambridge: Cambridge University Press. pp. 525–539.

Jackson, P.L. (1978) *An Investigation of the Spatial Aspects of Tornado Hazard and Mobile Housing Policy in Kansas*, Ann Arbor, MI: Xerox University Microfilms.

Jacoby, L.L. and Dallas, M. (1981) 'On the relationship between autobiographical memory and perceptual learning', *Journal of Experimental Psychology*, 110: 306–340.

Jarillo, C. (1988) 'On strategic networks', *Strategic Management Journal*, 9: 31–41.

Jenkins, J.G. (1933) 'Instruction as a factor of "incidental" learning', *American Journal of Psychology*, 45: 471–477.

Jick, T. (1979) 'Mixing qualitative and quantitative methods: triangulation in action', *Administrative Science Quarterly*, 24: 602–611.

Johnson-Laird, P. (1983) *Mental Models*, Cambridge: Cambridge University Press.

Jones, R.V. (1975) 'The theory of practical joking – an elaboration', *The Institute of Mathematics and its Applications*, University of Aberdeen, 11 (1): 10–17.

Jungk, R. (1961) *Children of the Ashes*, New York: Harcourt, Brace & World.

Kahneman, S.M., Slovic, P. and Tversky, A. (eds) (1982) *Judgment under Uncertainty: Heuristics and Biases*, New York: Cambridge University Press.

Kerr, M.R. (1992) *An Analysis and Application of Tacit Knowledge to Managerial Selection*, Ottawa: National Library of Canada.

Kets de Vries, M.F.R. (1991) 'Exploding the myth that organizations and executives are rational', in Kets de Vries et al., *Organizations on the Couch: Clinical Perspectives on Organizational Behavior and Change*, San Francisco: Jossey Bass.

Kiresuk, T.J. (1993) 'The evaluation of knowledge utilization: placebo and nonspecific effects, dynamical systems, and chaos theory', *Journal of the American Society for Information Science*, 44 (4): 235 ff.

Kirk, J. and Miller, M. (1986) *Reliability and Validity in Qualitative Research*, Qualitative Research Method Series, Newbury Park, CA: Sage Publications.

Kœnig, G. (1990) *Management stratégique. Vision, manœuvres, tactiques*, Paris: Nathan.

Koriat, A. (1993) 'How do we know that we know? The accessibility model of the feeling of knowing?', *Psychological Review*, 100 (4): 609–639. American Psychological Association.

Kotter, J.P. (1979) 'Managing external dependence', *Academy of Management Review*, 4: 87–92.

Kottkamp, R.B. (1990) 'Means for facilitating reflection', *Education and Urban Society*, 22 (2): 182–203.

Krackhardt, D. and Stern, R.N. (1988) 'Informal networks and organizational crises: an experimental simulation', *Social Psychology Quarterly*, 51 (2): 123–140.

Kuhn, T. (1962) *The Structure of Scientific Revolutions*, Chicago: University of Chicago Press.

Kuhn, T. (1972) 'Logic of discovery of psychology of research', in I. Lakatos and A. Musgrave (eds), *Criticism and the Growth of Knowledge*, Cambridge: Cambridge University Press.

Kunst-Wilson, W.R. and Jazonc, R.B. (1980) 'Affective discrimination of stimuli that cannot be recognized', *Science*, 207: 557–558.

Lacouture, J. (1961) *Cinq hommes et la France*, Paris: Editions du Seuil.

Lamourdedieu, M. (1990) 'Carnet de route', *Cahiers d'Histoire de l'Aluminium*, 6 (summer): 60–84. Paris: IHA.

Langer, E. (1978) 'Rethinking the role of thought in social interaction', in J. Harvey, W. Ickes and R. Kidd (eds), *New Directions in Attribution Theory*, Vol. II, Hillsdale, NJ: Erlbaum. pp. 35–58.

Langer, E., Blank, A. and Chanowitz, B. (1978) 'The mindlessness of ostensibly thoughtful action: the role of "placebic" information in interpersonal interaction', *Journal of Personality and Social Psychology*, 36: 635–642.

Lant, T.K., Milliken, F.J. and Batra, B. (1992) 'The role of managerial learning and interpretation in strategic persistence and reorientation: an empirical exploration', *Strategic Management Journal*, 13: 585–608.

Lanzara, G.F. (1983) 'Ephemeral organizations in extreme environments: emergence, strategy, extinction', *Journal of Management Studies*, 20: 71–95.

Larrue, J. (1990–91) 'Fria en Guinée: des aspects humaines d'une industrialisation différente', *Cahiers d'Histoire de l'Aluminium*, 7: 37–49.

Lave, J. and Wenger, É. (1991) *Situated Learning. Legitimate Peripheral Participation*, Cambridge: Cambridge University Press.

Leibniz, G.W. (1697) 'De l'Origine radicale des choses', in L. Prenant (ed.) (1975), *Oeuvres de Leibniz*, Paris: Aubier-Montaigne. pp. 338–345.

Leibowitz, M. (1993) 'The identity crisis at Indosuez US: when patrician French bankers collide with brash ex-Drexel swappers, guess what emerges?', *Investment Dealer's Digest*, 59 (16), 19 April: 20–26.

Leonard-Barton, D. (1990) 'A dual methodology for case studies: synergetic use of a longitudinal single site with replicated multiple sites', *Organization Science*, 1 (3): 248–266.

Lewicki, P. (1986) *Nonconscious Social Information Processing*, New York: Academic Press.

Lichtenstein, E.H. and Brewer, W.F. (1980) 'Memory for goal-directed events', *Cognitive Psychology*, 12: 412–445.

Lifton, R.J. (1967) *Death in Life: Survivors of Hiroshima*, New York: Random House.

Lincoln, Y.S. and Guba, E.G. (1985) *Naturalistic Inquiry*, Beverly Hills, CA: Sage.

Linsky, L. (1983) *Oblique Contexts*, Chicago: University of Chicago Press.

Locke, J. (1894) *An Essay Concerning Human Understanding*, ed. A.C. Fraser, Oxford: Clarendon Press.

Lorenz, E.L. (1963) 'Deterministic non-periodic flow', *Journal of Atmospheric Science*, 20: 130–141.

Lovell, M.C. (1983) 'Data mining', *Review of Economics and Statistics*, 65: 1–12.

McAndrews, M.P. and Moscowitch, M. (1985) 'Rule-based and examplar-based classification in artificial grammar learning', *Memory & Cognition*, 13: 469–475.

McAuliffe, K. (1990) 'Get smart: controlling chaos', *Omni*, 12 (5): 42–49.

Mace, W.M. (1974) 'Gibson's strategy for perceiving: ask not what's inside your head but what your head's inside of', in R. Shaw and J. Bransford (eds), *Perceiving, Acting and Knowing*, Hillsdale, NJ: Erlbaum.

Machlup, F. (1983) 'Semantic quirks in studies of information', in F. Machlup and U. Mansfield (eds), *The Study of Information*, New York: John Wiley.

McLaughlin, B.P. and Oksenberg-Rorty, A. (eds) (1988) *Perspectives on Self-Deception*, Berkeley: University of California Press.

Mandler, J.M. and Parker, R.E. (1976) 'Memory for descriptive and spatial information in complex pictures', *Journal of Experimental Psychology: Human Learning and Memory*, 2: 38–48.

Mannheim, K. (1936) *Ideology and Utopia*, New York: Harcourt.

Mansfield, E. (1961) 'Technical change and the rate of imitation', *Econometrica*, 29: 741–766.

Marcel, A.J. (1983) 'Conscious and unconscious perception: experiments on visual masking and word recognition', *Cognitive Psychology*, 15: 197–237.

March, J.G. (1978) 'Bounded rationality, ambiguity, and the engineering of choice', *Bell Journal of Economics*, 9 (3): 587–607.

March, J.G. (1991) 'Exploration and exploitation in organizational learning', *Organization Science*, 2 (1): 71–87.

March, J.G. and Olsen, J.P. (1976) *Ambiguity and Choice in Organizations*, Bergen: Universitetsforlaget.

March, J.G. and Shapira, Z. (1992) 'Variable risk preferences and the focus of attention', *Psychological Review*, 99 (1): 172–183.

March, J.G. and Simon, H. (1956) *Organizations*, New York: McGraw-Hill.

March, J.G., Sproull, L.S. and Tamuz, M. (1991) 'Learning from samples of one or fewer', *Organization Science*, 2 (1): 1–12.

Marchandise, J. (1990–91) 'Extra muros: histoire de Fria', *Cahiers d' Histoire de l'Aluminium*, 7: 84–6.

Markus, H. (1977) 'Self-schema and processing information about the self', *Journal of Personality and Social Psychology*, 35: 63 ff.

Marquardt, M.J. and Engel, D.W. (1993) 'HRD competencies in a shrinking world', *Training & Development*, 47 (5): 59–65.

Medio, A. (1992) *Chaotic Dynamics: Theory and Applications to Economics*, Cambridge: Cambridge University Press.

Merleau-Ponty, M. (1963) *The Structure of Behaviour*, trans. A. Fisher, Boston: Beacon Press.

Meyer, J.W. and Rowan, B. (1977) 'Institutionalized organizations: formal structure as myth and ceremony', *American Journal of Sociology*, 83 (2): 340–363.

Miles, M.B. and Huberman, A.M. (1984) *Qualitative Data Analysis*, Beverly Hills, CA: Sage Publications.

Milgram, S. (1974) *Obedience to Authority: an Experimental View*, New York: Harper and Row.

Miller, D. (1990) *The Icarus Paradox*, New York: HarperCollins.

Miller, D. and Friesen, P.H. (1980) 'Momentum and revolution in organizational adaptation', *Academy of Management Journal*, 23: 591–614.

Miller, D. and Friesen, P.H. (1984) *Organizations: A Quantum View*, Englewood Cliffs, NJ: Prentice-Hall.

Milliken, F.J. and Starbuck, W.H. (1988) 'Executives' perceptual filters: what they notice and how they make sense', in D. Hambrick (ed.), *The Executive Effect: Concepts and Methods for Studying Top Managers*, Greenwich, CT: JAI Press. pp. 35–65.

Mino, H. (1983) 'KAL tragedy provides insight into Soviet military preparedness', *Business Japan*, 28: 22–26.

Mintzberg, H. and Westley, F. (1992) 'Cycles of organizational change', *Strategic Management Journal*, 13: 39–59.

Mitroff, I.I. and Lyles, M.A. (1980) 'Organizational problem formulation: an empirical case study', *Administrative Science Quarterly*, 25: 102–119.

Mitroff, I. and Mason, R. (1982) 'Business policy and metaphysics: some philosophical considerations', *Academy of Management Review*, 7: 361–371.

Mitroff, I.I. and Pauchant, T.C. (1990a) 'Crisis management: managing paradox in a chaotic world', *Technological Forecasting and Social Change*, 38 (2): 117–135.

Mitroff, I.I. and Pauchant, T.C. (1990b) 'Corporations that prepare for disaster', *Business and Society Review*, 75: 78–79.

Moingeon, B. and Edmondson, A. (eds) (1996) *Organizational Learning and Competitive Advantage*, London: Sage Publications.

Morin, E. (1980) *La Méthode II: la vie de la vie*, Paris: Editions du Seuil.

Morin, E. (1986) *La Méthode III: la connaissance de la connaissance*, Paris: Editions du Seuil.

Morin, E. (1992) *The Nature of Nature*, trans. J.L. Roland Bélanger, New York: P. Lang.

Moullet, M. (1992) *Le Management clandestin*, Paris: InterEditions.

Newell, A. and Simon, H.A. (1972) *Human Problem Solving*, Englewood Cliffs, NJ: Prentice-Hall.

Nisbett, R.E. and Ross, L. (1980) *Human Inferences: Strategies and Shortcomings of Social Judgment*, Englewood Cliffs, NJ: Prentice-Hall.

Nisbett, R.E. and Wilson, T.D. (1977) 'Telling more than we know: verbal reports on mental processes', *Psychological Review*, 84: 231–259.

Nonaka, I. (1988a) 'Creating organizational order out of chaos: self-renewal in Japanese firms', *California Management Review*, 30: 57–73.

Nonaka, I. (1988b) 'Self-renewal of the Japanese firm and the human resource strategy', *Human Resource Management*, 27: 45–62.

Nonaka, I. (1988c) 'Toward middle-up-down management: accelerating information creation', *Sloan Management Review*, 29: 9–18.

Nonaka, I. (1990a) 'Managing innovation as a knowledge creation process'. Presentation at New York University, Stern School of Business, International Business Colloquium.

Nonaka, I. (1990b) 'Redundant, overlapping organization: a Japanese approach to managing the innovation process', *California Management Review*, 32: 27–38.

Nonaka, I. (1991a) 'Managing the firm as information creation process', in *Advances in Information Processing in Organizations*, Vol. IV, Greenwich, CT: JAI Press. pp. 239–275.

Nonaka, I. (1991b) 'The knowledge-creating company', *Harvard Business Review*, 69 (6): 96–104.

Nonaka, I. (1992) 'A management theory of organizational knowledge creation', research paper, original version of Nonaka (1994).

Nonaka, I. (1994) 'A dynamic theory of organizational knowledge creation', *Organization Science*, 5 (1): 14–37.

Nonaka, I. and Hedlund, G. (1991) *Models of Knowledge Management in the West and Japan*, Institute of International Business at the Stockholm School of Economics, Research Paper 9.

Nonaka, I. and Johansson, J.K. (1987) 'Market research the Japanese way', *Harvard Business Review*, 65: 16–18.

Nonaka, I. and Kenney, M. (1991) 'Towards a new theory of innovation management: a case study comparing Canon, Inc. and Apple Computer, Inc.', *Journal of Engineering and Technology Management*, 8: 67–73.

Nonaka, I. and Sullivan, J.J. (1986) 'The application of organizational learning theory to Japanese and American management', *Journal of International Business Studies*, 17: 127–147.

Nonaka, I. and Takeuchi, H. (1995) *The Knowledge Creating Company*, New York: Oxford University Press.

Nyíri, J.K. and Smith, B. (eds) (1988) *Practical Knowledge: Outlines of a Theory of Traditions and Skills*, New York: Croom Helm.

Nystrom, N.C. and Starbuck, W.H. (1984) 'To avoid organizational crisis, unlearn', *Organizational Dynamics*, Spring: 53–65.

Ohmae, K. (1989) 'The global logic of strategic alliances', *Harvard Business Review*, 67 (2): 143–154.

Oksenberg-Rorty, A. (1988) 'The deceptive self: liars, layers, and lairs', in B.P. McLaughlin, and A. Oksenberg Rorty (eds), *Perspectives on Self-Deception*, Berkeley: University of California Press.

Osgood, C.E. (1953) *Method and Theory in Experimental Psychology*, New York: Oxford University Press.

Osterman, K.F. (1990) 'Reflective practice: a new agenda for education', *Education and Urban Society*, 22 (2): 133–152.

O'Toole, J. (1993) *Tornado! 84 Minutes, 94 Lives*, Worcester: Databooks.

Parkhe, A. (1991) 'Interfirm diversity, organizational learning, and longevity in global strategic alliances', *Journal of International Business Studies*, 22: 579–601.

Peach, J.T. and Webb, J.L. (1983) 'Randomly specified macroeconomic models: some implications for model selection', *Journal of Economic Issues*, 17: 697–720.

Perlmutter, H.V. and Heenan, D.A. (1986) 'Cooperate to compete globally', *Harvard Business Review*, March–April: 136 ff.

Perrow, C. (1972) *Complex Organizations*, New York: Newbery Award Records.

Perrow, C. (1984) *Normal Accidents: Living with High-risk Technologies*, New York: Basic Books.

Peters, J. (1991) 'Strategies for reflective practice', in R. Brockett (ed.), *Professional Development for Educators of Adults*, San Francisco: Jossey-Bass.

Pettigrew, A.M. (1973) *The Politics of Organizational Decision Making*, London: Tavistock.

Pfeffer, J. and Salancik, G.R. (1978) *The External Control of Organizations: A Resource Dependence Perspective*, New York: Harper & Row.

Piaget, J. (1980) *Experiments in Contradiction*, trans. D. Coltman, Chicago: University of Chicago Press.

Piaton, R. (1955) 'Pechiney et la concurrence internationale'. Interview with the president of the administrative council of the Compagnie de Produits Chimiques et Électrométallurgiques Pechiney, Paris, *L'Économie*, 481 (11th year), 24 February: 4–6.

Pinfield, L.T. (1986) 'A field evaluation of perspectives on organizational decision-making', *Administrative Science Quarterly*, 31 (3): 414–450.

Poincaré, H. (1993) 'New methods of celestial mechanics', Woodbury, NY: American Institute of Physics.

Polanyi, M. (1966a) *Personal Knowledge: Toward a Post-critical Philosophy*, Chicago: University of Chicago Press.

Polanyi, M. (1966b) *The Tacit Dimension*, Garden City, NY: Doubleday.

Polanyi, M. (1969) *Knowing and Being*, London: Routledge & Kegan Paul.

Pondy, L.R., Boland, R. and Thomas, H. (1988) *Managing Ambiguity and Change*, New York: Wiley.

Porac, J.F. and Howard, T. (1990) 'Taxonomic mental models in competitor definition', *Academy of Management Review*, 15 (2): 224–240.

Porac, J., Baden-Fuller, C. and Howard, T. (1989) 'Competitive groups as cognitive communities: the case of Scottish knitwear manufacturers', *Journal of Management Studies*, 26 (4): 397–416.

Priesmeyer, H.R. (1992a) *Organizations and Chaos: Defining the Methods of Nonlinear Management*, Westport, CT: Quorum Books.

Priesmeyer, H.R. (1992b) *Strategy [computer file]*, Cincinnati, OH: South-Western Pub.

Priesmeyer, H.R. and Baik, K. (1989) 'A potential new planning tool: discovering the patterns of chaos', *Planning Review*, 17: 14–21.

Quinn, J.B. (1980) *Strategies for Change: Logical Incrementalism*, Homewood, IL: Irwin.

Quinn, R.E. and Cameron, K.S. (eds) (1988) *Paradox and Transformation*, Cambridge, MA: Ballinger.

Ramanan, T. (1992) 'The Bhopal tragedy revisited', *Risk Management*, 39: 62–63.

Ransom, H.H. (1973) *Strategic Intelligence*, Morristown, NJ: General Learning Press.

Raphals, L. (1992) *Knowing Words: Wisdom and Cunning in the Classical Traditions of China and Greece*, Ithaca, NY and London: Cornell University Press.

Reber, A.S. (1967) 'Implicit learning of artificial grammars', *Journal of Verbal Learning and Verbal Behavior*, 6: 317–327.

Reber, A.S. (1969) 'Transfer of syntactic structure in synthetic languages', *Journal of Experimental Psychology*, 81: 115–119.

Reber, A.S. (1993) *Implicit Learning and Tacit Knowledge: An Essay on the Cognitive Unconscious*, Oxford Psychology Series no. 19, New York and Oxford: Clarendon Press and Oxford University Press.

Reber, A.S. and Lewis, S. (1977) 'Toward a theory of implicit learning: the analysis of the form and structure of a body of tacit knowledge', *Cognition*, 5: 333–361.

Reber, A.S. and Millward, R.B. (1965) 'Probability learning and memory for event sequences', *Psychonomic Science*, 3: 341–432.

Riveline, C. (1986) 'L'enseignement du dur et l'enseignement du mou', *Gérer et Comprendre*, 5, Paris: Ecole des Mines.

Rose, A. (1992) 'Framing our experience: research notes on reflective practice', *Adult Learning*, 3 (4): 5.

Rosset, C. (1977) *Le Réel: traité de l'idiotie*, Paris: Editions de Minuit.

Rosset, C. (1985) *Le Réel et son double: essai sur l'illusion*, Paris: Gallimard.

Rosset, C. (1991) *Principes de sagesse et de folie*, Paris: Editions de Minuit.

Ruddick, W. (1988) 'Social self-deceptions', in B.P. McLaughin and A. Oksenberg Rorty (eds), *Perspectives on Self-Deception*, Berkeley: University of California Press. pp. 380–389.

Ruelle, D. and Takens, F. (1971) 'On the nature of turbulence', *Communications of Mathematical Physics*, 20: 167–192.

Ruthen, R. (1993) 'Adapting to complexity', *Scientific American*, 268 (1): 130 ff.

Ryle, G. (1945) 'Knowing how and knowing that', *Proceedings of the Aristotelian Society*, 46 (1945–46), pp. 1–16, reproduced in Ryle, *Collected Papers*, London: Hutchinson, 1971. See also Ryle, *The Concept of Mind*, London: Hutchinson, 1949.

Sandelands, L.E. and Stablein, R.E. (1987) 'The concept of organization mind', *Research in the Sociology of Organizations*, 5: 135–161.

Sanders, A.F. (1988) *Michael Polanyi's Post-critical Epistemology: a Reconstruction of Some Aspects of 'Tacit Knowing'*, Amsterdam: Rodopi.

Savit, R. (1988) 'When random is not random: an introduction to chaos in market prices', *Journal of Futures Markets*, 8 (3): 271–290.

Savit, R. (1989) 'and chaotic effects in options prices', *Journal of Futures Markets*, 9: 507–518.

Savona, D. (1992) 'When companies divorce', *International Business*, 5: 48–51.

Scarborough, D.L., Gerard, L. and Cortese, C. (1979) 'Accessing lexical memory: the transfer of word repetition effects across task modality', *Memory and Cognition*, 7: 3–12.

Schank, R.C. and Abelson, R. (1975) *Scripts, Plans, Goals, and Understanding*, Hillsdale, NJ: Erlbaum.

Schelling, T.C. (1960) *The Strategy of Conflict*, Cambridge, MA: Harvard University Press.

Schelling, T.C. (1978) *Micromotives and Macrobehavior*, New York: Norton.

Schön, D. (1983) *The Reflective Practitioner*, New York: Basic Books.

Schön, D. (1988) *Educating the Reflective Practitioner*, San Francisco: Jossey-Bass.

Schoorman, F.D., Bazerman, B. and Atkins, R. (1981) 'Interlocking directorates: a strategy for the management of environment uncertainty', *Academy of Management Review*, 6: 243–251.

Schut, J.H. (1993) 'Managing Murphy's Law: lessons learned from World Trade Center bombing and from other major disasters', *Risk Management*, 40: 58–60.

Schwartz, H.S. (1987) 'On the psychodynamics of organizational disaster: the case of the space shuttle *Challenger*', *Columbia Journal of World Business*, 22: 59–67.

Schwenk, C.R. (1986) 'Information, cognitive biases and commitment to a course of action', *Academy of Management Review*, 11 (2): 298–310.

Schwenk, C.R. (1989) 'Linking cognitive, organizational and political factors in explaining strategic change', *Journal of Management Studies*, 26 (2): 177–187.

Schwenk, C.R. and Lyles, M.A. (1992) 'Top management, strategy and organizational knowledge structures', *Journal of Management Studies*, 29 (2): 155–174.

Schwenk, C.R., Miceli, M.P. and Near, J.P. (1991) 'Who blows the whistle and why?', *Industrial Labor Relations Review*, 45 (1): 113–130.

Scott, W.R. (1981) *Organizations: Rational, Natural and Open Systems*, Englewood Cliffs, NJ: Prentice-Hall.

Scribner, S. (1986) 'Thinking in action: some characteristics of practical thought', in R. Sternberg and R.K. Wagner (eds), *Practical Intelligence: the Nature and Origins of Competence in the Everyday World*, Cambridge: Cambridge University Press. pp. 13–30.

Shenkar, O. and Zeira, Y. (1992) 'Role conflict and role ambiguity of chief executive officers in international joint ventures', *Journal of International Business Studies*, 23 (1): 55–75.

Shlesinger, M. et al. (eds) (1987) *Perspectives in Biological Dynamics and Theoretical Medicine*, New York, NY: New York Academy of Sciences.

Shrivastava, P. (1985) 'The lessons of Bhopal', *Business and Society Review*, 55: 61–62.

Shrivastava, P. and Siomkos, G. (1989) 'Disaster containment strategies', *Journal of Business Strategy*, 10: 26–30.

Sigurdson, J. and Tågerud, Y. (eds) (1992) *The Intelligent Corporation*, London: Taylor Graham.

Simmel, G. (1906) 'The sociology of secrecy and of secret societies', in *Soziologie* (in German) Chapter 5, pp. 337–402, trans. in *American Journal of Sociology*, 11 (4): 441–498.

Simmel, G. (1955) *Conflict*, trans. K. Wolff, Glencoe, IL: Free Press.

Simon, H.A. (1991) 'Bounded rationality and organizational learning', *Organization Science*, 2 (1): 125–134.

Simon, H.A. and Simon, P.A. (1962) 'Trial and error search in solving difficult problems: evidence from the game of chess', *Behavioral Science*, 7: 425.

Smircich, L. (1983) 'Organizations as shared meanings', in L.R. Pondy, P.J. Frost, G. Morgan and T.C. Dandrige (eds), *Organizational Symbolism*, Greenwich, CT: JAI Press. pp. 56–65.

Smircich, L. and Morgan, G. (1980) 'The case for qualitative research', *Academy of Management Review*, 5 (4): 491–499.

Spender, J.C. (1989) *Industry Recipes: The Nature and Source of Management Judgment*, Oxford: Basil Blackwell.

Spender, J.C. (1992) 'Workplace knowledge and the nature of competitive advantage'. Rutgers University, Graduate School of Management, unpublished research paper.

Spender, J.C. (1993) 'Competitive advantage from tacit knowledge: unpacking the concept and its strategic implications', *Proceedings of the Academy of Management Annual Meeting*, Atlanta.

Spender, J.C. (1994) 'Workplace cognition: the individual and collective dimensions'. Research paper for the 2nd International Workshop on Managerial and Organizational Cognition, Brussels.

Stacey, R. (1993) 'Strategy as order emerging from chaos', *Long Range Planning*, 26: 10–17.

Stambler, I. (1991) 'Chaos creates a stir in energy-related R&D', *Research & Development*, 33: 16 ff.

Starbuck, W.H. (1981) 'Organizations and environments', in P. Nystrom and Starbuck, W.H. (eds), *Handbook of Organizations Design*, Oxford: Oxford University Press.

Starbuck, W.H. (1982) 'Congealing oil: inventing ideologies to justify acting ideologies out', *Journal of Management Studies*, 19 (1): 1–27.

Starbuck, W.H. (1983) 'Organizations as action generators', *American Sociological Review*, 48: 91–102.

Starbuck, W.H. (1988) 'Surmounting our human limitations', in R. Quinn and K. Cameron (eds), *Paradox and Transformation: Toward a Theory of Change in Organization and Management*, Cambridge, MA: Ballinger.

Starbuck, W.H. (1992a) 'Learning by knowledge-intensive firms', *Journal of Management Studies*, 29 (6): 713–740.

Starbuck, W.H. (1992b) 'Strategizing in the real world', *International Journal of Technology Management*, Special publication on technological foundations of strategic management, 8 (1/2): 77–85.

Starbuck, W.H. (1993a) 'On behalf of naïveté', Research Paper, New York University.

Starbuck, W.H. (1993b) 'Watch where you step! or, Indiana Starbuck amid the perils of academe (rated PG)', in A.G. Bedeian (ed.), *Management Laureates: A Collection of Autobiographical Essays*, Vol. III, Greenwich, CT: JAI Press.

Starbuck, W.H. and Hedberg, B. (1977) 'Saving an organization from a stagnating environment', in H.B. Thorelli (ed.), *Strategy + Structure = Performance*, Bloomington: Indiana University Press. pp. 249–258.

Starbuck, W.H. and Milliken, F.J. (1988a) 'Executive's perceptual filters: what they notice and how they make sense', in D. Hambrick (ed.), *The Executive Effect: Concepts and Methods for Studying Top Managers*, Greenwich, CT: JAI Press. pp. 35–65.

Starbuck, W.H. and Milliken, F.J. (1988b) '*Challenger*: fine-tuning the odds until something breaks', *Journal of Management Studies*, 25 (4) (July): 319–340.

Starbuck, W.H. and Webster, J. (1988) 'Theory building in industrial and organizational psychology', in C.L. Cooper and I. Robertson (eds), *International Review of Industrial and Organizational Psychology*, Chichester: Wiley. pp. 93–138.

Sternberg, R.J. (1988) *The Triarchic Mind. A New Theory of Human Intelligence*, New York: Viking.

Stevenson, W.B. and Gilly, M.C. (1993) 'Problem-solving networks in organizations: intentional design and emergent structure', *Social Science Research*, 22: 92–113.

Stewart, A. and Gnyawali, D.R. (1994) *An Integrative Framework of Organizational*

Learning: Content, Process and Outcomes. Working Paper Series 732, Joseph M. Katz Graduate School of Business, University of Pittsburgh.

Teece, D.J. (1987) 'Profiting from technological innovation', in D.J. Teece (ed.), *The Competitive Challenge*, Cambridge, MA: Ballinger. pp. 185–219.

Thiétart, R-A. (1990) *La Stratégie d'entreprise*, Paris: McGraw Hill.

Thiétart, R-A. and Forgues, B. (1993) 'Chaos theory and organization science', *Organization Science*, 6 (1): 19–31.

Thomas, T.S. (1980) 'Environmental scanning – the state of the art', *Long Range Planning*, 13 (1): 20–28.

Thomas, W.I. and Znaniecki, F. (1918) *The Polish Peasant in Poland and America*, New York: Alfred A. Knopf.

Thomas, W.I. and Znaniecki, F. (1974) *The Polish Peasant in Europe and America*, New York: Octagon Books.

Thorndike, E.L. and Rock, R.T., Jr. (1934) 'Learning without awareness of what is being learned or intent to learn it', *Journal of Experimental Psychology*, 1: 1–19.

Tiller, J.W. (1983) 'An interpretation of the epistemology of Carlos Castaneda'. Doctoral thesis, New York University.

Toma, L. and Gheorghe, E. (1992) 'Equilibrium and disorder in human decision-making processes: some methodological aspects within the new paradigm', *Technological Forecasting and Social Change*, 41: 401–422.

Torbert, W.R. (1972) *Learning from Experience: Toward Consciousness*, New York: Columbia University Press.

Torbert, W.R. (1976) *Creating a Community of Inquiry: Conflict, Collaboration, Transformation*, New York: Wiley.

Torbert, W.R. (1989) 'Modeling organizational meaning systems', in R.W. Woodman and W.A. Pasmore (eds), *Research in Organizational Change and Development: an Annual Series featuring Advances in Theory, Methodology and Research*, Vol. III, Greenwich, CT: JAI Press.

Tranter, R.A.F. (1989) 'Some lessons from the October 17 quake', *Public Management*, 71: 2–4.

Turner, S.P. (1994) *The Social Theory of Practices: Tradition, Tacit Knowledge and Presuppositions*, Chicago: University of Chicago Press.

Tushman, M.L. and Romanelli, E. (1985) 'Organizational evolution: a meta-morphosis model of convergence and reorientation', in L.L. Cummings and B.M. Staw (eds), *Research in Organizational Behavior*, Vol. VII, Greenwich, CT: JAI Press. pp. 171–222.

Tvede, L. (1992) 'What chaos really means in financial markets', *Futures*, 21: 34–36.

Uleman, J.S. and Bargh, J.A. (1989) *Unintended Though*, New York: Guilford.

Vancil, R.F. (1979) *Decentralization, Managerial Ambiguity by Design: a Research Study and Report*, Homewood, IL: Dow Jones-Irwin.

Vinten, G. (1992) 'Thriving on chaos: the route to management survival', *Management Decision*, 30 (8): 22–28.

Vygotsky, L.S. (1962) *Thought and Language*, Cambridge, MA: MIT Press.

Wagner, R.K. (1991) *Tacit Knowledge Inventory for Managers: Test Booklet*, San Antonio, TX: Psychological Corp. and Harcourt Brace Jovanovich.

Walsh, J.P. (1988) 'Selectivity and selective perception: an investigation of managers' belief structures and information processing', *Academy of Management Journal*, 31 (4): 873–896.

Walsh, J.P., Henderson, J. and Deighton, J. (1988) 'Negotiated belief structures and decision performance: an empirical investigation', *Organizational Behavior and Human Decision Process*, 42: 194–216.

Watzlawick, P. (1976) *How Real is Real?: Confusion, Disinformation, Communication*, New York: Random House.

Watzlawick, P. (1984) *The Invented Reality: How do We Know What we Believe We Know? Contributions to Constructivism*, New York: Norton.

Watzlawick, P., Weakland, J. and Fisch, J. (1974) *Change: Principles of Problem Formation and Problem Resolution*, New York: W.W. Norton.

Wegner, D.M. and Vallacher, R.R. (1977) *Implicit Psychology: An Introduction to Social Cognition*, New York: Oxford University Press.

Weick, K.E. (1979) *The Social Psychology of Organizing*, Reading, MA: Addison-Wesley.

Weick, K.E. (1989) 'Theory construction as disciplined imagination', *Academy of Management Review*, 14 (4): 516–531.

Weick, K.E. (1990) 'The vulnerable system: an analysis of the Tenerife air disaster', *Journal of Management*, 16: 571–593.

Weick, K.E. (1995) *Sensemaking in Organizations*, Thousand Oaks, CA: Sage Publications.

Weick, K.E. and Roberts, K.H. (1993) 'Collective mind in organizations: heedful interrelating on flight decks', *Administrative Science Quarterly*, 38 (3): 357 ff.

Wicker, L.J. (1990) *A Numerical Simulation of a Tornado-scale Vortex in a Three-dimensional Cloud Model*, Arbor, MI: University Microfilms.

Wilensky, H.L. (1967a) 'Organizational intelligence', in *International Encyclopedia of Social Sciences*, New York: Macmillan and The Free Press. pp. 319–334.

Wilensky, H.L. (1967b) *Organizational Intelligence*, New York: Basic Books.

Williams, D. (1993) 'A shrewd and cunning authority', *Antioch Review*, 51 (2): 214 ff.

Williamson, O.E. (1975) *Markets and Hierarchies: Analysis and Antitrust Implications*, New York: Free Press.

Winter, S.G. (1987) 'Knowledge and competence as strategic assets', in D.J. Teece (ed.), *The Competitive Challenge*, Cambridge, MA: Ballinger. pp. 159–184.

Yates, B. (1983) *The Decline and Fall of the American Automobile Industry*, New York: Vintage Press.

Yin, R. (1984) *Case Study Research: Design and Methods*, Applied Social Research Method Series, Vol. V, Beverly Hills, CA: Sage Publications.

You, Y. (1993) 'What can we learn from chaos theory? An alternative approach to instructional systems design', *Educational Technology Research and Development*, 41 (3): 17.

Zand, D.E. (1981) *Information, Organization and Power: Effective Management in the Knowledge Society*, New York: McGraw-Hill.

Ziman, J.M. (1987) 'The problem of "problem choice"', *Minerva*, 25: 92–106.

Case Study References

Qantas, or collective wisdom

Anonymous, 'Australian Airlines loses identity', *Aviation Week & Space Technology*, 139 (19): 35 (8 November 1993).

Anonymous, 'Qantas considers cutting 1,835 jobs', *New York Times*, section D: 4 (19 January 1993).

Anonymous, 'Qantas names new managing director', *Aviation Week & Space Technology*, 139 (6): 36 (9 August 1993).

Bryant, A., 'British Airways tumbles by 57.4% net', *New York Times*, section D: 4 (19 May 1993).

Cromie, A., 'At the top, a man obsessed', *Business Review Weekly*, 11 December 1992: 41–42.

Deans, A., 'Flight to a merger: Australia's main airlines to form a mega-carrier', *Far-Eastern Economic Review*, 1993.

Feldman, J.M., 'Where the action is', *Air Transport World*, 28 (8): 64–73 (August 1991).

Findlay, I., *The Australian Airline Industry*, Sydney: First Boston, June 1992.

Grosvald, S.A., 'The inside story', *Frequent Flyer*, November 1992: 28–39.

Karos, P.P. and Honsvald, G.M., 'Qantas's position in globalizing airline industry', *First Boston Equity Research*, Sydney, 16 September 1992.

Kyung-Mi, S., 'Korea attracts retinue of foreign carriers', *Business Korea*, 8 (10): 52–57 (April 1991).

Shenon, P., 'Asians seek to restrict US airlines', *New York Times*, section 1: 39 (10 July 1993).

Shenon, P., 'Australia asks for air accord', *New York Times*, section D: 21 (24 June 1993).

Stevenson, R.W., 'European airlines nearing decision on possible merger', *New York Times*, section D: 7 (29 March 1993).

Vizard, M., 'Qantas takes off with notes', *Computer World*, 27 (45): 49 (8 November 1993).

Westlake, M. and Jeffries, B., 'Aviation 1991: airborne uncertainty', *Far-Eastern Economic Review* (Hong Kong), 151 (20): 31–54 (16 May 1991).

Woolsey, J.P., 'All Nippon's international-growth barriers', *Air Transport World*, 29 (5): 58–62 (May 1992).

Young, S., 'Foreign airline systems face uphill battle', *Business Korea*, 8 (8): 44–47 (February 1991).

Organizations

BDW Aviation Services, Asia Pacific Aviation and Tourism Consulting Pty, PO Box N777, Grosvenor Place, Sydney, NSW 2000, Australia.

CS FIRST BOSTON Australia Equities Limited, Level 21, 60 Margaret Street, PO Box N686, Grosvenor Place, Sydney, NSW 2000, Australia

DEPARTMENT OF TRANSPORT AND COMMUNICATIONS, Aviation Division, GPO Box 594, Canberra, ACT 2601, Australia.

THE ABC WORLD AIRWAYS GUIDE, The Australian Broadcasting Commission, Customer Services, Reed Travel Group, Church Street, Dunstable, Bedfordshire LU5 4HB, United Kingdom.

Archives and documents

The Qantas Story: A History of Australia's International Airline, Qantas, 1996.
Weekly Schedule Performance Report, 13 April 1993.
PLANET Prototype for Schedule Planning.
1993/94 Business Plan – CIO Mandate, CioPlan/081/March 1993.
Cabin Crew Operating Patterns, Bid Period 0031, 31 May 1993 to 25 July 1993.
General flow chart, department charts, reports and memos.

Indigo, or navigating in the tacit

Ackermann, R.K., 'Intelligence aims to amassing overt information', *Signal*, August 1993.

Allen, T.B. and Polmar, N., *Merchants of Treason: America's Secrets for Sale*, New York: Delacorte Press, 1988.

Baram, M.S., 'Trade secrets: what price is loyalty', *Harvard Business Review*, November 1988: 66–74.

Baumard, Ph., 'Economic cultures, economic intelligence, and national economies of scale'. Address at the 1993 OSS Symposium on National Security and National Competitiveness. Available from Open Source Solutions, 1914 Autumn Chase Court, Falls Church, VA, 22943–1735.

Baumard, Ph., 'Must one see without being seen?', *Social Intelligence*, 1 (2). London: Taylor Graham, 1991.

Dedijer, S., 'Secrecy in the life of the product: a design for product secrecy management', Research Policy Institute, Lund University, research paper, 1976.

Ewing, L.J., 'Keeping the lid on secrets', *Risk Management*, 29 (11), November 1992: 18–25.

Goleman, D., *Vital Lies, Simple Truths: The Psychology of Self Deception*, New York: Simon & Schuster, 1985.

Sigurdson, J. and Tågerud, Y. (eds), *The Intelligent Corporation: The Privatisation of Intelligence*, London: Taylor Graham, 1992.

Simmel, G., 'The sociology of secrecy and of secret societies', *American Journal of Sociology*, 11 (4) 1906: 469.

Steele, R. (ed.), *National Security and National Competitiveness*, Washington: Open Source Solutions Second Annual Symposium Proceedings, 1993.

Indosuez, or elusive know-how

Anonymous, 'Acquisitions expert leaves', *Wall Street Journal Europe*, section 19: 1 (28 March 1990).
Anonymous, 'Banque Indosuez has hired Richard Sandor to run a new risk management subsidiary, Indosuez International Capital Markets Corp', *Wall Street Journal Europe*: 16 (15 March 1990).
Anonymous, 'Compagnie de Suez SA: bank unit's six-month net increased nearly fourfold', *Wall Street Journal*, section B: 4B (13 September 1993).
Anonymous, 'Compagnie de Suez unit announces appointees at Carr brokerage firm', *Wall Street Journal*, section A: 11 (13 September 1993).
Anonymous, 'Corporate Report: Compagnie de Suez: chairman tells shareholders that '92 may be "difficult"', *Wall Street Journal*, section A: 12 (18 June 1992).
Anonymous, 'Indosuez sacks its brokers', *The Economist*, 328 (7829): 84 (18 September 1993).
Anonymous, 'Indosuez wins entry to Vietnam', *Wall Street Journal*, section A: 16:2 (20 January 1992).
Anonymous, 'Moody's cuts rating on long-term debt of two French banks', *Wall Street Journal*, section A: 6 (17 May 1993).
Anonymous, 'Morgan Grenfell – unwelcome attention', *The Economist*, 313 (7628): 102 (11 November 1991).
Anonymous, 'S&P may downgrade French banks', *American Banker*, 28 January 1993: 12.
Anonymous, 'Three French banks are downgraded', *American Banker*, 17 March 1993: 20.
Clifford, M., 'A slap for Indosuez', *Far Eastern Economic Review*, 154 (40): 56–57 (3 October 1991).
Evans, J., 'Banque Indosuez to increase stake in Morgan Grenfell', *American Banker*, 30 October 1989: 7.
Henriques, D.B., 'Banque Indosuez adds risk-management post', *New York Times*, section D: 4–5 (14 March 1990) (recruitment of Richard Sandor from Drexel Burnham Lambert).
Holland, K., 'Citicorp loses six officials in LDC debt trading unit', *American Banker*, 1 March 1991: 2.
Kraus, J.R., 'Banque Indosuez forms investment bank in US', *American Banker*, 20 April 1992: 13.
Kraus, J.R., 'Banque Indosuez makes big gains by staying small', *American Banker*, section 3A: 1 (19 April 1993).
Leibowitz, M., 'The identity crisis at Indosuez US: when patrician French bankers collide with brash ex-Drexel swappers, guess what emerges?', *Investment Dealer's Digest*, 59 (16): 20–26 (19 April 1993).
White, D., 'Jean-Jacques Picard of Banque Indosuez', *Banking World*, 8 (6): 6–9 (June 1990).

Indosuez internal documents

Jeancourt-Galignani, A., 'General management', No 92/06, 31 December 1992. Directive from Antoine Jeancourt-Galignani, President of Banque Indosuez on the reorganization of the bank. 12 pages.

Jeancourt-Galignani, A., 'Indosuez positions in North America strengthened', 1986 annual report (64 pages), pages 8–9.

Jeancourt-Galignani, A., 'Strategic directions', in 1987 annual report (75 pages), page 2.

Jeancourt-Galignani, A., 'Strategic directions', in 1988 annual report (72 pages), Chairman's Message pages 3–4.

Jeancourt-Galignani, A., 'Strategic directions', in 1989 annual report (88 pages), Chairman's Message pages 4–6 and 7–16.

Jeancourt-Galignani, A., 'Strategic directions', in 1990 annual report (95 pages), Chairman's Message pages 5–7 and 8–19.

Jeancourt-Galignani, A., 'Strategic directions', in 1991 annual report (107 pages), Chairman's Message pages 7–11 and 12–21.

Jeancourt-Galignani, A., 'Strategic directions', in 1992 annual report (119 pages), Chairman's Message pp. 7–8, and 12–25.

Pechiney, in a too explicit world

Barrand, P. and Gadeau, R. (eds) *L'Aluminium*, 2 vols. Paris: Eyrolles, 1964.

Berry, M., *Une Technologie invisible? L'impact des instruments de gestion sur l'évolution des systèmes humains*. Paris: Centre de Recherche en Gestion de l'École Polytechnique, June 1983.

Bocquentin, J., 'Problèmes de relations entre Européens et Africains sur le chantier de Fria (1957–1960)', *Cahiers d'Histoire de l'Aluminium*, winter 1994–95: 78–117.

Bradley, R. and Curtis, A. (executive producers) 'Black power'. London: BBC. Ninety-minute documentary on the experience of Kaiser in Ghana from 1958 to 1969.

Cailluet, L., 'Stratégies, structures d'organisation et pratiques de gestion de Pechiney des années 1880 à 1971'. Thesis in contemporary history, Université Louis-Lumière-Lyon II, 1995.

Camara, S-S., *La Guinée sans la France*. Paris: Presses de la Fondation Nationale des Sciences Politiques, 1976.

Gignoux, C.-J., *Histoire d'une entreprise française*. Paris: Hachette, 1955.

Lacouture, J., *Cinq hommes et la France*. Paris: Editions du Seuil, 1961.

Lamourdedieu, M., 'Carnet de route ou l'histoire d'un alliage: le Duralumin', *Cahiers d'Histoire de l'Aluminium*, 6 (summer 1990): 60–83.

Larrue, J., 'Fria en Guinée: des aspects humains d'une industrialisation différente', *Cahiers d'Histoire de l'Aluminium*, 7 (winter 1990–91): 37–49.

Le Roux-Calas, 'Recherche scientifique et innovation technique dans l'industrie de l'aluminium en France aux XIXe et XXe siècles', EHESS-CNAM, mémoire de DEA d'Histoire des Techniques, 1988.

Marchandise, J., 'Extra muros: histoire de Fria', *Cahiers d'Histoire de l'Aluminium*, 7 (winter 1990–91): 84–6.

Marseille, J., *Empire colonial et capitalisme français*. Paris: Calmann-Lévy, 1983.

Martin, R., *Patron de droit divin*. Paris: Gallimard, 1984.

Morsel, L., 'Louis Marlio, position idéologique et comportement politique d'un dirigeant d'une grande entreprise dans la première moitié du XXe siècle', *Cahiers d'Histoire de l'Aluminium*, 2 (winter 1987–88).

Oury, J.M., *Économie politique de la vigilance*. Paris: Calmann-Lévy, 1983.

Piaton, R., 'Pechiney et la concurrence internationale'. Interview with the president of the Conseil d'administration de la Compagnie de Produits Chimiques et Électrométallurgiques Pechiney, Paris: *L'Économie*, 481 (11th year), 24 February 1955: 4–6.

Riveline, C., 'L'enseignement du dur et l'enseignement du mou', *Gérer et Comprendre*, 5 (December 1986).

Riveline, C., Moisdon, J.C. and Berry, M., 'Qu'est ce que la recherche en gestion?', *Revue Informatique et Gestion*, September–October 1979.

Archives Pechiney

La Revue de l'Aluminium dont la collection complète est conservéee aux Archives, et contenant des informations concernant les relations entre Pechiney et les États-Unis.

Cote 00–01–20036: Congrès de 1939 à 1957, qui permirent d'étudier le flux continuel d'informations sur la technique que Pechiney maintient dès l'après-guerre.

Cote 00–01–20046 et 00–01–20047: Relations de Pechiney avec les pays étrangers.

Cote 00–08–11343: 'L'histoire d'une entreprise française' de C.J. Gignoux, manuscrit original.

Cote 00–08–20567: Rapport de l'Institut Battelle de Genève de 1966 sur l'organisation de Pechiney.

Cote 00–10–10018: Pour découvrir comment l'organisation gérait son information, notes d'organisation qui ont précédé la Seconde Guerre Mondiale, le schéma d'organisation de 1933, l'organisation du bureau d'exportation de 1934.

Cote 00–10–10019: Collection Historique de titre général Organisation qui permirent d'étudier la création du Bureau Central d'Études qui eut lieu en 1940, ainsi que le rapport sur ce même bureau de M. Massé, daté de 1943. Ce carton d'archives contient également une note d'organisation de Pierre Jouven datée de 1948.

Cote 00–10–10020: Rapport d'organisation de K.B. White, en livres reliés, de 1948 qui fait le point sur les perspectives d'amélioration de la Compagnie au lendemain de la Guerre. Il contient notamment une étude sur les jeunes ingénieurs de l'entreprise qui donne des informations sur les critères de recrutement en vigueur à l'époque.

Cote 00–10–10021: Projet de réforme de la Compagnie de 1945, et note sur les responsabilités de la Haute Direction vis-à-vis des techniques modernes, et sur l'évolution des idées en matière de gestion des entreprises (1953–1955) contenues dans la collection historique.

Cote 00–15–20444: de la Collection historique de Pechiney, contenant les notes de voyage d'études aux États-Unis de 1939 à 1946 m'ont permis une partie de l'étude de l'acquisition de connaissances externes aux États-Unis.

Cote 00–15–20450: concernant les voyages d'études aux États-Unis de 1964 à 1967.

Cote 00–15–20451: Collection historique, elles couvrent la période 1923–1956. Elles ne couvrent malheureusement pas les périodes difficiles qui débutèrent à ce moment-là. Il est dommage que les archives historiques ne contiennent pas de sources objectives sur l'affaire guinéenne pour la période 1956–1966.

Cote 540/2–12–28964: Elles contiennent les exemplaires de la revue HOROYA qui fournit des informations complémentaires à celles des Archives historiques sur une période s'étendant jusqu'en 1969.

Index

Matter, Jean, 178, 179, 180–82, 183
mechanistic organizations, 25, 200,
   222, 229
memory, 8, 9, 58, 62, 86–7, 151–2, 193,
   194, 208, 214
Mencius, 69
mental models, 12, 14–15, 24, 59
Menuhin, Yehudi, 43–4
Merleau-Ponty, M., 63
Messud (at Pechiney), 90, 94
mètis, 21, 53–5, 64–72, 75, 76, 101
Meyer, J.W., 12
Michelin, 218–19
Microsoft, 1
Miles, M.B., 98, 99, 102, 107, 112
Milgram, S., 83
Miller, M., 102
Milliken, F.J., 12, 38–9, 57, 81, 84, 137,
   224
Millward, R.B., 54
mining, see Pechiney (case study)
mobilization (knowledge), 103–4,
   106–7, 114, 117, 153
Moch, M.K., 82
modes of knowing/knowledge, 3,
   29–30, 64, 92, 101–8, 172–4, 200,
   227–8
Moingeon, B., 212
Montaigne, Michel de, 81–2
Moore, Allan, 121–2, 129–30, 131,
   133
moral wisdom, 69–71, 75
Morgan Grenfell, 157, 163
Morin, E., 81, 111, 136–7, 224, 227,
   229
Moscowitch, M., 56
Moullet, M., 61, 67–8, 137, 226
musical intelligence, 43–4
mutable knowledge, 67, 68–9, 149–50

NASA, 39–40, 41, 50, 52
Nasser, Gamal Abdel, 170
Native Americans (anticipatory
   knowledge), 64, 72–4, 75
natural disasters, 35–8, 52
network effect (in banking), 159–60
Newell, A., 8, 65
Nisbett, R.E., 54
non-capitalization of tacit knowledge,
   213–14
non-codifiable knowledge, 20–22, 77,
   222

non-expressed, 76, 78–118
non-intentional, implicit and, 57–8
non-linear dynamics, 42, 44–6, 47,
   49–50
non-observable (limitations), 110–17
non-partisan observers, 145
non-perceived, 84
Nonaka, I., 7, 8, 23–9, 32, 48, 82, 88, 93,
   101–2, 112, 133, 135, 150, 153, 172,
   209, 228
Norburn, D., 23
Normand, Georges, 182
North-West Airlines, 124
null hypothesis, 86, 91, 95
Nummi, 213
Nystrom, N.C., 136

O-ring problem (Challenger), 39–40
oblique knowledge, 67
observable actions, 102–8
observation
   challenge for observant, 92–6
   direct, 4, 98–108
observers, non-partisan, 145
Ohmae, K., 4
opportunism, 82
Order of Malta, 146–9 passim, 151
organic organizations, 25, 200–201,
   229
organizational culture, 26–7
organizational learning, 9, 15, 22, 27,
   54, 75–7
organizational structure, 25, 197,
   200–201, 222–3, 229
organizations
   competitiveness, 229–30
   knowledge withing, 7–33
   puzzled, 3, 34, 41–2, 49–50, 117, 218,
      229
   tacit foundations of, 197–223
Osaka International Hotel, 27, 101
Osgood, C.E., 56
Osterman, K.F., 91, 96
others, fear of, 82–3
O'Toole, John, 36
Oury, J.M., 180

panoptic prison, 25–6
Parisot (Governor of Guinea), 181,
   189
Parker, R.E., 151
Parkhe, A., 4